Christopher Priest: The Interaction

Edited by
Andrew M. Butler

Foundation Studies in Science Fiction, 6

The Science Fiction Foundation 2005

Published by the Science Fiction Foundation, Registered Charity 1041052.
Patrons: Sir Arthur C. Clarke and Ursula K. Le Guin

The Science Fiction Foundation was set up in 1971 by George Hay to promote science fiction in all its forms. It established a research library, which is now housed at the University of Liverpool, and began publishing a journal in March 1972. Over thirty years later, and now under the editorship of Farah Mendlesohn, *Foundation: The International Review of Science Fiction* continues to publish a lively mix of articles and reviews by critics, scholars, fans and authors. In addition to publishing books, the SFF also organises conferences and sponsors events at conventions.

For information on joining the SFF and receiving Foundation see
http://www.sf-foundation.org

23 Ranelagh Road
Bruce Grove
London
N17 6XY

Foundation Studies in Science Fiction (Series Editor: Farah Mendlesohn)
1. *The Parliament of Dreams: Conferring on Babylon 5* (1998)
    (edited by Edward James and Farah Mendlesohn)
2. *Terry Pratchett: Guilty of Literature* (2000)
    (edited by Andrew M. Butler, Edward James and Farah Mendlesohn)
3. *The True Knowledge of Ken MacLeod* (2003)
    (edited by Andrew M. Butler and Farah Mendlesohn)
4. *A Celebration of British Science Fiction* (2005)
    (edited by Andy Sawyer, Andrew M. Butler and Farah Mendlesohn)
5. *Parietal Games: Critical Writings by and on M. John Harrison* (2005)
    (edited by Mark Bould and Michelle Reid)

Hardback: ISBN 0-90307-06-1
Paperback: ISBN 0-90307-07-X

Contents

Acknowledgements

Thanks are due to Nick Gevers for his help and advice in the early stages of this project and to the Science Fiction Foundation committee. Special thanks go to Feòrag NicBhrìde, Edward James, Farah Mendlesohn, Graham Sleight, Bridget Bradshaw and all the contributors for their patience, efficiency and hard work on the production of this volume, and especially to Colin Odell for the cover.

Gilles Dumay, Paul Kincaid, Rob Latham, Mark Plummer, Andy Sawyer (in his capacity as librarian of the Science Fiction Foundation Collection) and Maureen Kincaid Speller all provided materials written by Christopher Priest without which this volume could not have been completed.

In addition to the people noted above, the editor would like to give personal thanks for life-support to Mark Bould, Robert Edgar, everybody at the Doves (top of the league!), Javier Martinez, Xavier Mendik, the Prefab Four, Sherryl Vint, Neil Whiffin and Nathan Woods.

Most importantly we owe an immense debt to Christopher Priest both for his works and his tolerance of this project, as well as for agreeing to the appearance of the interview with Gilles Dumay.

All proceeds from this book go to the Science Fiction Foundation, Registered Charity 1041052.

List of Abbreviations

A	*The Affirmation* (1981)
DA	*The Dream Archipelago* (1999)
DW	*A Dream of Wessex* (1977)
E	*The Extremes* (1998)
eX	*eXistenZ* (1999)
FDI	*Fugue for a Darkening Island* (1972)
G84	*The Glamour* (1984)
G85	*The Glamour* (1985)
G96	*The Glamour* (1996)
I	*Indoctrinaire* (1970)
IS	*An Infinite Summer* (1979)
IW	*Inverted World* (1974)
P	*The Prestige* (1995)
QW	*The Quiet Woman* (1990)
RTW	*Real-Time World* (1974)
S	*The Separation* (2002)
SM	*The Space Machine* (1976)

Introduction: The Interaction

Andrew M. Butler

There is a moment in a review of the excellent *Cambridge Companion to Science Fiction* (2003) when science–fiction novelist Adam Roberts notes an omission: "Christopher Priest, a very major figure indeed, gets nary a mention in the index: a very troubling absence indeed" (Roberts 2003). He was not the only reviewer to do so, and it is not the only place to lack his presence. Andy Sawyer, Farah Mendlesohn and I noted that his work was not covered by *A Celebration of British Science Fiction* (2005) when we were in the early stages of preparing it for publication.[1] Indeed, there is relatively little existing criticism on Priest's work, the most substantial being a number of articles by Paul Kincaid (1991, 1999b, 2000) and one book-length monograph, Nicholas Ruddick's *Christopher Priest* (1989). In 1989 Priest was so neglected academically that the editors of the various journals had problems finding suitable reviewers – *Science Fiction Studies* used their own reviews editor (Mullen 1991) and *Foundation* cheekily but helpfully asked the subject of the volume to do it (Priest 1990a). So why this reluctance to engage with one of the most important post-war British science-fiction writers?

For a start there is the issue of whether he is a science-fiction writer at all, and whether some of his critical statements about the genre have somehow let the side down or frightened the horses. In 1985, twenty years ago, he wrote that "What once seemed to me an attractively adventurous place to be a writer now seemed to be very conformist indeed..." (Priest 1985b: 9) – and twenty years before that, he began to show signs of boredom at the science-fiction magazines. Surely someone saying things like that has elected to leave the ghetto behind, like a British Kurt Vonnegut.

Certainly it would be difficult to argue that Priest is *central* to science fiction – and he is all the better for that. He inhabits the margins, the corners, and I can quite understand why he was overlooked in the *Cambridge Companion*, which inevitably – and I write as a contributor to the volume – needed to lay out the genre's middle ground. But Christopher Priest did get most of his breaks in science fiction, he has been published as a science-fiction writer, he has won science-fiction awards and he has felt that "what I write is most intelligently perceived by science fiction readers" (Priest 1985b: 9). Despite the first sentence of this paragraph, I would maintain that he is an important science-fiction writer, precisely because he is a one of a kind. Not only is there no one else quite like him writing within the genre, but also in many ways Christopher Priest does not write like himself, at least not for a third or fourth time.

There is certainly the sense that he interacts with science fiction, with each of his novels readable as a new variation on science-fictional ideas – *The Separation* (2002), for example, is a novel that focuses on the moment an alternate world branches off, rather than the much more common representation of a looking-glass world some decades or centuries later. This interaction takes the form of a forty-plus year engagement with the genre, as I explore in my chapter in this book. He also engages with H. G. Wells – most notably in *The Space Machine* (1976), less obviously in *The Glamour* (1984, 1985, 1996) – and, as Nick Hubble and Andy Sawyer discuss in their contributions to this volume, with John Wyndham and the British tradition of the cosy catastrophe. He even, according to Nicholas Ruddick's chapter, offers a parallel to Mary Shelley. There's a thread running through British science fiction from Thomas More's *Utopia* (1516) to J. G. Ballard's *Concrete Island* (1974) and beyond, that of the island, as Nicholas Ruddick explored in his *Ultimate Island* (1993). We are an island nation, after all, and Paul Kincaid examines the phenomenon of the insular, whether literal or metaphorical, within Priest's fiction. Insularity – what Nick Hubble helpfully locates in his chapter as "separation" as far back as *Indoctrinaire* (1970) – is clearly the flipside of interaction. Meaning is not necessarily to be found in choosing one state over another, but rather in the interaction by the individual between the two.

So is Priest actually part of the mainstream or general fiction? In 1983 the Best of Young British Novelists promotion, sponsored by the British book industry and publicised in *Granta*, selected Priest, along with Martin Amis, Pat Barker, Julian Barnes, Ursula Bentley, William Boyd, Buchi Emecheta, Maggie Gee, Kazuo Ishiguro, Alan Judd, Adam Mars-Jones, Ian McEwan, Shiva Naipaul, Philip Norman, Salman Rushdie, Clive Sinclair, Graham Swift, Lisa St. Aubin de Terán, Rose Tremain and A. N. Wilson as the leading novelists of their age and time. Certainly there are books written by some of those authors which would profitably be read alongside Priest's work since the 1970s, in particular Martin Amis and Ian McEwan's – and Victoria Stewart mentions McEwan's *Atonement* (2001) in her chapter.[2] He shares with them an awareness of the politics of the contemporary world, coupled with an interest in technology or its use as a metaphor, and Amis, Barnes, Emecheta, Gee, McEwan and Rushdie all have entries in Clute and Nicholls's *The Encyclopedia of Science Fiction* (1993). But whilst many of the others have achieved mainstream acclaim, perhaps Priest's previous twenty years of science-fiction writing held him back from respectability.[3] It is the mainstream's loss.

Writing back in 1991, Paul Kincaid suggested that Priest was a writer interested in fantasy, psychology and politics. It is hardly surprising then that at least two of our contributors use psychoanalysis as part of their critical toolkit. Both Nick Hubble and Matthew Wolf-Meyer explore, in differing ways, the ways in which Priest's protagonists attempt to heal themselves through the course of their narratives, and the reliving/relieving of trauma and amnesia that runs through Priest's fictions; indeed the theme of psychology runs through most of the pieces here. It falls to Graham Sleight to examine the importance of politics (and power) within Christopher Priest's narratives, though he observes a sense of healing too.

Thomas Van Parys and Victoria Stewart bring us up to date: Thomas Van Parys examines that often disregarded genre of the novelisation, and focuses on Priest's adaptation of David Cronenberg's *eXistenZ* (1999), a case of the literary interacting with the commercial, where a text intended to promote a product is also meant to stand as a literary artefact. Victoria Stewart analyses *The Separation*, Priest's latest novel at the time of writing, and one which was his first paperback original after more than thirty years – but a volume which triumphed at the award ceremonies.

In their discussions of Priest's work, both Nicholas Ruddick and Thomas Van Parys use the term "*Unbestimmtheit*" (uncertainty or indeterminability). Nicholas Ruddick is drawing upon Werner von Heisenberg, and his famous principle (cf. Ruddick 2001, especially n.4). Thomas Van Parys takes it from Wolfgang Iser (1988), who uses the term to refer to the gaps in and omissions from any narrative which force the reader – if she is to fully comprehend the work – to interact with the text and in part write the story for herself. In an age where everything is painfully spelt out – "You mean she was actually dead and they're being haunted by the living?" – Christopher Priest's understatement is at the very least refreshing. *Unbestimmtheit* is nowhere more apparent than in his endings – it is only after I had closed the covers of *The Prestige* (1995) and *The Separation* that the revelations struck me, and the pennies dropped that... well... the pay offs were there, if you fitted the pieces together. Equally the resolutions of *The Affirmation* (1981), *The Glamour* and *The Quiet Woman* (1990) require an interaction with the text that few other writers within the science-fiction field demand. The ending of *The Glamour* is perhaps so subtle, that Priest has had to rewrite it several times to get it just right.

Interpretation is made more challenging by the unreliable narrators that Priest often favours, along with the shifting viewpoints which are not always declared. It is not that his narrators are necessarily lying to us; to paraphrase a former British prime minister, they were sincere at the time. When memory cannot be trusted, when perceptions are misleading, when reality is subject to revision, when we cannot trust our eyes, we are on tricky grounds. Priest is a magician, a master of sleight of hand, a practitioner of legerdemain – a term which David Wingrove used in relation to Priest's fiction way back in 1979, comparing him to "a conjurer whose legerdemain focuses upon the unimportant so that he might obscure the essential" (Wingrove 1979: 3). The magician, of course, never reveals his secrets; not only does not say what he does, but he does not do what he says.

This is not to imply that Priest is just some sideshow attraction, that he is another tableau in the postmodern funhouse – although Nick Hubble and Matthew Wolf-Meyer may disagree. True, he can play those metafictional games of books within books and oscillations between levels of reality as well as any other writer, and he might be accused of sometimes maintaining a distance from some of his characters, displaying a waning of affect. But those levels of "realities" interact to a purpose, to say something about our attitudes towards the world, not least a fascinated abhorrence of violence in various forms. The misdirection enables him to make his points without sliding into propaganda. He is political without necessarily being party political.

Too many writers are content to perform the same old tricks. Priest's tight-rope act is to continue without repeating himself, to reinvent himself between novels, to be a writer from whom we expect the unexpected. Not for him the tenth book in an endless series, the easy pleasures of the consoling volume per year just in time for the Christmas market or the awards season. To padlock him in a straitjacket of science fiction, metafiction, postmodern fiction, magic realism, slipstream, post-New Wave, even – spare us – the interstitial or fables of exogamy, is to miss the point. We should take our cue from the French who simply see him as a writer – and read him, and interact with his work.

Notes

1. By that time we had already decided to produce this volume, although we did pursue some options over commissioning a piece for the *Celebration*.
2. See also Kincaid 1991: 44, but note Priest's comments on Amis, McEwan and Ishiguro: "I've got nothing in common with them. I don't want to have anything in common. It's another bloody orthodoxy [...] I'm closer to William Boyd" (Kincaid 1999a: 8).
3. In 1993, Iain Banks was listed for the *Granta* promotion; in 2003, in an indication of how (little) times have changed, newspapers like *The Observer* were able to write articles asking "Whatever happened to Christopher Priest?" and the new list excluded (what the judges saw as) genre writers: "Louise Welsh's *The Cutting Room* is a fine crime novel set in Glasgow. China Miéville is an extraordinary writer of dark fantasy. In the end we rejected both. Personally, I was sorry to see Welsh go" (Jack 2003: 11).

"Don't Believe in these Dreams": Power and Story in the Novels of Christopher Priest[1]

Graham Sleight

Christopher Priest is not an author who preaches. There are not many times in his work when the reader senses that a character, or a chunk of third-person narrative, is passing down the author's views from on high. But once in a while, one comes across a passage like the following, from his novel *The Separation* (2002). It is the transcript of Joe Sawyer's speech on May 7 1941 which persuades Churchill to sign an armistice with Nazi Germany. Churchill has just made the assertion that "History this time demands we deal effectively with Hitler", and Sawyer responds:

> On the contrary, history shows that war always defeats its own object. No war in recorded history has produced a result that is in accordance with the stated aims of the victor. This is because stated aims are either disingenuous, or if sincerely meant they are undermined by the violence inherent in war.

> Democracies say they fight wars with the stated intention of righting wrongs or of establishing peaceful relations between peoples, but in reality their motives are the protection of vested interests, financial investment and the pursuit of political power. Wars are fought by tyrants ostensibly to settle a dispute or to recapture lost territory, but in practice they wish to maintain illegal control over their people (S 5: 20: 411).

It is always dangerous for a critic to assume that a character is parroting the author's views, but I think that here one can make that case. *The Separation* amounts to an argument against the consensus wisdom of the Second World War as a necessary and moral war – that Hitler needed to be, in Churchill's terms, dealt with. The alternate world that it presents is neither Nazi-dominated nor tainted by the Holocaust; and the crucial moment which helps to bring this more benign history into place is the meeting at which Joe makes his speech. There is further corroboration from an interview between Priest and Nick Gevers:

> *The Separation* is a book of ideas, with no particular agenda to pursue, other than my own general anti-war sentiments.

> The so-called appeasers in the British government of the 1930s were all veterans of the First World War, who had seen the horrors at first hand

and who were determined that nothing like that must ever happen again. To me, that's an honourable instinct, not a despicable one. Appeasement only became discredited after it failed, after war broke out, after Churchill took over. History is written by the victors, and history is now against appeasement.

As a novelist, I don't give a stuff about historical consensus. I took the pacifist point of view that maybe there was, after all, something to appeasement (Gevers 2002).

This point-of-view is, to put it mildly, arguable: David Brin (2004) has contested it in detail, accusing Priest among other things of anti-Americanism and, as it were, rigging his alternate history to accord with his prejudices. Whether one agrees or disagrees with the historical argument represented by *The Separation*, it is clearly (Brin's word, and one that Priest, given the interview, would likely agree with) a "prescriptive" book. The prescription, though, should not be surprising. As the Joe Sawyer quotation makes clear, war is the attempt by one group of people to assert power over another; and this is a strand that has run through Priest's work from the beginning.

In this essay, I want to suggest that there are two deeply linked themes in Priest's work. The first, perhaps more obvious one, is a preoccupation with the creation of stories. A story is a way of perceiving or making sense of the world, or oneself, or others. It may in some respects rewrite experience into a more useful or appealing form. (It may lie, in other words.) It may use the tools of the fantastic to make its point, and so may also constitute a critique of the fantastic. It may help to structure one's life or, corrosively, it may impinge on the life of another. The second theme takes up from that last point: stories can be used to assert power over others. To take a real-world example, as Priest says in the interview above, history tends to be written by the victors, and so the British politicians who advocated appeasement in the 1930s have had their story subsequently marginalised by Churchill's view of the necessity of British rearmament in the 1930s – to the point where it becomes difficult to see how anyone of intelligence and good faith could have been an appeaser. However, Priest is primarily concerned by the stories told by individuals, not groups – many of his books boil down to a dynamic between three or four characters, and one could argue that *The Affirmation* (1981) is a one-character book. And he is concerned with far more radical rewritings of the world than the pendulum-swing of historical revisionism.

Being very schematic about it, Priest's novels can be seen as falling into three rough periods. The books up to *The Space Machine* (1976) gradually home in on the themes I have outlined above, while at the same time marking Priest's closest use of the devices of science fiction. The novels from *A Dream of Wessex* (1977) to *The Quiet Woman* (1990) are where these two themes are explored most repeatedly and obsessively, often with motifs (and even character names) shared back and forth between books. The subsequent books – from *The Prestige* (1995) onwards – represent a broadening of his concerns, certainly in terms of subject matter, although not to the exclusion of the ideas which had preoccupied him before. If Priest is only now consistently gaining something like his due in awards and acclaim, it is not because of any lack of competence or depth in the novels he wrote in the late 1970s or 1980s. But a book like *The Prestige* is more deeply engaged in and fascinated with the workings of the world than any of its predecessors, and so is more approachable – perhaps even more likable – than the Möbius-strip solipsism of, say, *The Affirmation*. To put it another way, Priest tended in the earlier part of his career to concentrate on enclosed environments: a walled city on rails, a small group of researchers in a castle, or simply the inside of one man's head. He has more recently given us books which suggest that such communities always exist in relation to an outside, which may be as worthwhile to describe as the world within the wall (and see especially Kincaid in this volume for more on the trope of the insular).

The fractious and intimate walled community is where we are plunged within a few pages of starting Priest's first novel, *Indoctrinaire* (1970). The first section depicts a surreal nightmare of prison camp life into which the protagonist, Wentik, is abducted. The camp seems to be located in the remote Planalto region of the Brazilian jungle. Wentik enters it by stepping into a perfect circle of stubble etched into the ground – anticipating the crop circle mania of two decades later, which Priest alludes to in *The Quiet Woman* (3: 16-19). *Indoctrinaire* presents a number of striking images in its early pages – the stubble circle, a disembodied animate hand emerging from a tabletop, a vast maze concealed within a tiny wooden hut – and then progressively justifies them through a time-travel plot. In other words, it uses the characteristic sf strategy of explaining itself as the novel goes on. It's difficult not to feel that this weakens the book, and Priest evidently did too – see, for instance, his interview with Paul Kincaid (1999a). His next several novels can be seen, among other things, as experiments in form and how best to match the content of story with its structure.

If *Indoctrinaire* is most striking when it is depicting the rigidly structured community life in the prison camp, then *Fugue for a Darkening Island* (1972) is about the opposite: the progressive breakdown of a community. The community in this case is British life – in particular, British middle-class life – under pressure from waves of refugees from the developing world. Some of the novel's implications are pretty troubling now that, in 2005, the issue of immigration is being used so widely for political capital by proponents of particularly ugly racist views. *Fugue* could be read as a cautionary tale about the implications of escalating racial tensions, much of whose outlook is defined by its first line, "I have white skin" (FDI 9). But it is clear that, although Priest's first-person narrator is blinkered and foolish about his predicament, the reader is meant to see other perspectives as the book progresses. Thus, for instance, we're given a close sense of the views of the narrator's wife or the "Afrim" (African Immigrant) commander whom he falls in with. The more benign interpretation to be put on *Fugue* is that Priest was intending to write a novel that depicted the fragility of "civil society"; and that his point is that when civilisation breaks down, everyone regardless of race will tend to behave more brutally. As Paul Kincaid said, the book's ending "suggests that to try to identify a party-political bias in the work would only reveal Priest's ambiguity on the subject, just as he is ambiguous on the subject of feminism and pornography" (Kincaid 1991: 46). One can see that as a novel, *Fugue* served two purposes for Priest. The first was to explicitly and savagely rewrite the "cosy catastrophes" which were pervasive in post-war British science fiction into something altogether darker and more realistic – as Sawyer discusses in his chapter in this book. The second was to experiment with a particular narrative technique – in this case, a fragmentation of the narrator's story – to convey the dislocation which he experiences.

Fugue's formal experiments are apparent on the first page, as the first of many jump-cuts take us from a "civilised" to a "barbaric" version of the narrator. By contrast, *Inverted World* (1974) initially conceals both its narrative tricks and its science-fictional content. It is the first Priest novel to use alternating third-person and first-person narratives, a device which even here is far from formal trickery and which later becomes part of the architecture of some of his greatest books. In *Inverted World*, the spine of the story told by Helward Mann is straightforward enough. He is coming of age in a peculiar city that travels on rails through a largely uninhabited landscape.

(It is worth saying that *Inverted World* is particularly fine at conveying a sense of place and depicting the sunlit Mediterranean landscape through which the city moves. It is a trait shared with, for instance, the Dream Archipelago stories or the Riviera-like alternate Dorchester in *A Dream of Wessex*. When Priest sets works in the United Kingdom – particularly the South of England – his landscapes tend to have a washed-out greyness to them, as if the land was one where it is extremely difficult to find new stories: reviewing *The Quiet Woman* in 1990, John Clute argued that this represents a covert attack on the damage Thatcherism did to the UK (Clute 1995: 215). Priest's characters often leave this terrain for freer and sunnier climes – whether to visit Tesla in Colorado or to holiday in the South of France with invisible lovers – but return to England to conclude their stories. Staying in the sunshine, as at the end of *A Dream of Wessex*, is a retreat from reality. By the same token, *The Quiet Woman* remains solely in the terrain of England's internal exile and is Priest's darkest book.)

In any case, in *Inverted World* Helward's bright summer of young manhood is also an exploration of the strange world he inhabits. It becomes clear that the city's guild system, of which he is a junior member, is both repressive and necessary in holding together their community's fragile collective enterprise: unless the city keeps moving towards an ever-receding "optimum", its inhabitants will not survive. The book gradually proceeds to its famous revelation: that Helward's world is shaped like the graph of $y=1/x$, and so is, literally, inverted. (One of the book's many fine touches is that the city itself is called Earth: an inversion within an inversion.) Rereading *Inverted World* after many years, I was surprised to find that the revelation about the world's shape comes as early as half-way through. The rest of the book places this science-fictional conceit within an even richer framework: a story of altered perceptions. Here is where the reader sees the point of the third-person sections that alternate with Helward's story. Towards the end of the book, Helward is told but does not believe that his city is on Earth (*IW* 4: 4: 216), that everyone but the city's inhabitants still perceives the planet as a sphere, and that their city's founder carried out the experiments that led to a global crash. The third-person material reinforces the sense that these two modes of perception coexist but are utterly different, and thus that the city's predicament would be all but inexplicable to the rest of the world. Even a community as rigidly organised and successful in its own terms as the city is helpless in the brute facts of the world; the novel ends, most strikingly, with the city perched at the edge of the Atlantic with the optimum it must pursue receding westwards like the setting sun.

After the superb architectural complexity of *Inverted World*, *The Space Machine* (1976) seems something of a romp or a relaxation. Its pastiching of H. G. Wells is amiable enough, and Priest has some fun commenting on Victorian society and, for instance, its treatment of women. There is certainly a sense of darkness in the book, not just in the Martian invasion sequences, but also in the protagonist's explorations of the Martian slave-city. Equally, there's a reforming zeal in some passages as when the protagonist is reunited with his adored Amelia and she tells him – almost offhand – that "I have established a new social order for the slaves" (*SM* 14: I: 209). Amelia is by far the strongest and most complex female character in Priest's novels up to this point, and her moral clearsightedness is one of the most striking aspects of *The Space Machine*.

Historians sometimes play the counterfactual game of asking how we would view Winston Churchill's career if he had died before the Second World War – or, more specifically, if the car which struck him in New York in 1931 had killed him. The answer usually is that we would see him as a flawed but colourful minor character of politics, whose brilliance and potential were fulfilled only in flashes. I have a similar feeling in looking at Priest's career to 1976, with one unarguably great novel and three others of interest behind him. Over the next fourteen years he would publish four novels which, for many readers, exemplify his strengths, his concerns, and his ambivalent relationship with genre science fiction.

For me, at least, Priest's concerns click into focus with *A Dream of Wessex* (1977) – specifically on page sixty-five. Up to that point, *A Dream of Wessex* seems in many ways an orthodox piece of science fiction. Julia Stretton, the protagonist, works for a near-future project based in Maiden Castle in southwest England which is developing the "Ridpath projector". She and a group of other academics are engaged in a kind of collective dreaming, bringing into being through the projector an idyllic shared virtual reality. This collective dream uses the same terrain that they inhabit in the real world, but is set a couple of centuries on. In this future, seismic disruptions have split Wessex away from the mainland of the country, and Dorchester is now a quasi-Mediterranean seaport. Slowly, the "rules" of the interaction between these two worlds become clearer, as one would expect of an sf novel. Julia and the other dreamers each have a matching persona in their dreamworld. Dreamers in the simulation are retrieved by messengers carrying circular mirrors, which trigger off quasi-hypnotic reactions and allow safe awakening. When one member of the simulation dies (*DW* 8: 48), he vanishes from the simulated world. So it becomes clear that the simulation is malleable in ways which the outside world is not: one supposes that a sufficiently strong persona could reshape it radically.

Julia's initial assignment is to retrieve David Harkman, who has been inside the simulation for two years and who has resisted attempts to retrieve him. After a first sortie into the simulation (*DW* 3: 14-9: 58), she returns to reality and goes through the everyday routines of picking up the mail which has accumulated during her time away. Then, on page sixty-five, her former lover Paul Mason appears in a doorway, and a tremor runs through the book.

In his interview with Priest, David Langford describes a phenomenon which he calls the "Priest effect" (Langford 1995). He is referring to moments in books like *The Affirmation* or *The Glamour* (1984, 1985, 1996) when the certainties which the reader has had up to that point are suddenly and shockingly undermined. In both those cases, the shock is due to a fantastic effect calling into question basic certainties about the narrative. But, I would argue, Julia's reaction to Paul's arrival is of exactly the same kind: "The sight of [Paul] was so wholly unexpected that Julia froze in mid-step. She pressed herself back against the wall. Looking at him, seeing his confident, smiling face, Julia wanted to run. She felt a total compulsion to return to Maiden Castle at once, to bury herself in the future forever" (*DW* 10: 65). One feels, along with Julia, that the enclave of life and story which had so far been protected is now vulnerable, a house of cards which could collapse when this arrogant godling flicks his fingers. And so it proves.

Paul, it becomes evident, is both deeply exploitative and extremely plausible. (Before he comes onstage, he sends Julia a note (*DW* 2: 11) which is a masterpiece of understated threat. One feels unnerved by its creepiness, and then that such a reaction is irrational and Paul is the reasonable one – doubtless the effect that Priest intended.) Paul rapidly insinuates himself into the Wessex project, persuading the authorities that he should participate in the simulation. At the same time, he makes plain to Julia that he wants to resume the earlier relationship with her that she ended. Paul's central scene of confrontation with her (*DW* 18: 105-110) sees him making clear his desire to assert his power over both the project and her, and culminates in an attempted rape that Julia only narrowly averts. So the violation which Julia fears from Paul is made concrete in the most personal way.

In any case, Paul's charms have worked on the project's leaders and he becomes one of the dreamers. When he begins to assert control over the simulation, it starts to change. From its initial state as an unspoiled idyll, oil refineries and pipelines begin to appear. The sea is sick with pollution, and Dorchester is now "oil-town, spoil-town, used and usurer" (*DW* 24: 151). The one card which Julia has is her knowledge – which Paul does not share – of a relationship she has conducted with Harkman inside the simulation. Knowledge, too, is power. Julia's passionate adherence to Harkman, to the story of her and him, drives the last section of the book – even though she knows the story is conducted within a fiction.

Eventually, a confrontation between Mason and Harkman takes place in the simulation (*DW* 25: 168). Julia is pulled out of the simulation, but elects to return to it and the now restored (that is, Paul-free) idyll of Dorchester. Even though she knows the simulation may be shut down, she seeks out Harkman and is reunited with him. They acknowledge that, "Neither of us is real, but it doesn't matter" (*DW* 27: 185). The novel ends with a failed retrieval, as the messengers with circular mirrors fail to pull Julia and Harkman out of the simulation. They prefer, in short, a solipsism of love to the less malleable real world. A happy ending such as this, Priest seems to be saying, is a retreat, a refusal to deal with complexity; but at the same time, we come to understand why someone as sympathetic as Julia might make that choice, might choose to become only a fiction.

Priest's own sense of the importance of this novel to his development as a writer is confirmed in Paul Kincaid's 1999 interview with him. When Kincaid asks about the recurrent use of the sexual triangle in Priest's work, Priest responds that this "is hardly unique to me. It's one of the great engines of literature." Kincaid points out that it was not there in the novels before 1977. Priest then says:

Ah, now you're touching a different point. You see, A Dream of Wessex was the key novel, that's where it changes. You can actually see the process changing. That's the point where science fiction starts being subverted, where I'm saying that you mustn't take this stuff too seriously, because that's what A Dream of Wessex is all about: don't believe in these dreams. [...] After [The Space Machine] I was simply taking on more adult themes. It seems to me that stories are best told through character, and engagement of sex is one way (Kincaid 1999a: 5).

Priest's disavowals of originality about the sexual material in his later novels should be taken with caution. He uses these tropes in consistent and distinctive ways across several books. Firstly, the sexual triangle in his novels is always uncomplicatedly heterosexual. Secondly, it always comprises one woman, a "bad" man and a "good" man. The bad man is a former lover of the woman, or believes himself to be; he is also a compulsive writer/rewriter of his own and others' stories. His attempts to force himself on the woman culminate in a sexual assault, attempted or actual (and possibly only conducted in his head). He also attempts to assert control over the woman, and the world more generally, by a control of the fictions in which they both find themselves locked – an assertion which is played out in the architecture of the book. The woman, while sympathetic, on some level recognises why she might be attracted to the man. The good man only begins a liaison with the woman some way through the book and is often a more shadowy presence. Nevertheless, as with Harkman's intervention in A Dream of Wessex, he may be crucial to bringing about the final resolution.

This triangle is played out again in Priest's 1990 novel The Quiet Woman. As I mentioned earlier, it is set entirely in England, and remains Priest's darkest novel both in the society it depicts and in the personal story it tells. Priest has been dismissive of the book, saying he puts it with Indoctrinaire and The Space Machine as "three novels I'm not very happy with at all" (Kincaid 1999a: 6). And indeed, Kincaid – who is the most prolific and insightful critic of Priest's work we have – while interviewing Priest, suggested that it "looked like a story you weren't very comfortable writing [...] With the exception of possibly Indoctrinaire I think it's the weakest story you've done" (Kincaid 1999a: 5). I have to disagree with these assessments. Although The Quiet Woman is a very uneasy book, its depiction of its protagonists' damagingly intertwined lives is superbly controlled and devastating.

The premise of The Quiet Woman is simpler than almost any of Priest's other books. Alice Stockton, a writer living in Wiltshire, is working on a biography of six women, including her elderly neighbour Eleanor Hamilton. Eleanor is found murdered, and shortly afterwards Alice is visited by a man called Gordon Sinclair (or, sometimes, Peter Hamilton) who says that he is Eleanor's son. The novel is told alternately in the third-person, from Eleanor's point-of-view, and in the first by Gordon/Peter. He attempts to befriend and, ultimately, seduce Alice but is rebuffed. Meanwhile, the south of England is under quarantine from a leak from a French nuclear power station. Alice cautiously begins a relationship with Tom Davie, a civil rights activist who helps with her attempts to get her book freed from government strictures on secrecy. As the novel progresses, Sinclair/Hamilton begins to reveal his loathing of his mother, his work in "information management" for the government's secret services and in particular his belief that he and Alice have met before. At one point, he recounts a meeting with Alice at a party where she drunkenly tried to force him to have sex with her (*QW* 22: 138-140). He claims that she subsequently became obsessed with him.

To say the obvious: Sinclair/Hamilton is very close in character to Paul Mason, though his fantasies are spelt out far more clearly. In *The Quiet Woman*, his ability to affect others' stories is made even more explicit. Through his work for the intelligence services, he has access to files on Alice and Eleanor; moreover, he has the ability to alter them. When he does so, his language is deliberately ambiguous: is he changing the record or the reality?

> The coroner's verdict on David Andrew McLennan became open, with cross-referenced implications to Alice's file in the Police National Computer for potential drug abuse. She was refused a visa for the USA [... H]er driving licence was cancelled following a conviction for dangerous driving. She became HIV positive (*QW* 31: 207).

In this book's triangle, Tom Davie is even more of a transient presence than Harkman was in *A Dream of Wessex,* and the central emotional scenes of the book are played out between Alice and Sinclair/Hamilton. Given the latter's tendency to fantasy, the reliability of his narratives becomes a problem. (This is apparent from his first section of narration in the book, when he describes driving towards Alice's house and seeing a UFO creating a crop circle (*QW* 3: 16-19).) In particular, the last two chapters of the book (*QW* 31: 207-212; 32: 213-216) present contrary versions of how the story could end. In the first, Sinclair/Hamilton describes Alice arriving at his office. She very quickly becomes as sexually wanton as she was in the earlier party scene, and the chapter ends with him murdering her in a particularly harrowing and sexual way. (Sex and power, the two poles in the dynamic between Priest's characters for control of their stories are here linked with the inevitable third, death.) In the second chapter, Alice's book is freed from government suppression, Gordon is arrested on suspicion of his mother's murder, Alice's relationship with Tom is blossoming, and a large cheque arrives for her from a previously unknown European institution. Clearly, these two accounts are mutually exclusive, and the reader's instant reaction is to accept the latter as being more rooted in reality. But if the first is Hamilton/Sinclair's fantasy ending, then the second can also be read as wish-fulfilment for Alice. As John Clute suggests in his review of *The Quiet Woman,* it is too neat to be fully believable (Clute 1995: 215). If it is more believable than its predecessor, that merely reflects the fact that Alice is a more stable person. Both Alice and Gordon, like any of us, play out aspirations for the future as a means of making the chaos of life into something storyable. (Alice's work as a biographer is a cue to this stratum of the novel.)

The Quiet Woman, I would argue, thus comes clearest as an examination of the costs of turning lives – one's own or others' – into stories. Its refusal to grant the reader any stable reading models the difficulty of doing so, even if one is as sane as Alice. All of Priest's novels have at their heart a kind of stubbornness, a refusal to accede to exterior demands – whether they are the demands of genres or of readers. *The Quiet Woman* is perhaps the stubbornest of all his books, and this may account for the lukewarm reception it has had even among Priest's most thoughtful readers. Kincaid, for instance, suggests that the sudden revelation of Gordon's arrest for his mother's murder is a technical flaw, a too-neat tying up of loose ends (Kincaid 1991: 57; cf. Clute 1995: 214). If my argument about the status of the book's ending is valid, then this neatness is deliberate and serves a larger purpose: it underlines Alice's need, or weakness, for closure. As with Julia's solipsism at the end of *A Dream of Wessex,* Priest's happy ending here seems almost sarcastic.) So *The Quiet Woman* is, I would suggest, a uniquely disturbing and powerful work; the cost of this, which Priest surely realised, is that it is a difficult book to feel affection for.

Certainly, more than any of his other novels, *The Quiet Woman* provides fewest cues about how to judge its material, and not only the ending. It is easy, therefore, to be chilled by Priest's distant (and, as ever, technically perfect) depiction of appalling material. But just because Priest does not tell the reader how to feel about what happens in his books does not mean that reading them is an unemotional experience. I'm reminded of similar criticisms about supposed emotional distance in the films of Stanley Kubrick, and Michael Herr's eloquent rebuttal in his memoir of Kubrick. Herr recounts the film critic Anthony Lane's assertion that since Kubrick's early film *The Killing* (1956), "his subsequent career has been the slow and maniacal banishment of that young man's riskiness, to the point where feeling, like rainfall, can be measured by the inch." Herr responds:

> So how many inches for Charlotte Haze's hunger and confusion, or for Humbert's unending torture? How much for the loneliness verging on desperation of a space that's empty beyond conception, and even emptier for the presence of a few humans?...What about the living hell of Jack Torrance's madness/possession, or the truly unbearable suffering of Marine recruit Pvt. Pyle in *Full Metal Jacket.* Not even Bergman or Bresson showed more suffering in their films. Merciless is not the same as pitiless (Herr 2000: 36-37).

No, merciless is not the same as pitiless, but both Kubrick's and Priest's characters can at times seem trapped in a web of story so deliberately constructed by the author that its technical perfection comes to seem more to the point than either mercy or pity. This is never truer than in Priest's 1981 novel *The Affirmation*, regarded by many as his finest and most characteristic work. To be blunt: critics' theories are always too neat for the works they describe, and that is a problem for critics and no-one else. *The Affirmation* does not easily fit into the template I have put forward, that Priest is centrally concerned with depicting power – the assertion of one person's control over another, often in ways rooted in sexuality. The reason for this is that *The Affirmation* can, in many ways, be regarded as a one-character novel. Its protagonist Peter Sinclair tells stories about himself only for his own benefit. The two narratives of *The Affirmation* – the one set in "our world" and the other in Priest's recurring setting of the Dream Archipelago – are intimately close, like M. C. Escher hands drawing each other. But this recursion leaves no room for other rounded human presences, let alone the sexual triangle I have described as occurring in other books. Peter's ex-lover Gracia/Seri is a shadowy presence on the margins of his (re-)writing of his life. The novel's extraordinary reversals, its undermining of every certainty about the status of its truth-claims, gain their effectiveness from their solipsistic intensity not, as in *The Quiet Woman*, from a clash between two different world-views.

The Affirmation was cited by Jonathan Lethem as one of the founding examples of his proposed genre of "amnesia fiction", and rightly so (Lethem 2000: 326). The motif of amnesia was, I would suggest, even more potently used in Priest's next book, *The Glamour*. *The Glamour* weds all the streams of Priest's work I have been discussing: the use of genre tropes to critique the tricks of genre; the power-games of a sexual triangle played out at the deepest levels of the novel's structure; and the resulting unreliability of the stories it contains. Its reality-games are so complex that a detailed synopsis may be of some help.

Part One of *The Glamour*, told in the first-person, is brief and tells of the narrator's childhood. There are recollections of an enforced absence from school, of being given a camera and through it taking on a solitary observer's life. Part Two, told in the third-person, recounts the convalescence of a man called Richard Grey, who was injured and became amnesiac in an IRA bomb. Since he was previously a television cameraman, it is a reasonable guess that he was also the author of Part One. Richard's psychiatrists attempt to recover his memories by a variety of means, including hypnosis, and during a trance Richard seems able to speak French (G84 2: viii: 53/G96 2: 9: 54), something he had not recalled. Meanwhile, Richard is visited by a woman called Susan Kewley, who believes that she had a relationship with him. But it is unclear – certainly Richard does not remember – how long they were together. Evidently, they broke up some time shortly before the bomb attack, due to the influence of a third person named Niall. Susan asks whether Richard remembers an incident with a cloud: he does not.

We then move onto Part Three, Richard's first-person narrative of the summer before the bomb. He recounts a holiday in France, a first meeting with Susan on a train, their sudden attraction, and her description of her life in London, with a "sort-of writer" named Niall who is a "parasite" (G84 3: ii: 68/G96 3: 2: 70). Although their romance progresses quickly, Richard has a number of questions, over whether Susan is really travelling alone, or whether they are somehow being shadowed by Niall. At one point, almost sardonically, Richard sends a postcard to Susan's address in London marked "Wish you were here. X" (G84 3: vii: 91/G96 3: 7: 94). After the holiday in France, Richard and Susan return to London but Niall's presence continues to haunt them, culminating in a scene where, although Richard and Sue seem to be the only people in a room, another man's laughter is audible (G84 3: xvii: 122/G96 3: 17: 123). Richard walks away, and shortly thereafter into the bomb attack. (It is worth noting that Richard, like every single one of Priest's first-person narrators, is not telling the truth. Whether they tell their stories to lie to themselves, or to others, and whether they do it knowingly or not, each Priest character who tells his own story (they are almost all male) is to some extent a deceiver.)

The brief Part Four, told in the third-person, undermines almost every assumption the reader has gathered so far. It begins with Richard and Susan driving away from the convalescent home after the events of Part Two and returning to Richard's flat in London. But to Richard, the flat seems somehow wrong: possessions seem to have been moved, and a room he remembers is no longer there. He talks with Susan about the memories he has recovered of their meeting in France. But Susan denies that that this had ever happened, saying that she has never left the UK. Moreover, she says, a different secret lies at the heart of their relationship: she shows Richard what she calls the "glamour". Standing a few feet from him, she summons what she thinks of as a "cloud" about herself, and becomes invisible (G84 4 iii: 143/G96 4: 3: 150). As David Langford points out, this is a psychologically-induced rather than "scientific" invisibility which is far closer to Chesterton's story "The Invisible Man" than Wells's more famous novel of that title (Langford 1992: 32).

Part Five, Susan's first-person narrative, unpacks some of the consequences of this revelation. She recounts first meeting Richard in a London pub when she was with her then-boyfriend Niall. Niall and Susan share a talent for invisibility as do, it transpires, a number of others who form an unseen subculture. The invisibles largely exist by stealing; they are able to recognise each other but (rather like the underclass in John Sladek's *Love Among the Xoids* (1984)) tend to be ignored by society. So they live marginalised lives, stealing what they need and often heading towards mental instability and early death. In this narrative of Richard's and Susan's relationship – which clearly contradicts that given in Part Three – invisibility is at the heart of their understanding from the start, as is the worry that Niall may somehow be haunting them. This first becomes a real threat when Richard and Susan are driving through Norfolk and Susan realises that Niall is in the car with them (G84 5: xi: 199/G96 5: 11: 213). She makes Richard stop the car, saying that she feels sick. At this point, the choice which she faces in the sexual triangle is made clear: "To live the normal life I craved I had to put Niall behind me forever. I could not go back to the morbid, vagrant life of the glams" (G84 5: xi: 200-201/G96 5: 11: 215). Although Richard has the same talent for invisibility as Niall and Susan, he represents the chance for what Susan recognises is a fully human life: one which rejects the fantasy of the glamour. Niall then confronts Susan and beats her (G84 5: xii: 205/G96 5: 12: 219-220). Returning to Richard, she senses that Niall has won a victory: "I called out to you but you did not hear. I realised that in my wretchedness I had slipped back into invisibility, another of Niall's victories over me" (G84 5: xii: 206/G96 5: 12: 221). The next night, when Richard and Susan are making love, the invisible Niall anally rapes her (G84 5: xiii: 209-210/G96 5: 13: 223-224). Once again, and more clearly than ever, a personal violation stands for all the horrors inflicted on the woman by the man who cannot stand to see her leave his life. Susan and Richard return to London, but Niall now seems to be absent. Indeed, he sends Susan a postcard from France marked "Wish you were here. X" (G84 5: xix: 229/G96 5: 19: 241). In this version, it is Niall who informs Susan of Richard's injury in the bomb (G84 5: xxi: 242/G96 5: 21: 259).

Part Six, which closes the novel, is mostly narrated in the objective-sounding third-person. It picks up Richard's story after the car-bomb, with him taking a piece of filming work in Liverpool. Richard recognises that the memories of France – that is, the narrative of Part Three – "were mostly false, projected on his mind by some quirk of the unconscious" (G84 6: i: 247/G96 6: 1: 265). But Susan's story from Part Five also seems difficult to believe, a fiction told about someone else. Richard begins digging into Susan's past, and eventually goes to meet her again. Doubting his own half-memories about invisibility, he asks her to prove the reality of invisibility, which she does (G84 6: vi: 276-285/G96 6: 6: 300-305). But then come a series of revelations. Susan receives a manuscript from Niall (G84 6: viii: 295/G96 6: 9: 317), which turns out to comprise the objective-sounding third-person narrative of Part Two. So has Niall been writing the story himself? Is he, like any objective sounding third-person narrator, just an invisible voyeur of the events he describes? Then, the narrative of Part Six slips into the first-person (G84 6: viii: 297/G96 6: 9: 320) and Niall is there in the room with Richard and Susan. He tells them to freeze, like an author telling his characters what to do, and they obey: "We are all fictions: you are one, Susan is another, I am also one to a lesser extent. I have used you to speak for me" (G96 6: 11: 324).

This coup prompts so many questions that the book's eventual resolution, with Richard beginning a relationship with his hypnotist from the hospital and sending Susan a postcard, seems almost a formality. Invisibility and authorship, voyeurism and reading, power and story: all now marry in an instant. Niall may be a solipsist trying to create a fictive world to keep himself sane, or he may be a delusional manipulator trying to justify his marginalisation by people and society as a whole. But we see the power that story-telling allows him to exercise, and as readers are complicit in his exercise of that power.

My admiration for the structure and execution of *The Glamour* should be evident; its wedding of two distinct tropes on the borders of the fantastic, invisibility and amnesia, seems utterly right. (To my mind, the only substantial flaw in the book is Priest naming his protagonist Richard Grey: a too-obvious hint about his half-kinship with the world of the invisible.) It seems to me utterly clear that Paul Mason, Niall, and Peter Hamilton/Gordon Sinclair are avatars of the same figure, and that Priest finds this persona the most potent means he has of depicting what (to use an old-fashioned word) evil is. In a sense, Priest's view of evil has a fine liberal heritage: just as my right to punch another person stops where their nose starts, so my right to create stories becomes illegitimate once those stories start to impinge on others. Priest's refusal to offer secure, conventional restitution in his books may be offputting: although some of these characters, as I have noted above, seem to be defeated, the books' narratives offer no certainty on this point. We are left with just the stories, and Priest's insistence that we as readers do the work – moral and intellectual – of making sense of them.

To return to alternate-world scenarios, one could have imagined, in another world, a Priest career comprised of novels which continued down the path outlined by *The Glamour* and *The Quiet Woman*, in the same way that J. G. Ballard's books have obsessively pursued a relatively narrow range of icons, settings, and treatments. *The Prestige*, therefore, came as a shock and a most welcome one. Quite apart from being the most purely enjoyable Priest novel to date, it sees him for the first time since *Inverted World* and *The Space Machine* showing evident enthusiasm for the detail of a particular subculture and period – in this case to the world of stage magic. The narratives of the two stage magicians, Alfred Borden and Rupert Angier, are The heart of *The Prestige*. There is no sexual component to their rivalry, but each desperately wants to beat – to assert power over – the other.

To rephrase an argument put forward above: almost any of Priest's novels since 1977 can be read as being about the costs of the fantastic. They use their science-fictional devices precisely as critiques of science fiction. Borden and Angier presume that using "magic" will make their lives easier and more successful, whether the magic takes the form of Borden's Pact or Angier's Tesla machine. In fact, both of these devices exert terrible costs on the characters, those around them, and their descendents. Borden and Angier continue their feud because, ultimately, they are fantasists like Paul Mason or Niall who *do not know when to stop making up stories*. It is no surprise that in interviews Priest spends a good deal of time discussing his ambivalence about science fiction. One could say that technology or magic – the enabling tools of science fiction or fantasy – are desirable because they enable us to efface the drudgery of contemporary life. A teleporter saves you the trouble of having to get on the train to work, or a love potion compels the object of your desire without you having to take on the risks of rejection. And Priest's message to those who wish for such devices is, once again, don't believe in these dreams. Even if they look as if they will work or help you, they will leave you exploiting others and will render you into something less than fully human. This is graphically shown in the final section of *The Prestige*, where we see the family vault where Angier's prestiges are stacked. These inhuman husks stand as Priest's most potent image for the cost of trying too hard to make the world act like a story. Apart from the poignancy and excitement of its narrative, and its great structural ingenuity, the main impression left by *The Prestige* is that the author has once again decided that the world is worth talking about.

The Extremes (1998) also embodies this broadening of concerns. Like its predecessor, it features significant sections of narrative set in the USA, though its main setting is again southern England. Teresa Gravatt, a young woman recently widowed by the death of her FBI Agent husband in action, visits the small town of Bulverton. There, she finds herself drawn into its recent history of a massacre conducted by a gun-wielding maniac (Priest had in mind the very similar events of 1987 in the Thames valley town of Hungerford; see Priest 1999a or 1999b). Teresa also becomes increasingly addicted to the virtual reality scenarios provided by the company ExEx, which she knows from her own FBI training. She begins to suspect that the scenarios could provide her with a way to be reunited, at least in imagination, with her husband. In short, it is a return to much of the territory covered in *A Dream of Wessex*, with the difference that the technology is closer at hand, used by individuals rather than an academic collective, and already open to commercial exploitation. Indeed, the final resolution is almost identical: Teresa prefers a virtual reality solipsism of love to the real world. For this reason, and despite the novel's many virtues, I find *The Extremes* Priest's least satisfying novel in many years.

The Separation, however, is an extraordinary and ambitious work. Priest has always, among other things, had a most un-science-fictional concern with the state of the British nation, and the stresses which might pull it apart or corrupt it – from the obvious and violent dislocations in *Fugue for a Darkening Island* to the Tartan Army bomb in the first line of *A Dream of Wessex* and the IRA bomb which disables Richard Grey. *The Separation* is, explicitly, a novel about how Britain in 2002 got where it is, and how it might have taken a different and perhaps better course. As I suggested at the start of this chapter, it creates a historical argument which the reader can agree or disagree with; but the premises of Priest's views about war follow logically from everything else he has written. If it is immoral for one person to try to impose their will on another, then it is also for countries to attempt the same. Just as the Nazis attempted, as it were, to make the whole of Europe a part of their narrative of what the world should be like, so Churchill was trying through war to do the same. While Priest is always careful not to suggest that the two sides are morally equivalent, for instance by showing early on the terrible glamour of the Berlin Olympics, he is suggesting that another way could have been found which did not involve either side trying to compel the other.

So it is that Joe Sawyer concludes the novel in an ambulance with a Red Cross volunteer called Phyllida: "I clung to my life, forcing myself to breathe evenly, without anxiety, watching Phyllida sleep and dreaming of a better future" (S 5: 24: xxxi: 464). No other Priest novel, I would argue, ends with such earned peace, with such a convincing sense that its characters have successfully faced down their demons. There are not many times in Priest's work when we glimpse a genuinely loving couple: after all Priest's depictions of the self-consuming cost of power, it is deeply satisfying to be able to close one of his books on a note of grace.

Note
1. I'm grateful to Andrew M. Butler for his help in tracking down and providing secondary material, and to Iain Harris and Ben Richardson for a number of conversations about Priest's work.

Christopher Priest

Interviewed by Gilles Dumay (April, 2005)

1. You were born in 1943, during WW2. What was the life of your family at this time?

I was born on Bastille Day, 1943, so I must have been conceived at the end of October 1942. (My parents' wedding anniversary is 31st October, which probably explains a lot.)

In September 1939, when World War 2 was declared by Britain and France, my parents were living in south-west London. They had one baby child: my sister Jacqueline, who was born in 1938 (also on Bastille Day). They stayed in that area for a while, but when the Luftwaffe started bombing London the family moved to the north of England, first to Blackpool, then to the southern suburbs of Manchester. The bombing followed them, of course. There was nowhere safe in Britain at that time.

My father was originally a salesman, and the company made and sold weighing machines. As he got older he became a manager, first of one of the small branches belonging to the company, then later of all the branches in the area. (At the end of his career, in the 1970s, he was the managing director of the company.) My mother, orphaned as a small child, was trained for service, worked for a short period as a paid companion to woman in Woking, but after she married she never had a job again. She came from a vast Edwardian family. She was the youngest-but-one of 17 children. All but three of these emigrated to the USA. Because of this I currently have more than 500 relatives in the USA, none of whom is aware of me, I believe.

I was born in a village near Manchester called Heald Green. In those days it had countryside around it, but now it is just a suburb of the city. There was not much bombing damage in Heald Green, but other places close by had been hit.

2. What is your first memory and what judgment do you make about your childhood, life in England after the war?

When I was a child my family spent a lot of time in Frinton-on-Sea, Essex, because my grandparents were there. I have a clear memory of playing on the beach with my sister, and I've worked it out that it must have been during Easter of 1946. While the war was on, the beach at Frinton had been mined and defended, and of course a lot of shipping had been sunk. So I remember concrete emplacements, and big patches of crude oil on the beach. We used to hear naval guns being fired out at sea, presumably during exercises.

In the years when you're a child, you assume that what you see around you is normal. My immediate environment was a quiet village or suburb of a large city, but whenever we went into Manchester you couldn't avoid seeing the damage the war had caused. Vast areas of Manchester had been bombed and burnt out, and there were hundreds of hectares of broken rubble. It had a particular smell – a combination of burnt timber, chemicals, sewage, rotting wood, old bricks, plaster ... and flower scents. Wildflowers grew all over it. A glimpse now of loosestrife or rosebay-willowherb takes me back to those days.

Strangely, I have similar memories of Frinton. This is a small, quiet town for wealthy retired people, situated on one of the most boring bits of the British coast. During my childhood visits I was struck by the number of houses that had been destroyed during the war. I was fascinated to see the blown-up buildings, with wallpaper, staircases, bits of old furniture, hanging out in the ruins. Frinton, like most British seaside towns (including Hastings, where I live now) was subjected to hit-and-run bombing raids for most of the war. I can still go round Frinton today and pick out the houses which have been rebuilt or repaired since the war.

Probably the most significant childhood memory involves one of my aunts. She was the wife of my mother's brother, and she was bedridden with Bright's Disease: inflamed kidneys. My uncle worked as an administrator at a seminary for Methodist ministers. This was a large, rambling Victorian building, surrounded by ornamental gardens, situated in a valley in the heart of the Pennine moors. It was in a remote area of Derbyshire, a long way from any town and conditions were Spartan. My uncle and aunt, and their two sons, lived in a small house somewhere in the grounds, overlooked on all sides by steep, rocky crags. We used to make regular visits to see these people, about once every six weeks, for year after year. We would drive away from our conventional, bourgeois suburb and go up into the hills, getting further and further away from what I thought of as civilisation, then ending up in a damp, dark house dominated by the needs of an invalid. For two or three hours we would hear terrible stories about medical emergencies at midnight, and see braces and supports, bedpans and large instruments for doing horrific things, and much else. Every now and then one of the ministers would come in and assure her that everyone was praying for her.

Well, it made me into an agnostic! And it gave me nightmares, and years later it has provided an almost inexhaustible source of images and ideas for stories.

3. What was the life of the teenager Christopher Priest? (School, readings, family, friends, music.)

School.

I went to a "good" school, one I had to pass an examination to enter. It was in a huge Victorian building, about 100 years old when I was there (from 1951 to 1959), tall, forbidding, dark-bricked, with spires. You could see it from a long way away, because it looked like a cathedral. It was a mixed-sex grammar school, set up in the 19th century as a charitable foundation for the bereaved children of poor-but-honest working families. It was also, therefore, an orphan school. When I was there, it was known as Cheadle Hulme School, named after the village in which it was situated, but the real name was Warehousemen and Clerks' Orphan School. However, I was there in comparatively modern times, and although there were a number of orphans in the school, most of the children were bright kids from the neighbourhood who had passed the entrance examination. We were segregated on class lines. The orphans (we called them residents, or "rezzies") wore a different uniform from the day pupils and were usually streamed into the lower-achievement groups. They beat the shit out of the day boys whenever no teacher was looking. But the system seemed to work. The orphans were given a much better education than they would have received elsewhere. The other thing I would say in praise of the school was that the principles on which it worked were on the whole enlightened, modern, reformist, liberal, and so on.

My personal experience of the school was poor. Although I easily passed the entrance exam and was obviously clever, I disliked my time there, made no effort to do well and couldn't wait to be old enough to leave.

Readings.

I grew up at a time when books were relatively expensive and hard to come by, because of paper shortages after WW2. I read constantly, working through the usual canon of children's writers of that period. When I reached my early teens, two things happened. The first was that I grew tired of reading fiction; the second was that cheap paperback books started to become available. By the time I was about 14 I was reading non-fiction almost exclusively, in paperbacks which I bought and kept (several of which I still possess). Non-fiction is of course subject-focused, so many of the books reflected the interests of a 14-year-old boy: making model aircraft, explorations and discoveries, astronomy, and so on. I was also interested in books about WW2 – stories about air attacks, prison-camp escapes, tank battles in the desert, and so on.

I was notorious in my family for being a constant reader. Neither of my sisters was much interested in books, although they could and did read. My father never read books. My mother read lightweight books: detective stories, showbiz biographies, etc. I didn't discover science fiction until I was about 19, when I began reading it in earnest.

Family.

In social terms I come from a stable family background. My parents were only ever married to each other, and they stayed together all through my childhood. I have two sisters: one five years older than me, the other three years younger. We lived in a house that was big enough for all of us (but by no means a large or affluent house), in a safe neighbourhood. I didn't realise how stultifying this was until it was over. For years I used to envy other writers, who all seemed to come from broken homes, had been buggered by sports masters, suffered the hell of boarding school, etc., building up subject-matter for their books as they went along. None of this happened to me.

Friends.

I made no special friends in childhood, just other kids at school, some of whom I got on with quite well. I really mean what I said about school. When I left it in 1959 I felt I was walking out of a phase of my life I never wanted to go back to, and slammed the door behind me. My real life began a short while after leaving school, when I began to make friends with people whom I still know.

Music.

The answer is in one word. (Or three!) Rock 'n roll! When I was small there was non-music around me. My parents played dance bands, light classical, crooners. British radio then was dreadful! The American influence in Britain was huge. There were hundreds of thousands of American servicemen in the country, and so Britain was flooded with American music. The days of swing and jazz were over: this was the time of Rosemary Clooney, Teresa Brewer, Frank Sinatra and Nat King Cole ... Eisenhower music! (I still hate this kind of music with a real venom.) However, one day I heard a song called "Shake Rattle and Roll", and in common with millions of other kids I discovered real music. I was about 13 or 14. Soon, it was Bill Haley, Jerry Lee Lewis, Gene Vincent, Little Richard, Buddy Holly ... the familiar roll-call of the greats of the 1950s. (But not Elvis – never Elvis.)

Then, later, just as rock started being commodified, mainstreamed, Elvised, and just as I was starting to feel disillusioned, I went in 1962 to Liverpool and by luck was taken to the Cavern Club where I heard the Beatles playing live. That was a moment when life changed forever. It's amazing how powerful an influence music can be.

My parents were anti-culture, so classical music barely existed in my life as a child. It wasn't until I was in my twenties that I began to take an interest, but then the music of Bach, Mozart, Beethoven, Haydn, etc., took over. These days I have almost no interest in rock music, except occasionally. My musical interest now is broadly divided 75% classical or serious music, 25% jazz or swing from the 1940s. Artie Shaw is my preferred choice of light music now.

4. When did you begin to write fiction and why?

After I left school in 1959 I went to London and my father found me a job as a trainee accountant in the City of London. Within a few days of joining the accountancy firm I realised I was in the wrong place. I hated accountancy! Never got the idea.

But there were a few advantages. Accountants travel around a lot, so I was always being sent to remote parts of the country, and would spend a month living in some provincial hotel and learning the wicked ways of the world. That was good. (It was on one of these trips that I went to Liverpool and saw the Beatles playing at the Cavern Club.) I was also discovering girls, and that was better. But the overall sense of boredom was crushing, and it was from this background that I discovered science fiction. It was a revelation to me.

I began reading science fiction in early 1962. By the end of that year I had made the biggest decision of my life, which was to give up my job and become a writer. I thought that the ideas of science fiction were so enthralling and original that they made me see the world in a completely different way. I soon realised that that was how I had always seen the world myself, but had never found a way of expressing it.

By the middle of 1963 I had started my first few stories. They were of course terrible and have never been published. But I was lucky, or else I learned quickly – I only wrote about 5 or 6 stories before I began selling. I sold my first story ("The Run") in 1964, and followed that up with two or three more. I didn't write or sell much, but everything I wrote was obviously better than the one before. In late 1967 I wrote a story called "The Interrogator", which I sold to John Carnell for *New Writings in SF*. In 1968 I wrote a sequel, called "The Maze", but Carnell rejected it and it was never published.

All through this period I was still working as the worst accountant in the world, and of course I was always being fired from my job. I kept getting more jobs (I had to have the money), but it was obvious I was running out of options. In the summer of 1968 I was fired from my last job, so I decided to give the whole thing up and try my luck as a freelance writer. My luck held.

I took "The Interrogator" and "The Maze" and rewrote them as a single work. I pretended they were the first chapters of a novel I was writing (I wasn't) and made up a synopsis of how the story was going to develop (in truth I hadn't the faintest idea). My agent began offering it. Gollancz swiftly rejected it (a big disappointment), but much to my amazement I received an offer from Faber in January 1969. This was a breakthrough, but of course it also meant I had to write the non-existent novel. I rushed through the drafts. Within 9 weeks I had completed the book, and called it *Indoctrinaire*. Faber accepted it without any changes being asked for, and it was published in the summer of 1970. I didn't get much money from it (£150 paid in three instalments). Even then it wasn't enough to live on, so I carried on with whatever hackwork I could find for a bit longer, but it gave me a solid psychological footing. The following year I wrote my second novel, *Fugue for a Darkening Island*, and a couple of years later *Inverted World*.

5. You published stories in *New Worlds* – what was the new wave scene for you?

During the last years that *New Worlds* was being edited by John Carnell, it was a mediocre British sf magazine, publishing stories that were weak imitations of American science fiction. But *New Worlds* was all we had, the only market for sf short stories. As I started writing in the early 1960s, I saw it as the natural place where I would hope to publish when I was good enough. This was because as well as all the mediocre fiction, *New Worlds* was regularly publishing two writers I found intensely interesting. They were Brian Aldiss and J. G. Ballard, who were both nurtured by Carnell at the beginning of their careers.

I was hugely influenced by them both. Ballard's work thrilled me with his surreal, nightmarish images, and all those mysterious but fascinating obsessions with time and entropy and glamour. A unique writer. Brian Aldiss was just as interesting, but for different reasons. Aldiss was a much better and more varied stylist. Also, he was noticeably *British*. His work made few if any concessions to American writing. But at the same time, his work was just as exciting, imaginative and thoughtful as the best American writers.

These two writers made explicit for me what it was possible to do with science fiction and other forms of speculative literature. You manifestly did not and *should not* write boring and repetitive "planetary exploration" stories to be a British science fiction writer (90% of the rest of the fare in *New Worlds* at the time).

In 1963 it was announced that *New Worlds* and its sister magazines were going out of business, a matter of disappointment to me. Then it was revealed that the titles had been bought by another firm, and that new editors had been appointed: *Science Fantasy* would be edited by Kyril Bonfiglioli, *New Worlds* by Michael Moorcock. I'll never forget the feeling of betrayal when I heard this news. I knew nothing about Bonfiglioli, but Moorcock was a hack writer who had been clotting the pages of *Science Fantasy* with his dreadful Robert E. Howard imitations.

Anyway, in fairness to Mike Moorcock, let me say that I soon swallowed my thoughts and words. When his first issues of *New Worlds* appeared, it turned out (most unexpectedly, I might add) that he was a big admirer of Ballard and Aldiss, and not only intended to go on publishing their work, which he did, but was actively looking for newer and younger writers who were prepared to work in a more personal literary vein. This interested me greatly, because I felt it described me.

Let me stress that I was young, inexperienced, unpublished and eager to please. What burned in me was the need to get my stuff into print. Consequently, at first I took Moorcock's propaganda on board more or less uncritically. I began crafting my stories towards what I thought the "new wave" of sf wanted. It turned out that that was an easy trick to turn. I soon had a couple of stories published in *New Worlds*. I blush to remember them now, because they are so derivative of the stuff that was then current.

As well as trying to write like a *New Worlds* writer, I was trying to act like one too. Pretty difficult in my case because I spent most of my time dressed up in a business suit, and failing at accountancy! I came to know Moorcock personally, and I met many of the other writers who were in and around *New Worlds* at that time. At first, I found it more exciting and stimulating than I could ever have thought possible.

But I was growing up too, and starting to develop my own inner voice as a writer. I was reading more widely. I'd grown restless after reading science fiction for a couple of years, and was branching out into more challenging modern fiction.

I also profoundly disliked the attitude of many of the people within those circles. Moorcock had a habit of attracting acolytes, hangers-on. Whenever I saw Mike he was surrounded by these obnoxious sycophants, who laughed dutifully at his jokes and praised all his stories and utterances. Like all parasites they had a nasty side to them. Whenever anyone left Moorcock's apartment to go home, these toadies invariably launched into a vicious attack on whoever it was. (Mike too, I'm sorry to say.) You'd be surprised at some of the people who got this treatment. Good writers like John Sladek, Keith Roberts, John Brunner. They'd get up to leave what had felt until then like a pleasantly relaxed conversation or party, and a couple of minutes later everyone was attacking them. I hated that, and found myself staying later and later, wanting to be the last person to leave so no one could say terrible things about *me*. But then I realised a funny thing: everyone else was staying on as long as possible, too. Probably for the same reason! So I not only began to loathe these people, I realised I was in danger of becoming like them.

I clearly remember the moment when this insight landed on me. It was a shocking experience, but also a great revelation. It made me feel sick. As soon as I had realised it I knew I had to cut myself loose from the whole *New Worlds* thing. It was a moment of growing up. I was only 21, 22, which is a young age to be writing. But I had suddenly discovered I wanted independence as a writer more than I wanted anything else. I couldn't stand the thought of those sniggering Moorcock cronies disapproving of what I was writing, or, even worse, *approving* of it.

So I went my own way, and have never had a single reason to regret it. The *New Worlds* thing staggered on for a few more years, but for me the energy in it had dispersed long before.

Whenever anyone asks me about that period of my writing, I always find it difficult to describe, because it is for me such a complicated part of my life at a time when change was swift. I try to be honest, not only about the importance to me of what was going on then, but also to try to convey the reality of those days.

It's very difficult to isolate the *New Worlds* business from the rest of my life at that time. So many other things were happening. For instance, at the beginning of 1966 I was involved in a car accident, which traumatised me for several months, putting me out of action as far as writing was concerned. I was having a tough time in my job, hating every minute of it and trying to find some other way of making a living before I could survive as a writer. Sex, and the hunt for it, was a preoccupation. I was still living at home with my parents, and desperate to get out and find a place of my own. (Eventually I did move into an apartment in London.) I was always short of money and could never find enough time to write. It was also a time of immense social change, in Britain, all over Europe, and in the USA. The Vietnam War was going on. The old order was being kicked out. Everything was changing.

None of this is particularly unusual, but it's the general context I was living in while the *New Worlds* stuff was going on. It was an important period, but not a crucial one as it turned out. Some of it was good, and some good writers emerged: John Sladek, Tom Disch, Samuel R. Delany from the USA – me, M. John Harrison and Keith Roberts in Britain. All the rest fell by the wayside, including every one of those Moorcock cronies, whose names no one can even remember now.

Some of the propaganda was good. It was right to throw out that mediocre stuff from the 1940s that people in science fiction call the "Golden Age". It was right to try and put science fiction in a literary context, so that writers had some way of measuring how good they were, or how not-so-good. It was right to encourage young and new writers, and allow them to try out fresh approaches. But the *New Worlds* thing soon became an orthodoxy, with A-lists of people they approved of and shit-lists of those they didn't, a lot of hypocritical backbiting about good writers who wouldn't fit into their mould, and the whole thing propped up by their own dismal efforts, everyone writing Jerry Cornelius stories, and that kind of thing.

At the beginning we had Elric and spaceships; at the end we still had Elric and spaceships. Plus ça change …

Priest's Repetitive Strain

Nick Hubble

Introduction: Literary Judgements and Other Political Fictions

> "[...] the book is extremely badly written. It's too long for its subject matter. The depiction of the characters is sketchy, and only the most shallow of motives are attributed to them to explain their actions. Your storytelling ability is not strong. The text changes direction unexpectedly. You do not acquit yourself well in the writing [...] Your vocabulary is restricted and there are too many repetitions" (QW 29: 199).

The above justification is given by Gordon Sinclair, the head of a shadowy private company delegated to handle censorship for the Home Office, as the reason for the suppression of Alice Stockton's manuscript in *The Quiet Woman*, Christopher Priest's 1990 novel of a near-future Britain. Little does it avail Alice to complain "'But those are literary judgements! [...] this is nothing to do with the book being subversive'" (QW 29: 200), the subtext is that such judgements are always political. It is not by accident that the verdict reads like a satirical description of one of Priest's own novels. The capacity of his characters to fade from visibility or consciousness or even the text itself, as conventional narrative is thwarted at every turn, is matched only by his own apparent invisibility – despite winning several notable prizes – within the public sphere and to the eyes of academia in particular. One way of explaining this lack of recognition for undoubtedly one of the finest British writers over the last thirty years would be to employ terminology from his own fiction: he is simply too "glamorous" to be noticed. That is to say that Priest's public invisibility is not simply a product of the well-known perfidy of mainstream critics and cultural commentators, but has also become a matter of choice concomitant with the years of diligent practice spent honing to perfection a natural talent for misdirection. The most explicit fictional acknowledgement of this interpretation can be found in *The Prestige* (1995), his mesmerising story of feuding turn-of-the-century stage magicians, which is also discussed by Ruddick in this volume. Consider the following tantalising passage in which one of the main protagonists, Alfred Borden, compares the act of writing with that of staging an illusion:

> I have misdirected you with the talk of truth, objective records and motives. Just as it is when I show my hands to be empty I have omitted the significant information, and now you are looking in the wrong place.
>
> As every stage magician well knows there will be some who are baffled by this, some who will profess to a dislike of being duped, some who will claim

to know the secret, and some, the happy majority, who will simply take the illusion for granted and enjoy the magic for the sake of entertainment.

But there are always one or two who will take the secret away with them and worry at it without ever coming near to solving it (P 2: 1: 38).

Not surprisingly, this challenge of "solving" Priest's "secret" meaning has proved irresistible to critics. For example, David Wingrove has contended that Priest's unifying theme is "the idea of Man separated and at a distance from reality" (Wingrove 1979: 3), only to be disputed by Paul Kincaid: "Priest's theme is not to show Man separated from the real world, but to show the psychological effects of such a separation. Throughout his work [...] a healthy mind [...] is consonant *only* with an involvement in the real world" (Kincaid 1991: 43). Yet what are these "themes" and "realities" but the "talk of truth, objective records and motives" that Priest warns us against? Such judgements are also political. How then can we read Priest without falling into these traps? The approach taken here will be to consider the developments in Priest's fictional practice across his career as attempts to avoid exactly those traps and, therefore, as providing a model that we can adapt towards a practice of active readership.

The Question of Separation
The question of "separation" is explicitly addressed by Priest in his most recent novel, *The Separation*, in which twin brothers Joe and J. L. Sawyer "separate" into alternate historical tracks during the Second World War. While the book is dedicated to Kincaid, it flatly contradicts his thesis that Priest's theme is the necessity for involvement in the real world, by depicting history – and specifically British war and postwar history – as a constructed "reality" that not only must be escaped, but also remade (see Hubble 2005b). Hence the bomber pilot, J. L., repeatedly wakes from a crash – which is fatal to him in Joe's universe – to successively modified futures (S 2: 7: 46; 2: 9: 58; 2: 12: 76) before he finds himself in the world where the Allies won the war, while pacifist Joe's repeated awakenings from his own accident (S 5: 11: i: 303; 5: 11: iii: 308) – fatal in J. L.'s universe – and after other events such as the bombing of Coventry (S 5: 11: v: 315; 5: 11: vii: 318), can be seen as an eventually successful attempt to wake up to the peace which emerges in his world with the signing of an armistice between Britain and Germany in May 1941. However, in the final twist, J. L. rejects even this alternate history of peace, as the book closes with him "dreaming of waking to a better future" (S 5: 24: xxxi: 464), which by implication is outside history (see also S 5: 10: 302).

This process of repeatedly working through scenarios until they are mastered bears a striking resemblance to the process of "repeating and working-through" that Sigmund Freud regarded as central to psychoanalysis, where the challenge facing the analyst is to bring to consciousness that which has been repressed by the patient. The analyst treats repression by inducing a compulsion to repeat so that the patient "acts" out what has been repressed as a "piece of real life" (Freud 1958a: 150-152). A cure can be achieved by having the patient continue this repetition under analysis until the point when what has been repressed no longer represents a threat to ego stability. It can be seen that Priest's protagonists undertake something like a self-analytic process by submitting to their own compulsions to repeat.

Freud generally allowed fiction to be a form of wish-fulfilment falling completely within the field of the pleasure principle – the corrective mechanism which acts to keep the level of excitement and agitation resulting from external or internal stimuli to as low and stable a level as possible, exemplified by the pleasure of the sexual act which resides in the "momentary extinction of a highly intensified excitation" (Freud 1984b: 336-337). In the well-balanced individual, the pleasure principle is supposed to be subordinate to the reality principle, which postpones immediate satisfaction in favour of greater satisfactions in the long term. Yet it is still the pleasure principle which forms the primary defence mechanism for protecting the ego from trauma by repressing those internal excitations which would otherwise overrun it. Thus, it is the resistance of the pleasure principle that has to be circumvented by the compulsion to repeat during the psychoanalytic encounter in order to effect the cure to the trauma. Freud explained how this was possible by arguing that the compulsion to repeat was an infantile stage of ego defence mechanism that was normally superseded in maturity and only resurfaced if the pleasure principle was overwhelmed. This developmental argument can be illustrated by the classic example of the child who compensates for the mother's absences by staging the disappearance and return of toys within his reach. The repetition of a distressing moment does not accord with the pleasure principle but rather allows the child to attain an active rôle in place of his normal passive position. Freud concluded that this infantile stage was a necessary precursor for the subsequent adoption of the pleasure principle and, later still, the reality principle. What he did not consider was the alternate possibility that this mastery through repetition might be preferable to the developmental stages that are supposed to succeed it. This is the radical idea that has been developed by Priest in his most recent fiction, where the goal is not just to escape from history but from all forms of "reality".

It was not always so. While the condition of separation has affected Priest's fictional protagonists since 1970 and his first novel *Indoctrinaire* (see I 1: 7: 47; 1: 11: 103; 2: 19: 174; 3: 25: 216), it was initially depicted as a form of wish-fulfilling escapism and, as Kincaid argues, the stance of the early books (although, as we shall see, it is only strictly true of the first two novels) was implicit criticism of these characters for their lack of commitment. The key to understanding this transition, from a condemnation to a celebration of separation, is to be found in the way that the condition is associated with a specifically British experience. For instance, *The Encyclopedia of Science Fiction* suggests that the "haunted lassitude" (Clute and Nicholls 1993: 960) expressed by the hero of *Inverted World* is characteristically British. In this vein, it is possible to read Priest's early novels as an indictment of Britain for itself existing in a state of separation from history or as having become detached from the reality principle. His creation of alternate histories in the 1970s – especially *Fugue for a Darkening Island* (1972) and *A Dream of Wessex* (1977) – represented an acting out of what had been repressed and can be seen as an attempted analytic cure designed to jolt history back on track and re-establish the possibility of British agency. A version of this idea is still evident as late as *The Quiet Woman*, where the separation of biographical writer Alice from the outside world is gradually revealed as she comes to realise that she has been drawing "on the events of history without involving herself with the idea that history actually had to be made" (*QW* 15: 91). However, Alice's attempts to regain agency are mirrored by those of the monomaniac Gordon and the novel's parallel endings suggest that the liberal solution of "only connect" – perhaps implied in the earlier novels (see Kincaid 1991: 43-44) – is no longer sufficient to resolve the British problem. It is this ongoing concern with the state of the nation that has led to the major shift in the psychological and philosophical underpinnings of Priest's fiction so that separation is no longer a problem to be cured but a point of departure.

Priest has acknowledged this development in his fiction, albeit in typically backhanded manner: "Although I seek to avoid categorisation of my books, slipstream can be a useful identifier" (Priest 2003a). He has variously identified slipstream as "an interest or obsession with thinking the unthinkable or doing the undoable" (Priest 2003b: 31) and "a different way of inquiring into the familiar" (Priest 2003a). But it might also be described as a type of fiction that does exactly what Freud thought impossible in the aesthetic field by going beyond the pleasure principle to those compulsive and repetitive "tendencies more primitive than it and independent of it" (Freud 1984b: 287). Such a transition involves crossing the boundary identified by Brian McHale in *Postmodernist Fiction* as that where "intractable epistemological uncertainty becomes [...] ontological plurality" (McHale 1989: 11). McHale illustrates this transition by citing the poet Dick Higgins's examples of epistemological questions – "How can I interpret this world of which I am a part? And what am I in it?" – and ontological questions – "Which world is this? What is to be done in it? Which of my selves is to do it?" (McHale 1989: 9-10). McHale's intention is to differentiate between the respective dominant concerns of modernist and postmodernist fiction, but it is his correlative examples of popular genres that are of particular relevance to us here: "the detective story is the epistemological genre *par excellence*", but "science fiction [...] is the ontological genre *par excellence*" (McHale 1989: 16). While McHale seeks to show the staged transition of modernist concerns into postmodern ones across the individual careers of different writers such as Samuel Beckett, Alain Robbe-Grillet and Thomas Pynchon, it is possible to demonstrate a comparable transition for Priest: firstly, from epistemologically orientated genre science fiction to ontologically orientated science fiction and then, secondly, beyond science fiction itself, where we find not the mainstream but the slipstream.

Epistemologically Orientated Science Fiction: Anxiety Fantasies

Brian Aldiss coined the term "cosy catastrophe" (Aldiss 1973: 293-294) to refer to the British postwar disaster novel epitomised by John Wyndham's *The Day of the Triffids* (1951). The problem with the term is that too many of the books it is supposed to refer to, including Wyndham's, are far too ambiguous to warrant the generalisation. Even Aldiss uses the term as a kind of imaginary bench mark from which the magnitude of deviation can be measured. Thus he describes John Christopher as "semi-cosy" (Aldiss 1973: 295) and Priest's *Fugue for a Darkening Island* as "far from being a cosy catastrophe" (Aldiss and Wingrove 1986: 376) – and Andy Sawyer discusses the issue in his chapter in this volume. *Fugue for a Darkening Island* was Priest's second novel, in which a suburban family disintegrates amidst the savage civil war triggered by the arrival of two million African boat people in England (see Hubble 2005a). However, its predecessor *Indoctrinaire* had also incorporated elements of the disaster genre. Specifically, the Third World War breaks out in July 1979 (*I* 2: 15: 140-141), with England being destroyed by nuclear weapons on 22 August 1979 – a fate which the hero, Elias Wentik, deliberately chooses to share.

The distance travelled across the genre from the imaginary Wyndhamesque template can be illustrated by examining some different representations of the stock moment of the hero awakening in a hospital bed: Wyndham's Bill Mason peels off his bandages to find himself sighted and sane in a blind and insane world, before venturing out manfully; J. G. Ballard's Donald Maitland, in *The Wind from Nowhere* (1962), hallucinates himself as blind and in hospital and then realises that he is in fact sighted and sane and not in hospital; Priest's Wentik comes round to find himself two hundred years in the future in Brazil and has sex with the nurse. Of course, it is this wish-fulfilment fantasy that Wentik ultimately rejects by deciding to go back and die with England. The logic behind this is that to live in the cosy future would be to accept the destruction of his family and the "whole set of memories and impressions and images" which made up his identity (*I* 3: 21: 195) and, therefore, it would be "to condone the removal of a part of himself": exactly that condition of separation which haunts Priest's oeuvre. But this is "just one half of a two part problem" – the other being whether Wentik can choose to believe that his world is still going on regardless of the fact that he has been told otherwise: "To have a belief indoctrinated externally is one thing, but can a person indoctrinate himself by simply *wishing* to believe something?" (*I* 3: 21: 195) This is the central question of the book – hence the title – and it is also one that runs throughout Priest's subsequent work. Here, the answer is firmly in the negative and a position which we know is endorsed, albeit in a modified form, in his later fiction is identified squarely with Jexon, the principal character of the future society: "the man was a meritocrat-advocate, interpreter and delineator of a society he had abstracted himself" (*I* 3: 25: 219). Against this, Wentik's "main pre-occupation was to get back to what he knew as a normal life" (*I* 1: 11: 100). The qualification "what he knew as" merely serves to indicate the limits of an epistemological framework which is still determined in the last instance by rationality. Within the confines of such a framework, the only means of avoiding the alienated condition of separation is through death. Priest's early fiction is characterised by uncosy resolutions to epistemological impasses, thanks to its rejection of wish-fulfilment.

While this confirms our dissatisfaction with the "cosy catastrophe" paradigm, it does fit with Aldiss's alternative and less well-known designation of the disaster subgenre as "anxiety fantasies" (Aldiss 1973: 295). This phrase contains a very fruitful ambiguity. If we think of fantasies as being analogous to dreams, it is possible to take anxiety fantasies as either fantasies that fulfil wishes (such as the cosier kind of catastrophe) or fantasies that master the unconscious to a different end by drawing on psychical resources preceding the establishment of the pleasure principle (see Freud 1984b: 303-305). While both strands are often in evidence, it is clear that the sub-genre as a whole follows the Freudian model of "repeating and working through": with the breakdown of the reality principle, compulsion resurfaces and eventually sufficiently masters chaos to the point that a new reality principle forms, as in *The Day of the Triffids* for example.

In Priest's work, this compulsion is perhaps most clearly present in the symbolically named Helward Mann, the hero of *Inverted World*, in which a city has to be kept moving relentlessly across hostile terrain by a continuous process of laying down and taking up huge rails, supervised by "guilds". This starts like a classic coming-of-age story in which the young apprentice masters a number of setbacks through sheer doggedness and thus proves himself to his guild superiors as sufficiently driven and determined to be accepted as an equal. However, confounding our expectations, he remains true to this code even when it becomes obvious to everyone else in the city that there is no need for it to keep on moving, which has in any case become no longer possible. Ironically – considering this subversion of a classic plotline – the novel has been described as "pure" (Clute and Nicholls 1993: 960), or even "first-rate hard" (Aldiss and Wingrove 1986: 337), science fiction. This is to miss the point that although the counter-intuitive physics, in which an infinite world resides within a finite universe, is brilliantly realised, the sf is neither predominantly pure nor hard but distinctively metaphorical and psychological. The subtext of the physical inversion of planet Earth – the origin of the expeditionary forces from which the inhabitants of *Inverted World* are apparently descended – is a political inversion of colonialism. Whereas on Earth, civilisation depended on a system of economic inequality which allowed the rich and powerful to monopolise commodities, in the novel it is a surplus of food, fuel and raw materials which allows the civilised mobile city to exploit "native" manpower: "the process was inverted, but the product was the same" (*IW* 3: 4: 168). The apparent physics of the world, in which the city must keep moving because otherwise a perpetual southward drift will move it so far from "the optimum" that it will be subject to spatial and temporal distortion, naturalises the compulsive drive behind civilisation and colonialism. This analogy is particularly cleverly brought out through the final initiation rite undertaken by aspiring guildsmen: they must escort "native" women back "down past" to their home villages after the spells they have spent in the city for breeding purposes. The unspoken element of the initiation rite – and therefore of becoming a man – is the sexual exploitation of the women, which is portrayed as a natural outcome of the physical distortions encountered, as they spontaneously burst from their clothes: "Rosario split the seat of her trousers. One of Lucia's buttons popped off [...] and Caterina tore the fabric of her shirt down both seams below her armpits" (*IW* 2: 6: 131). More specifically, the book can be read as a metaphorical portrayal of postwar Britain. The guilds are the public-school establishment, driven by their ideal of service; the armed attacks on the city carried out by the native "tooks" represent the various independence movements across the Empire, filtered through the imagery of Vietnam; and the internal dissident movement of "terminators", who want to stop the city, are the 1968 generation.

What Mann resents most is the way that the combination of external and internal attacks lead to a loss of self-belief: "Now the tracks were being built in spite of the situation with the tooks, rather than in the way I now understand the motivation of the city to be derived, from an internal need to survive in strange environment" (*IW* 3: 2: 161). Therefore, Mann's position can be seen as one that privileges inner compulsion over the external demands of "reality". The famous twist in the novel serves to make this clear. It transpires that the city is in fact on Earth, having been founded by a British particle physicist and set on a course starting in China some two hundred years previously, following a "natural window of potential energy" across the surface of the Earth which serves to power an artificial energy field around the city. However, we also learn that this "translateration generator" has the side-effects of altering perception and creating genetic defects. When these facts become known, the people of the city turn off the generator and allow their perceptions to revert back to the reality principle. Ontological uncertainty seems to be resolved back into an epistemological framework with only one problem: Helward Mann. He alone refuses this alternative and instead dives off the unfinished bridge, which the city guilds have been trying to build across the Atlantic. As with the ending of *Indoctrinaire*, the logic is that destruction is preferable to the state of separation (from all previous impressions, memories and identity) which would follow from having to accept a different "reality". However, there is one final twist in the last sentence: "As darkness fell I swam back through the surf to the beach" (*IW* 5: 4: 255). Although ambiguous, this is a more upbeat ending than those of the previous two novels and suggests that the choice confronting Mann is not simply that of old and new realities. Indeed, there is an alternative: the time Mann spends "up future" where the temporal distortion means that "a day spent lazily on the bank of a river wasted only a few minutes of the city's time" (*IW* 3: 9: 195). The attainment of this "terrain where time could almost standstill" is only achieved by the partial separation of being distanced from the "reality" of the city, without switching to the alternative "reality" of twenty-second century Earth, which would entail an irrevocable separation. This rather fragile possibility suggests a future beyond the "better an end in horror than horror without end" closing of *Indoctrinaire*.

The narrative device of the time loop, which features in various forms in all of Priest's early novels, is the great contribution of genre sf to the problem of how the complex potentiality of utopia can be represented. Priest's greatest success with this approach is *A Dream of Wessex*. Julia Stretton's desperation to escape the terrorism, police road blocks and traffic congestion which characterise the disintegrating Britain of the 1970s, motivates her participation in a collective projection of a future soviet Wessex. Here, she is caught between the fascinations of two compulsively driven males, David Harkman and Paul Mason, who represent alternative rejections of the reality principle. The complex resolution to the novel is achieved by a sophisticated time loop in which the participants of the future projection are talked into projecting themselves further into the future by Paul. Most of them return to the 1977 starting point, but Paul disappears into some future reality of his own while David remains in the projection, where Julia manages to rejoin him in an undeniably happy ending. The closing descriptions of David surfing through the drowned valleys of England are quite explicit in their demonstration of his achievement as a psychological one, as he experiences a sudden lapse:

> Beneath him, the wave, the cliffs and the sea had vanished. He was floating above countryside [...] There was a road down there, and he could see a line of traffic moving along it [...]. He felt he was about to fall, and he thrashed his arms and legs as if this would save him [...]. At once his motion ceased, and he was suspended again in the air, although noticeably lower than before. Now he could hear the traffic on the road [...] Harkman wished himself higher [...] and at once he felt the pressure of the wind on his back, and he soared upwards. When he had attained his former height, he made himself turn around again [...]

What he saw had no meaning for him: it was the product of some unconscious wish that he could not control [...]. It was something that had excluded him, something that he had in turn rejected. [...] Because it was from the unconscious past, unremembered, it was at once wholly intimate and voluntarily relinquished. It was the landscape of his dreams, a world that was not real, could not ever become real.

As once before, when he had unconsciously rejected this phantasm from his life, Harkman exercised a conscious option, and expelled the dream (*DW* 29: 197).

Therefore, rather than David and Julia's escape being a wish-fulfilment fantasy, it is "reality" that is shown to be the wish-fulfilment fantasy, as the limits of the epistemological are transcended in a fully ontological world and the stable projection of a utopian future becomes possible for the first time in Priest's fiction.

Ontologically Orientated Science Fiction: Writing Against "Reality"

Despite its utopianism, *A Dream of Wessex* remains ambiguous in one crucial respect: the narrative ends with Paul remaining in some future "reality" of his own. While the novel rejects this future on moral grounds as being characterised by monomania and insecurity, it cannot deny it the same ontological possibilities as the preferred alternative. The net effect was a prescient demonstration that postwar Britain could break down in two ways. History dictated that rather than utopianism, it was to be the ontological possibilities represented by Paul that prevailed as the basis for the Thatcherite "reality" of the 1980s – the background of Priest's next three novels. In the third of these, *The Quiet Woman*, the surveillance cameraman Gordon Sinclair's self-serving narration works brilliantly to map out the social-psychological history of the 1960s, 1970s and 1980s in terms of its ontological underpinnings:

I found in advertising the medium I had been seeking: the kind of campaigns I was best at created a fantasy world from elements of reality, heightened the fantasy to induce uncertainty and discontent in the audience, then satisfied those negative feelings with the advertised product.

Advertising used all the techniques I had discovered [...] It narrowed the frame, it filtered out the confusions of context, it selected clear targets, it emphasized its message with telling images, it rearranged reality to heighten reality.

But advertising turned out to be yet another transition. I did not find an outlet for my real skills until, in the early seventies, I formed my own small information management company. With this I finally discovered what I had been aiming towards all my life, and as the company grew and our influence spread, I receded to the heart of it, absorbed in what I was doing, narrowing the frame, removing from context, heightening the fantasy, and in doing so fabricating a new reality (QW 24: 167).

Thus, the anxiety fantasies of postwar Britain were first heightened and altered by consumerism and advertising during the 1960s, before undergoing the onto-logical transition into the postmodern world of "reality" fabrication. However, there was nothing neutral about the transition. While Sinclair's account dis-plays the Thatcherite mentality, the extract ultimately serves to acknowledge the uncanny horror of the 1980s: that they were enabled by those 1960s left and libertarian movements – including new wave sf – which broke with the "reality principle". The problem left at the end of *Wessex* was the need to square the circle: to break free from the wish-fulfilment of the "reality principle" with-out opening up the possibility of horror scenarios. What was needed was a ne-gation that was also an affirmation, as suggested by Priest's brilliant short story, "The Negation", in which there exists a book called *The Affirmation* (IS 111). This became inverted in the subsequent novel *The Affirmation*, in which there exists a book called *Renunciation* (A 7: 63). This paradox is contained within a time loop, which is now truly conterminous with the entire text – a fact recog-nised by Ian Watson's perceptive review claim that *The Affirmation* was its own sequel (Watson 1981: 83). The enabling background for this loop is no longer constructed from the stock components of genre sf as in Priest's earlier fiction, but represented as a consequence of the practice of writing, itself. In the words of the main protagonist, Peter Sinclair:

> I once thought that the emphatic nature of words ensured truth. If I could find the right words, then with the proper will I could by assertion write all that was true. I have since learned that words are only as valid as the mind that chooses them, so that of essence all prose is a form of deception. To choose too carefully is to become pedantic, closing the imagination to wider visions, yet to err the other way is to invite anarchy into one's mind (A 1: 1).

This balance is at best delicate in *The Affirmation* as the dichotomy between "inner life" and "external reality" becomes equated with the manuscript writ-ten by Peter in England about "The Dream Archipelago" and the manuscript written by Peter in the Dream Archipelago about "England". The apparent revelation that the manuscript written by Peter in England consists only of blank pages (A 22: 196) would seem to confirm the novel as critical of the effects of separation. However, the situation is more complex than this would allow, as can be seen from Peter's own realisation that his manuscripts can be read on three levels: the words written; the pencilled traces left by "Seri"; and the unwritten assumptions and omissions:

> In my words was the life I had lived before the treatment on Collago. In Seri's amendments was the life I had assumed, existing in quotes and faint pencil markings. In my omissions was the life I would return to.

Where the manuscript was blank, I had defined my future (A 23: 205).

These blank pages are at once the affirmation and the negation. They are the future, the way out of the oscillation between "end in horror and horror without end", which is at best only thwarted by a time loop; and, yet, at the same time, these blank pages are as difficult to look upon for the writer as the bottomless abyss. *The Affirmation* is Priest's breakthrough book, in which he escapes the circular limits of genre sf. This came at a cost, however, as he was later to acknowledge: "*The Affirmation* was to haunt me for years, and my writing was virtually immobilized for a half a decade afterwards" (Priest 1996).

The eventual successor was *The Glamour* (1984, 1985, 1996), which has probably succeeded in achieving a cult status and word-of-mouth reputation in excess of all his other work to date. As previously mentioned, the "glamour" itself is a form of invisibility and the main protagonist, Niall, is so glamorous that it is only in retrospect that we realise that he was in fact the main protagonist. This has led to one critic labelling Niall as the villain and the direct link between Paul Mason and Gordon Sinclair (Kincaid 1991: 53-54, 56) but it is the documentary cameraman, Richard Grey, who more clearly fits these criteria. By framing reality through his viewfinder, he clearly anticipates Gordon. The relationship between Richard and Niall explores the divergent possibilities of ontological freedom. Richard objectifies and makes real 1980s "reality", while Niall attempts to escape. As the introductory pages, which we subsequently realise to be written by Niall, admit, he is an infantile character but it is his refusal to grow up which frees him from the reality principle. He has the double-edged freedom of Peter Sinclair, but, unlike Peter, he not only becomes conscious of this through the practice of writing but also gains control over the process, enabling him to conclude to Richard: "We both threaten each other, you with your blundering ability to cause pain, I with my freedom to manipulate you. But now I am in control and you can stay as you are" (G85 6: viii: 210).

This assumption of control is not sinister but an acceptance of responsibility. This reading becomes much clearer in the revised edition of 1996, where Niall's "I am back in control, if only for a while" (G96 6: 10: 321) is less harsh sounding and his reference to Richard's "disconcerting, cameraman's gaze" (G96 6: 9: 320) is more specific than the merely "disconcerting gaze" of the 1985 version (G85 6: viii: 210). Furthermore, the distracting idea of Richard's independent reality sits awkwardly in the original – in Niall's phrases such as "Your real life does not concern me" (G85 6: ix: 211) and "You are real enough in your own life, but when you impinged on mine I took you and used you" (G85 6: ix: 212) – implying a sense of authenticity lingering in the "objective reality" with which Richard as a documentary cameraman is associated. When these phrases are removed – as they are in the 1996 revised edition – Niall's conclusion gains a fruitful ambiguity: "The urge to rewrite ourselves as real-seeming fictions is present in us all. In the glamour of our wishes we hope that our real selves will not be visible" (G96 6: 11: 324). This is a recognition of the "reality principle" as a fiction supported by a complementary process of wish-fulfilment and repression. The great irony of the book is that the only character prepared to let his full self be visible is Niall, the most outwardly invisible. Alone among the glams, Niall relishes his identity and is fit, handsome, clean and well-groomed. By not hiding his drives, he does not need to construct a false reality, far less drag others into it. Paradoxically, of course, he is forced to write a counter-reality in order to negate Grey's reality and affirm himself. Thus the book can be seen as a reworking of the themes of *The Affirmation*, but one in which Niall leaps the abyss of the blank page by writing his future. He is even generous enough to allow Richard a form of closure by returning him to the reality principle rather than leaving him in ontological limbo: "You will forget, induce a negative hallucination. You are no stranger to doing that, because for you forgetting is a way of failing to see" (G96 6: 11: 325). There is an edge to this of course in that it can also be seen as an address to the reader – those who simply demand wish-fulfilling entertainment are being treated with contempt: like Niall, Priest is "glamorous".

This hard-edged side of "the glamour" can be seen in Niall's relationship to Sue, which seems overbearingly possessive until it is realised that from the perspective of Priest's fiction, Sue's desire to leave the world of the glams and become "normal" like Richard is profoundly pathological. This association of female characters with everyday life is a running theme of Priest's fiction. While this association is simply treated as straightforward in the early books – in what can be seen as misogynist representations – by *A Dream of Wessex*, Julia is able to free herself from the grimy roadside cafés and terrorism by projecting and Sue is always able to escape everydayness because she is glamorous. *The Quiet Woman* begins with the old association once again intact as Alice hurries in from the rain, loaded down with shopping, running to answer the phone while desperate for the loo. Here, though, this very mundane everyday existence is explicitly associated with the stalled time aspect of her existence that sees her find the Wiltshire cottage she buys "as a consolation prize for the mess she had made of her life, a symbol of starting again [...] simply [become a] home, a symbol of neither past nor future" (QW 2: 8). Stranded in this manner, she is potentially prey to Gordon's mastery of fabricated reality – much as Julia was potentially prey to Paul Mason – and the book, through its multi-layered narrative, shows what the consequences of her allowing herself to be "written" by Gordon would be, even as it shows Gordon himself to be a reaction to having been "written" by his mother. However, Alice, unlike the earlier female protagonists of Priest's novels, is herself a writer and it is her achievement of being able to write herself – variously by reclaiming her impounded manuscript and writing an anonymous letter to the police accusing Gordon of murdering his mother – that presciently demonstrates, in a book published in 1990, the route out of the Thatcherite 1980s by using the ontological possibilities that enabled that particular "reality" against it.

Slipstream Fiction: Performance and Prestige

As we have seen, Priest was no longer generating these ontological possibilities structurally through the codes and conventions of genre sf, but poststructurally through the properties of language itself. Following J. L. Austin's work on performatives (Austin 1980) – acts of speech which make things happen in the world such as marriage vows and declarations of war – it is now generally accepted that no form of narrative can be neutral, that the act of narration changes the world by making things happen that otherwise would not. This is the source of the unease poststructuralists and postmodernists have with "grand narratives" or "metanarratives". Yet there are also positive contemporary responses to performativity such as Judith Butler's liberating work on gender as a form of identity that comes into being through performance rather than having anything to do with biological sex (Butler 1989, 1993). Priest's fiction should be seen as a contribution somewhere along this positive side of the spectrum as he shows the struggles of his characters to write themselves as beings in their own worlds rather than let themselves be written as things in someone else's. His most reflective work on this, and a novel that registers a significant development from the three books of the Thatcher years, is *The Prestige*. Here, it is the direct comparison between writing and stage magic, as noted at the beginning of this essay, which allows him to highlight the performativity of writing. A different section of the passage quoted in the introduction to this chapter serves to bear this out: "Already, without once writing a falsehood, I have started the deception that is my life. The lie is contained in these words, even in the very first of them. It is the fabric of everything that follows, yet nowhere will it be apparent" (P 2: 1: 38). The "very first of these words" are "I write in the year 1901" (P 2: 1: 35). In the context of the novel, this is a deception because Borden is one of a pair of identical twins who share the personal pronoun between themselves without distinction. Yet, in a more general sense, the personal pronoun is always a "grammatical fiction": performing a unity of subject that would not exist without it.

The fact that Borden is two identical people is the secret behind his most celebrated illusion, "The New Transported Man" and it is a secret which his rival Danton cannot work out. But this is simply another misdirection which lures us away from the real difference between the two, just as Danton's obsession with the hidden workings of tricks blinds him to Borden's understanding that "the wonder of magic lies not in the technical secret, but in the skill with which it is performed" (P 2: 6: 72). At one point in the book, Borden describes an illusion as consisting of three stages: the setup, the performance and the prestige. This latter is "the product of magic. If a rabbit is pulled from a hat, the rabbit, which apparently did not exist before the trick was performed, can be said to be the prestige of that trick" (P 2: 7: 73). While audiences, critics, fellow magicians and, especially, Danton are focused on the first two stages of "The New Transported Man", Borden simply states "for me, the performer, the prestige is the main preoccupation" (P 2: 7: 73). In other words, what is important to Borden and, by implication, to Priest as a writer, are the things that happen in the world as a result of performance. It is exactly these ontological possibilities that remain hidden from Danton in his blind epistemological desire to explain the unexplainable.

Of course, it is this stance so typical of genre science fiction which leads to Danton making a conceptual breakthrough in alliance with the electrical experimenter Nikola Tesla, as they discover a way of first projecting matter and, then, a human being through space. Danton happily employs this discovery in his stage act, allowing him to replicate Borden's transportation trick. The only drawback is that each time Danton performs the illusion, a prestige is produced: an unmoving, undecaying doppelgänger of Danton himself. This process suggests the Freudian notion of achieving ego development by adhering to the reality principle and rejecting the infantile narcissistic self (Freud 1984a), any reminder of which (via reflections, echoes, automata etc) will be likely to trigger an uncanny feeling in the subject (Freud 1990). Indeed, this is what happens to Danton as every time he creates a new reality, he simultaneously confirms his state of separation. For it is Danton's secret that he is actually Rupert Angier, The Earl of Colderdale: the aristocratic title signifying the sovereignty of the Self represented in the text by Danton.

It can be seen clearly how *The Prestige* displays the two qualities Priest ascribes to slipstream fiction: an obsession with thinking the unthinkable or doing the undoable and a different way of inquiring into the familiar. The Self is revealed as uncanny and reality is shown to be an illusion. Of course, slipstream would be merely another descriptive category, about as useful and satisfactory as "postmodernist fiction", if it were not for its political subtexts. A clue to the political subtext of *The Prestige* is provided by the name of the "contract worker" who initially introduces Borden to the performance of magic, "Robert Noonan". This is the real name of one of Priest's predecessors as a Hastings-based writer, Robert Tressell, author of the socialist classic *The Ragged Trousered Philanthropists*. In Tressell's novel, the socialist hero, Frank Owen, demonstrates to his workmates "The Great Money Trick" whereby the exchange of money enables the capitalist class to enrich themselves by extracting productive labour from the working class (Tressell 1965: 209-214). Translated into more theoretical terms, Tressell illustrates how money and the exchange process in general enables the prices resulting from a system of social relations (capitalism) to appear as the attributes of the things being sold thus obscuring the unjust and oppressive nature of those social relations. Amusingly, if somewhat heretically, the fictional Noonan is shown as fleecing his fellow workers at "Three Card Monte" every lunchtime (*P* 2: 2: 44-46), but this should not be allowed to misdirect us from the serious criticism of the capitalist exchange process provided by Priest. At one level, the Tesla machine represents exactly this exchange process and it is significant that every time Danton goes through the machine he takes five gold sovereigns through in his pocket and thus duplicates his money as well as himself. Therefore, the text can be seen to link separation with capitalism. In this context, it is fitting that the fictional Noonan is depicted as a trickster rather than a noble hero because the type of socialist politics he is intended to introduce to us, as well as to the "Borden" of the book, is not the traditional standpoint of opposing use-value to exchange-value that characterises Tressell's work, but a mode of practice that eschews any reduction to essence and, hence, the inevitability of being reinserted into the capitalist exchange process:

> One day, his painting work completed, Noonan left the yard and went out of my life. I never saw him again. He left behind him an impressionable adolescent boy with a compulsion. I intended to rest at nothing until I had mastered the art that I now knew (from a book I urgently borrowed from the lending library) was called Legerdemain (*P* 2: 2: 46).

This compulsion is none other than the compulsion to remember, repeat and work-through that allows the acting out of fantasy as "real life": a practice as central to the work of the stage illusionist as to the psychoanalyst. Such a practice, despite being beset with potential pitfalls, is shown by Priest's work to be the only means of combatting alienation in the modern world.

Conclusion: Beyond the Slipstream

As Priest has written, slipstream is about attitude (Priest 2003a). This attitude has been described by Bruce Sterling as one of "peculiar aggression against 'reality'" and its tendency is to "sarcastically tear at the structure of 'everyday life'" (Sterling). This attitude is seen at its clearest in *The Extremes*, where Priest's repetitive strain comes fully into its own. Here, Teresa Simons takes leave from the FBI and returns to her native Britain in order to investigate a Hungerford-style shooting in the south coast town of Bulverton, which occurred on the same day as her husband – also an FBI operative – was shot in Texas. Rapidly enmeshed in a shifting web of virtual-reality scenarios run by the Extreme Experiences Corporation, she comes to suspect that a leakage between virtuality and reality has brought about the two incidents on the same day and led to her husband's death. But by her own involvement in the scenarios she, herself, becomes fatally complicit in the process when she finds herself teaching the perpetrator of both massacres, Gerald Grove, how to shoot. This genre plot allows Priest to weave together a complex social fabric as Teresa initially tries to reconcile her American sense of featureless space with the British experience of "concentrated time": "history reaching behind her, the future extending before her, meeting at this moment of the present" (E 1: 9). However, her attempts meet with frustration as it becomes obvious that Bulverton, imprisoned by economic decline and benefits culture, has become stagnant: "it was just a dull, tired, unhappy seaside town, full of the wrong memories and with no conception of the future" (E 19: 190-191). It is this stasis in which people simply drift with no sense of purpose that Priest equates with social reality. Ironically, considering Priest's earliest fiction, this condition is depicted as analogous to that of being caught in a time loop. It is significant that when Teresa finds herself projected back into the past she rejects the explanation of time-travel and concludes that "linearity", or causality, has been given "a third dimension, made matrical" (E 36: 355). Thus, her response is neither passive acquiescence nor despair but the active construction of "the remainder of her life" (E 37: 376). With her hard-gained knowledge from FBI training that "interdiction scenarios were mastered only by repeated attempts to get them right" (E 37: 368), she repeatedly enters the scenarios again and again until Grove misses both times, allowing her to rescue her husband and transport him to an airliner soaring endlessly above Finland.

The psychological logic behind this repeating and working-through is explained by the objectionable Ken Mitchell, an executive with Extreme Experiences, who is concerned at all costs to protect the "linearity" of the Bulverton massacre so that it can be turned into a perfect virtual scenario for public consumption. A scenario must always have an edge where its "reality" ends because memory runs out, yet, as Mitchell warns Teresa, repeated interdiction scenarios introduce neural crossover because "successive experiences of the scenario alter your perception next time you go in" so that ultimately "linearity fades like yesterday" (E 23: 231-233). This is consistent with Freud's idea that memory-traces are left behind by unconscious processes and that, therefore, "consciousness arises instead of a memory-trace" (Freud 1984b: 296-297). Specifically, the possibility of dealing freely with stimuli depends on the existence of "freely mobile processes which press towards discharge" (Freud 1984b: 306) and these lines of cathexis (or neural crossover) can only be generated by repetition. Of course, as already discussed, we know that Freud considered these processes as infantile and only as a developmental stage on the way to a mature adherence to the pleasure and reality principles. However, Priest's point is that because memory is only linear while consciousness is multidirectional, it is possible for a fully conscious being to be able to transcend the linear limits of so-called social reality out of choice rather than simply as a temporary defence to trauma. For similar reasons, Walter Benjamin once wrote that "the production of a proper consciousness is the primary task of Marxism" (Benjamin 1998: 110).

In Freud's essay "Observations on Transference-Love", he argues that analysts should not sleep with their patients, because the love generated between the patient and analyst through induced repetition in the analytic process is something that must be treated as unreal because it "is entirely composed of repetitions and copies of earlier reactions, including infantile ones" (Freud 1958b: 166-167). This is advice that has sometimes been directed metaphorically at writers with respect to their characters and could easily be applied to readers as well. Regardless of these further crossovers, there is a case for arguing that the resolution to *The Extremes* is similarly unreal, not to say infantile, because Teresa and Andy are having sex across the seats of the airliner in what we know to be a virtual scenario that Teresa has earlier heard about from the porn actress "Shandy": "I play an air hostess on an aircraft, and me and the guy get down to it in a row of seats. Not very comfortable, but we put the arm-rests up" (*E* 27: 275). Yet, Freud's position is problematic because it cannot be both that repetition is unreal with respect to love and that the analytic process allows repressions to be worked through as "a piece of real life". In fact, he was forced to concede that every state of being in love reproduces infantile prototypes and that love was in fact pathological (Freud 1958b: 168). This renders his attempts to distinguish between "normal love" and "transference-love" unconvincing and calls into question any Freudian distinction between "real" and "unreal" situations. The obvious conclusion from this is that the analytic method could not and cannot ever reconcile patients with reality, it can only induce them to "act out", or perform, "realities" for themselves in the hope that they will eventually hit upon one that will allow them to successfully reintegrate with the "reality principle" governing society. It is exactly this endpoint that Priest's fiction has consistently sought to expose and reject. As we have seen, repetition is not just a theme but a practice he has developed towards achieving this aim and it is also a practice that we as readers need to develop. Freud pointed out that "it is hardly possible to persuade an adult who has very much enjoyed reading a book to re-read it immediately" (Freud 1984b: 307) and yet that is what Priest demands as it is only by repeated readings that the required neural crossovers can be developed that enable a full consciousness of his work. The postmodern celebration of virtuality and pornutopia that closes *The Extremes* is not a wish-fulfilment fantasy but the conclusion of that other type of anxiety fantasy in which the purpose of the repetition work is to master reality rather than seek accommodation with it and thus soar "out to the extremes where all memory ends and life begins anew" (*E* 38: 393).

Christopher Priest's Fractal *Fugue for a Darkening Island*

Andy Sawyer

"All prose is a form of deception". Although Christopher Priest is known for the games he plays with narrative, these are normally games played with language rather than structure. He misleads without failing to play perfectly square: the sleight of hand of a magician, as we find in *The Prestige* (1995) in which the solution to the complex layering of identities which is part of the novel can be found in a statement quite early in the book which means exactly what it says but which depends upon a fundamental but erroneous assumption hidden in an illusionist's explanation. Just as a stage conjuror misdirects his audience by stating the truth and withholding vital information, so a writer can be transparently honest and devious. And therefore "all prose," says Sinclair in *The Affirmation* (1981) "is a form of deception" (A 1: 1). *The Affirmation* itself suggests that this holds even (especially?) for autobiography. By the end of the novel it is difficult if not impossible to affirm (the choice of verb is deliberate) which is the "real" Sinclair, that of twentieth-century London or the Dream Archipelago, for both are fictional characters in this novel by a writer who is resolutely aware that he is manipulating the perceptions of a reader.

It is easy enough to talk the language of metafictions and postmodern dissociation in describing the way Priest's novels are so frequently novels of textual instability, of *trompe l'œil* effects, doublings and redoublings. Whether it is the difference between what we think we see the stage conjuror doing and what he actually does, a collective dream and the reality of the dreamers' world, the claims of the autobiographer for the facts of his life, or the possibilities of alternate histories inherent in the personalities of two twins, we are often unable to consider where, in a Priest novel, a baseline reality lies. But such complexities lie in the language of the storyteller rather than experiments with form. *Fugue for a Darkening Island* (1972), Priest's second novel, is his most "experimental" work, but it involves dislocation of narrative rather than shades of language. To return to Sinclair, "It seemed to me important that I should try to impose some sort of order on my memories", but *Fugue* weaves in and out of order. A fugue is, of course, a musical composition in which themes are stated, developed, and contrasted harmonically and contrapuntally. It is also a mental state, described in the *Collins New English Dictionary* as "an interval of flight from reality during which the individual assumes a personality and performs actions which are forgotten upon the return to normal consciousness." And "fugue", as Nicholas Ruddick points out, comes from the same root-word as "refugee", a term which applies both to the central character of the novel and his antagonists (Ruddick 1989: 15).

Fugue is also Priest's most controversial work. As well as the dislocations it applies to conventional narrative, its subject-matter is one which can easily be misread. The "Darkening Island" is of course Britain, and the most obvious surface-meaning of "Darkening" is the influx of African immigrants fleeing from a continent ravaged by war. It is possible to consider *Fugue* as a not-so-cosy-catastrophe variant which plays upon contemporary British fears of immigration from the West Indies and the Asian sub-continent, and the narrator's name (Whitman) is symbolic enough. But Whitman, who refers to the colour of his skin in the first sentence of the novel, is rather too ambivalent a personality to stand as identification-figure for a gung-ho racist readership. As Nicholas Ruddick implies (1989: 50) and as Paul Kincaid points out elsewhere in this volume, the first two paragraphs both present the narrator as the story opens and closes (the second paragraph is the thematic – though not "actual" – closing paragraph of the story: the rest of the text is how that position is attained) and establish that this is no coherent and reliable narrator. The shattered political climate and the shattered identity of the narrator are represented by the shattered narrative structure.

Pieced together from an a-chronological sequence of sections – ranging from a few lines to several paragraphs – the novel tells the story of Alan Whitman, a college lecturer in a near-future Britain where a right-wing government with racist leanings is in conflict with refugees from an Africa which has been devastated by a nuclear war. It is assumed, although not stated, that "Africa" is the sub-Saharan continent, and that at least one of "the two main powers" has been illegally supplying nuclear arms to African countries. The immigrants land throughout Europe, the Middle East, and America, but in Britain, because of the nature of the government, the problem is much greater. Whitman's marriage is failing, and he has had several affairs. Following the closure of the college, Whitman is forced to take a more menial job in a cloth factory. When the African immigrants (or Afrims) begin commandeering houses near their neighbourhood in London, Whitman, his wife Isobel and their daughter Sally flee from their home, intending to make for Bristol, where Isobel's parents live. They are forced to abandon car and possessions, and Whitman persuades his wife to continue to Bristol while he and Sally return to London. This proves more difficult that he imagined, in the context of what is in effect a civil war. Whitman and Sally join a group led by a man named Lateef, whom Whitman had come across once before, scavenging in a ruined village. Isobel has also taken refuge with this group but the reunion is only temporary – the women of the group are kidnapped by an Afrim detachment. Wandering with Lateef's group, Whitman is involved in action against the Afrims, and the group gradually becomes armed. Lateef tries to persuade Whitman to join him in a guerrilla army to take back what they have lost but, but fearing the chaos that would ensue, Whitman leaves to look for Isobel and Sally, following rumours that the Afrims have placed kidnapped women in a series of brothels catering for their troops. Following an interlude in a barricaded seaside town where the façade of normality is kept up (the Africans have been "kicked out"; the *Daily Mail* is still published, but from Northern France, with no mention of the Civil War), Whitman finds the bodies of his wife and daughter on a beach covered with oil-slicks. He murders a young African, steals his rifle, and heads for the countryside.

There are a number of ways in which this scenario might be seen as a prescient forecast of current British anxieties over "asylum seekers" or the expansion of the European Union which will allegedly send immigrants from Eastern Europe westwards in search of jobs. Waves of economic migrants from Africa fleeing proxy wars between superpowers, or the collapse into warring factions of a major European country seem more rather than less likely. At times, *Fugue* could be a weird fusion between the *Daily Mail* and the New Wave. It is certainly one of Priest's bleakest narratives; one in which form mirrors content in a way which constantly sends the reader back to the text to re-examine hasty initial readings.

The fractured structure forces us to read the narrative as a number of themes-and-variations in the musical manner and Nicholas Ruddick (1989: 21) identifies three sequences. The first, chronologically, is Whitman's childhood and career to the Afrim invasion; the second is the abandonment of the Whitmans' home to the abduction of Isobel and Sally; and the third, the wanderings with Lateef to the finding of the bodies. As befits the fugal form, there are occasional overlaps, and towards the end several sections appear in consecutive form, giving the impression of a crescendo, while the first two paragraphs, showing Whitman at beginning and end of his metaphysical journey, act as thematic reference, giving Priest the opportunity to state his theme as the character of the narrator rather than simply the events leading from paragraph one to paragraph two. The form also, if one can still use the word with a straight face, deconstructs the Wyndhamesque English disaster novel in a number of interesting ways. Just as we are not necessarily to consider Wyndham's narrator as being the central character – Bill Nighy's slightly irritating but enormously perceptive rendition of the narrator of *The Midwich Cuckoos* as "nice but dim" in the 2003 BBC Radio Four dramatisation underlined this – so *Fugue* shows us the detached, almost autistic, nature of Whitman's psyche, a trait to which he frequently draws our attention. As a member of the liberal intellectual classes, Whitman joins a society at his college which "professed" (a significant word) to be sympathetic to the plight of the immigrants, but the right-wing government led by John Tregarth seems to encourage populist protest movements and liberalism seems to be impotent. Whitman can commit himself neither to the personal (his marriage) nor to the political. He smiles politely when listening to appallingly racist jokes of which, he tells us, he disapproves. He is angered by the abduction of his wife and daughter, yet he himself uses a brothel staffed by African women for the benefit of English men, and had already abandoned Isobel, suggesting that she travel on her own, through possibly hostile country, to Bristol. He shoots down an Afrim helicopter, and, following Lateef's refusal to help the injured pilot, is unable to kill the man quickly neither out of ideology nor mercy but simply because "the physical act of pulling the trigger [...] was too positive an act ... one in which my commitment would be affirmed" (FDI 109).

There are a number of other sub-themes, of which the most important is the way sexuality is mirrored with race. Priest avoids the stereotypical mapping of sexuality with racial Otherness except for one significant area, a kind of ground-note to the main theme. The earliest memory which Whitman gives us of his childhood is when he is hiding in a barn, afraid of the "bogey" his brother has teased him with which he has visualised as "some monstrous being with black skin". He comforts himself with a "fantasy involving airplanes and guns", and then sudden movement makes him think of the "bogey" again. When he plucks up courage to look out from his hidey-hole, he observes a couple having sex (FDI 31-32).

Much later in his life – but several pages earlier – Whitman has told us about visiting a film with Louise, a woman he is having an affair with. The film is a sexually frank account of a "violently-resolved" affair between "a coloured man and a white woman". John Tregarth's right-wing government has been in power for three months, and the political climate is souring. Before the film ends, the cinema is raided by police. Whitman is carrying no identification, but gives a false name and address which is vouched for by Louise. When they return to Louise's room, the stress has made him impotent (FDI 18-19). Later in the novel, we discover two items of apparently unrelated information from separate strands which, simply because of their juxtaposition on the same page, reinforce a thematic significance. Whitman recalls meeting Laura, another former lover, who is of mixed race, one of the first victims of the Afrim situation, killed in the second London riot. Here we have a definite fusion of Whitman's love-hate relationship with sex and race. This section is immediately followed (FDI 124) by Whitman and Sally's encounter with the group led by Lateef, whose name we have seen frequently and may have wondered about (it is of Arabic/Egyptian origin) but who is now more firmly identified with racial otherness: "Because of the events of the time, I had grown to distrust anyone with coloured skin, however faint it might be." A third repetition of this sex/race theme is the sequence at Augustine's brothel, also fused with violent imagery – beneath the blankets on which Whitman is copulating with an African woman is the rifle which he later steals.

Despite the importance of race in British political discourse, British science fiction has tended to avoid an overt engagement with the topic. There are plenty of British science-fiction novels and stories which implicitly deal with the loss of Empire, to the point where this has become something of a cliché when the nature of British sf is discussed, and "loss of Empire" certainly signifies the loss of what is euphemistically called the "New Commonwealth" countries – the countries of the Indian sub-continent, the West Indies, and Africa. But these countries themselves, and specifically the people from them, who made up a high proportion of immigrants into post-war Britain, seem curiously absent, even by implication, from science fiction. Where British science-fiction writers have specifically mentioned race, it is often from that particular branch of social liberalism which seeks to deny, or smooth over, racial tensions. When Arthur C. Clarke, for instance, introduces a Black character in *Childhood's End* (1953), his language reads bizarrely in the context of present-day race relations; "A century before, his colour would have been a tremendous, perhaps an overwhelming handicap. Today it meant nothing. The inevitable reaction that had given early twenty-first century negroes a slight sense of superiority had already passed away. The convenient word 'nigger' was no longer tabu in polite society, but was used without embarrassment by everyone. It had no more emotional content than such labels as republican or Methodist, conservative or liberal" (Clarke 1953: 78).

It is easy enough to pillory someone for using the "wrong" terminology, and the carefully-articulated "negro" (usually capitalised as "Negro") with which writers known to have liberal, even radically so, views on race depict individuals of African, Afro-Caribbean, or Afro-American origin does read oddly today. It's less the fact that some writers "get it wrong" (whatever "right" may be) and more that consideration of race and racism is avoided as a kind of polite English assumption that a clash of cultures will result in a happy compromise in which injustices will be righted, attitudes will be adjusted, and the ruling castes will not actually lose anything in the process. It is not for nothing that in this bland, aimless utopia (which Clarke, it must be pointed out, is critiquing rather than celebrating) "the guard still marched in front of Buckingham Palace" (Clarke 1953: 93).

There are certainly stories from the mid twentieth century in which immigrants/refugees are featured. In John Wyndham's "Time to Rest" an Earthman (naturally an Englishman, Bert Tasser), is part of the remnant population of a destroyed Earth who have taken refuge on Mars. Wyndham points out that the first Earthmen on Mars saw the inhabitants as decadent, effete "natives" "to be kicked about and exploited whenever convenient" (Wyndham 1949: 85). In this pastoral, elegiac story Tasser is like the Englishman in the Far East who has "gone native", never to return to his own country: the story ends with him about to marry a Martian girl. In John Christopher's underrated novel *The Long Winter* (1962 aka *The World in Winter*) an ice age has sent the population of Europe fleeing to Africa, reversing the rôles of the races. Andrew Leedon, kindly if patronisingly taking a young Nigerian student under his wing in the early pages of the novel, is rescued from destitution by him, and the rôles are reversed. Christopher satirises English colour prejudice, albeit too easily by means of the most unthinkingly racist attitudes of the novel, being placed in the mouth of a shiftless working-class character who has come to power by means of the catastrophe, and the Nigerians coping with an influx of European refugees come across remarkably sympathetically. At the same time there is an uneasy presentation of Leedon as sympathetic viewpoint character: one of the reasons I have described *The Long Winter* as "underrated" is that it seems to be an interesting transition between the traditional "disaster" novel which focuses upon the struggle for survival and the Ballardian revision of the same in which the character heads *towards* the disaster as a kind of affirmation (or renunciation?) of identity. Leedon seems to accept his fate as a refugee, even as a second-class citizen, in a new land, but chooses, in the end, his Englishness in an Arctic waste rather than a position as a "White Nigerian".

Both Ray Bradbury's "And the Rock Cried Out" (1953) and Thomas M. Disch's "Casablanca" (1967) have Americans stranded in Third World countries following a catastrophe at home, positioned against the "natives" they have patronised and implicitly if not explicitly exploited. The sensibility here is less British unease and guilt – coupled with nostalgia – about Empire, as it is about American awareness of racial condescension and exploitation and the shock of reversal. The reader is forced to confront the possibility that "it could happen to us" but the "it" happens through the catastrophe of war. John Christopher's rapid "ice age" is, like Maggie Gee's later *The Ice People* (1998), a way of exploring the socio-economic entropic states of the country and political climate the writer is living in. Bradbury and Disch's Central American or Moroccan characters are presented with the people who have exploited them so efficiently that they do not really know that they have exploited them. The tables are turned. Christopher's Africans are engaged – it is *their* problem too. Their responses are coloured by post-colonial resentment, but schadenfreude is a luxury they cannot afford. Priest takes a less openly ironic stance, showing us only by implication anything like a viewpoint from the immigrants. His scenario is neither reversal (for everyone is a refugee) nor simple shock-effect. By presenting immigration in the context of the very real fears and bigotry at the heart of British politics during the time Priest was culturally positioned to write the book, he laid himself open to criticism. As he points out in *Foundation 50*, reviewing Nicholas Ruddick's book about himself, a novel which in 1972 was praised in *Time Out* for its potential to cause "soul-searching and disquiet" was condemned as racially inflammatory seven years later by the same magazine (Priest 1990a: 96).

Fugue, however, remains less about racial conflict as such, nor even the "clash of civilisations" rhetoric which rose to the surface after 9/11, than the disintegration of the white liberal into complicity with fascism, but like the above-mentioned stories it considers the psychology of Western racial attitudes, extrapolating from the future implied by Enoch Powell's notorious "rivers of blood" speech of 1968 (which was aimed, however, at West Indians and Asians rather than immigrants from Africa). It does use themes dredged from European/African relations to examine, within the psychology of an individual, questions of race, sex, power, and loss. True, this is a dangerous combination which could lead to clichéd treatment, but a racial bigot would, one feels, write a considerably more passionate novel. Priest's cut-up technique/fugal approach effectively avoids this. The distance between protagonist and plot avoids the "make-your-flesh-creep" *Battle of Dorking* approach. In his novel of 1871, Chesney deliberately drew upon inchoate invasion anxieties to raise genuine fears of German invasion. In *The War of the Worlds* (1898), Wells both wrote within the "future war" tradition and extended it by playing upon the contrast between "cosy" Englishness and the Otherness it feared by using the estranging effect of "vast and cool and unsympathetic" (Wells 2003: 41) invading Martians. In *Fugue*, Priest uses a less science fictional, but equally estranging approach, from which we can pick up some unusual ideas.

First, we notice a number of things which Whitman refers to almost in passing. There is a significant support for the displaced Africans. The police force, army, and air force divide into "Nationalist" and "Secessionist" factions. Whitman refers to the "incident in Dorset" (*FDI* 54-55) in which two shiploads of refugees attempt to land in the face of confrontation by the army. Thousands of people confront the army, and the Africans succeed in landing. There is an international element, with American marines supporting the Nationalists and a United Nations peace-keeping force. "Much later", Whitman records during his account of his wanderings with Isobel and Sally he learns that during this time "there was a large-scale welfare scheme being initiated by the Red Cross and the United Nations, which was attempting to rehabilitate all those people like ourselves who had been dispossessed by the fighting" (*FDI* 57). Behind Whitman's description of events there is a world-wide dislocation of which we get only a distorted snapshot, but the overall structure of Priest's plot is not a mere "Us" versus "Them" scenario. Whitman, whether he likes it or not, is a refugee like the Afrims; none of them are in control of their destinies. The narrow focus on Whitman prevents us from seeing the full picture, which is perhaps paradoxically both more terrible and more hopeful than we can guess. There is chaos, but there is also order. Whitman's departure for the "countryside" may prefigure a descent into guerrilla warfare and warlordism after Lateef's model, but all around there are islands of relative stability – which, in many cases, like the barricaded *Daily Mail*-reading South Coast community we are unable to fully believe in.

There are also those thematic oscillations of outer and inner turmoil. Just as the sections describing the last meeting with Laura and the second meeting with Lateef fuse images of race, violence and sexuality and suggest Whitman's own crumbling façade of liberalism and commitment, so the section in which Whitman refers to the offstage United Nations Welfare Scheme (which becomes discredited because of its manipulation by all participating sides) segues into the crumbling façade of his marriage, which, like the nation-state, has become "nothing more than a social convenience" (FDI 57). The breakdown of law and order which has seen Whitman beaten up by a policeman and he and his family wandering aimlessly in the countryside reflects the breakdown of the microcosmic "social order" which is the family. The structure of *Fugue* comes to resemble the way fractal designs remain the same whether blown up or scaled down. Human groups and their psychologies are seen to have a fractal-like relationship. From the largest (the nation-state) to the smallest (the individual in the form of Whitman) with the family somewhere in between, all seem, in this novel, to be mirrored in the others; divided and alienated.

So *Fugue for a Darkening Island* offers us not just a microcosmic and macrocosmic view of events, but something more complex. The "darkening island" is both Britain itself – and that symbolic representation of it which is Whitman. But as with any Christopher Priest novel we need to look again at the form in which this interpretation is offered to us. *Fugue* is an early novel in his oeuvre, and although some commentators have called it a masterpiece it has been relatively neglected in other quarters – not least by the author himself, who described it in 1985 in almost dismissive terms in as "another abstract novel" in "Leave the Forgotten to the Night" (Priest 1985b: 10) and in a 1995 interview with David Langford in *Critical Wave* 43 calls it a "period piece […] the one novel of mine where one hostile review wiped out any cheerful thoughts I ever had about the book, and I haven't been able to look at it since" (Langford 1995).

In the same interview, he calls it "the first book of mine about someone who misremembers things", and in "Leave the Forgotten to the Night" he noted "with hindsight" that the title's key word "fugue", in its sense of "dreamlike altered state, associated with amnesia" can be related to this process of forgetting or misremembering, which he associates in personal terms with a childhood accident (Priest 1985b: 10, and see the discussion in the interview contained in this volume). Elsewhere, in reviewing Nicholas Ruddick's *Christopher Priest*, he refers to having reassembled the fragments of non-linear narrative which makes up *Fugue* and, rewriting some, also composed an extra "joker" piece that "fits *nowhere* into any of the various strands" (Priest 1990a: 96). In conversation with this writer, he claimed to have forgotten which piece this was.

It is not my intention to "identify" this particular section although I am sure that with the necessary detective work it can be done (and at the time this essay was written I believed that I had identified it). But I would like to consider for the remainder of this chapter the question of misremembering or misinterpreting, because I feel that it offers some clues to the nature of Whitman's "lack of commitment" and moral vacuity.

Where does Whitman "misremember"? Following a retreat under fire from a barricaded village, Whitman feels a strong sexual urge for his abducted wife, "tormented by false memories of happiness together" (*FDI* 77). In the second section of the story, which we may read as the closing paragraph echoing the first, Whitman tells us "When I last saw my wife, I was cursing her" (*FDI* 9). Yet the relevant section of the narrative, the account of the abduction of the women from Lateef's group, does not show Whitman addressing Isobel in any way (*FDI* 139). Technically, the "last time" Whitman "saw" his wife, of course, could be when he sees the corpses of the women on the beach (*FDI* 147), but there he is careful to note for us his *lack* of reaction.

These opening sections are, though, set out of time: the second section cannot really be the end of the novel. Whitman is still considering his daughter Sally in the present tense. But, looking elsewhere, it is possible to see how unspecific Whitman is. He has problems with detail. Noting the wreck of a convoy: "I counted only seven [vehicles], though afterwards I heard Lateef say that there had been twelve" (*FDI* 122). Almost immediately, his description only emphasises the ambiguity of the text, the way chaos has replaced order:

[I]n this undeclared civil war, the opposing forces rarely displayed colours and it was unusual to see any kind of vehicle bearing identification-marks. Logically, the trucks had been driven by Nationalist or Loyalist troops, as the helicopters had been shown to be piloted by the Afrims, but there was no way of telling this for certain. I thought the trucks looked as if they had been American, but neither of us was sure (*FDI* 112).

Both these instances seem secure examples of the kind of *in*security of the text. But there are others which are more problematic and which lead us into the dangers of possibly over-interpreting a story which, by its very structure, is calling us to consider complexes of parallels, oppositions, and echoes of word and image. When we take into account, for example, the heavily sexual nature of Whitman's reminiscences, we may begin to wonder whether his inability on several occasions to fire his rifle is linked to his readiness to use his less symbolic phallic weapon. Is this counterpoint, or is Whitman protesting too much about his wife's frigidity? (On at least one occasion, we have seen, he has been impotent with one of his string of mistresses: on several others, he has difficulty reaching orgasm.) When he describes his motorbike rides with Isobel, he tells us: "It was rare for me, when by myself, to open up the cycle and take it to its maximum speed, though when Isobel was on the back she encouraged me to do it often" (*FDI* 80-81). Immediately after this, comes the scene where Isobel takes the sexual initiative and appears to be encouraging Whitman to, in the words of the passage just quoted "do it". What follows is short of intercourse but is a sexual assault in which Isobel's clothing is torn: "[S]he pulled away from me. On this occasion I was not willing to stop" (*FDI* 81).

The fugal structure perhaps imposes parallels where they may not exist. Only on the third time of reading did I realise that the "Laura", the mixed-race ex-lover whom Whitman comes across in a restaurant in a park (*FDI* 122) and who is killed in a race riot, was not the "Louise" with whom Whitman, after they dine in a restaurant, watches a film about a relationship between two lovers of different races which ends violently (*FDI* 18). Ironically, this particular case of misremembering seems to resonate with the story, bringing to light the fact that generally Whitman's lovers are indistinguishable ciphers, and this is perhaps how he recalls them. Laura is an important character. She is the only one of Whitman's lovers for whom (he says) he feels anything apart from physical desire; he has come "back to the restaurant in the park" (implying its importance to him) for some reason he cannot articulate. Once again, he avoids his motives: his memory is conveniently "inconveniently blank" (*FDI* 122). It is Laura who notes Whitman's weakness. His love for her is tinged with emotional masochism. But the confusion of characters is more than confusing two similar characters with superficially similar names. The verbal, thematic and descriptive echoes in the two encounters seem to pull them together. The parallels between the passages are clearly meant.

The structure, however, allows us to examine our understanding of exactly what kind of metaphorical interplay is going on in the novel. It is easy to consider Whitman's lack of emotional or political commitment and his damaged, predatory sexuality and map one on the other to conclude that one "means" the other. This reductive reading, however, overlooks the fractal structure and undermines the novel's richness. When Isobel and Sally are reunited with Whitman in Lateef's group, Whitman considers that they should re-establish a sexual relationship but "I was incapable of making the first move" (*FDI* 129). On the next page, he describes how Lateef despises him because "I was so evidently incapable of committing myself to a firm political viewpoint"(*FDI* 130). Whitman's incapacity is that of a small man, rudderless against the prevailing moral currents. Politically, he is in favour of the Secessionists and their humanitarian stance towards the refugees. "It was not morally right to deny the African immigrants an identity or a voice" (*FDI* 143). But although he distrusts and dislikes the Tregarth administration, it "appealed to me on an instinctive level. It had been the Afrims who had directly deprived me of everything I once owned." It seems as though Whitman's lack of a personal moral centre has affected his stance towards the wider world. As Ruddick points out, "[o]ur last glimpse of Whitman is of a divided self" (Ruddick 1989: 20), a division which has only been exacerbated by his horrific experiences. His account of the insularity of the barricaded community he stays with during the last few pages of the novel is revelatory. Kindly, hospitable, his hosts the Jefferys have turned their backs on the outside world. The price of groceries is rising because "It's the times changing" (*FDI* 142). The civil war is talked of as if it were a thousand miles away. Explosions are heard, but never mentioned. To Whitman, this is "an artificial restoration of life in an abnormal state" (*FDI* 144), yet he, too, despite his self-awareness and understanding of the wider context remains uncommitted almost until the very last.

The last couple of pages of *Fugue* are full of a laconic sense of distraction, of deferral of choice. Whitman, having decided to search for Isobel and Sally, walks through empty suburbia. He meets small groups of Afrim soldiers, but is undisturbed. He picnics on supplies from the Jefferys, carefully washing out his flask to save it for future use. He is invited to join a group of refugees setting out for France. The same man offers to guide him to the Afrim brothel. He declines, but walks towards the location it has been indicated to be in. Several times he tries to approach the building, but is ordered away. Returning to the shore, he sits on the beach in silence, watching the receding tide. Out to sea is a large warship, but he is unable to identify its type or nationality. Attracted by a squad of Afrim soldiers, he discovers the seventeen tarred or painted bodies amongst which are those of Sally and Isobel. Only then, after going through a spectrum of apathy, sadness, terror and hatred, does he take a stand and, armed with a murdered soldier's rifle, head back to the countryside. But even then, it is clear that Whitman's final commitment is one of despair.

Whitman's progress is a flight through the various meanings of "fugue" to this bleak shoreline. The "darkening island" of Great Britain is becoming more and more unstable, trying to dissociate itself from the rest of the world, to *not think* about the horror which has taken place in Africa. The novel's greatest irony is its "potential realism". It is situated against the complex or developing tradition of the British disaster novel. Wells's Martians or Wyndham's invading triffids, however; John Christopher's death of grass, J. G. Ballard's drowned, burning or crystal worlds: Christopher Priest avoids all this. The only science-fictional element of the novel is its displacement into future time. Take away the device of the nuclear explosions which wreck Priest's Africa, and we are still left with the anxieties voiced by so many British politicians and opinion-formers – the "flood of refugees". There is irony too in that it was written when the famines which caused the orgy of sentimental altruism which was Band Aid, the genocidal massacres at which the West stood helpless, and the phenomenon of "failed states" were some way in the future – but these responses are themselves part of the imperialist disdain with which the West has so often viewed Africa and the client states on its borders. We cannot award Priest a prize for forecasting a future which looks more likely now than it did then, but we can point out the discomfort with which we see the evasions and complacencies of what we can only call the "British psyche" exposed in the shape of Whitman. All Whitman can do on the personal level is to follow the example of his country, and in the end the breakdowns of Whitman, his family and his country are the same story. Images of impotence, insularity and alienation shift and coalesce throughout the narrative, attaching to different levels as the story shifts between them.

While the fractured – or fractal – nature of Whitman's account mirrors the psychological and sociological breakdown of inner and outer histories, Priest has turned in later works to more subtle ways of expressing this confrontation between realities, developing complex webs of meaning by means of twinning, doppelgängers and alternate or virtual realities. By using the way fiction itself depends on an uneasy relationship with truth – by both being (by definition) a lie and by affirming its truth, or by the various ways authors can deceive readers and yet play absolutely fair with them by using a narrator to construct a separate version of events to that which seems to be happening – Priest, as John Clute notes when reviewing *The Prestige*, has become one of our most adept manipulators of *story* (Clute 2003a: 130). Sinclair, in *The Affirmation*, attempts to impose order upon his memories. Whitman's account shows his memories weaving in and out of each other, imposing their own order upon the reality they ostensibly reflect.

"The Event" and "The Woman", or Notes on ~~the~~ Temporality ~~of Sex~~

Matthew Wolf-Meyer

Introduction

> He who, in the *epoche* of pleasure, has remembered history as he would remember his original home, will bring this memory to everything, will extract this promise from each instant: he is the true revolutionary and the true seer, released from time not at the millennium, but *now* (Agamben 1993: 105).

Christopher Priest's greatest contribution to literature and contemporary thought is the challenge that he offers to dominant conceptions of time, language, history and identity, which, bundled together, equate roughly to a minor theory of subjection and subjectivity.[1] My aim is to show how Priest's work offers alternative theories of subjection, based on minor conceptions of time and history in the Judeo-Christian West, which challenge dominant theories of the subject or self-identity in contemporary thought. Because the dominant conception of time and history is of the apocalyptic Christian tradition (Agamben 1993: 95), with time flowing in a directed progression, from past to present to some foretold future terminus at the end of this progression, contemporary theoretical models of the self or the subject use such historical thinking without interrogation, thereby severely limiting understandings of who we are and what we can be (e.g. Butler 1997). Priest's novels, particularly *A Dream of Wessex* (1977), *The Affirmation* (1981), *The Glamour* (1984, 1985, 1996) and *The Quiet Woman* (1990), present non-apocalyptic, non-messianic ideas of subjection. In this chapter I will trace the theories of time and the subject that he has laid out in order to counter contemporary dogmatic thought on the subject of subjection. Rather unwittingly, in the process of thinking through the model of poststructural subjection that Priest offers, I have retreated into the work of Giorgio Agamben, whose concern is the relationship between language, history and subjection. The following is, strangely, a mediated conversation or interaction between the work of Priest and Agamben, which provides odd illuminations of both, and centres, in the end, around sex and time, albeit non-psychoanalytically.

Psychoanalytic theories, especially those of Sigmund Freud and Jacques Lacan, stress the historicity of the subject, and that of all actions the subject is capable of making, he or she is most likely to replicate events from his or her past, most often to gain mastery of, or to suppress, traumatic events. More recently, scholarship on subjection – especially that of Judith Butler – stresses the political nature of performativity and how subjects may usefully disrupt gender hegemony by performing against or outside of their gendered subjectivities (Butler 1989), with the latter being both the product of and limited by historical processes (Butler 1997). Priest helps to show how this radical performativity may be achieved, largely through his emphasis on the mutability of time, language, history and identity, the four of which conspire to found memory. What Priest offers readers in his protagonists are subjects who have been divorced from their histories, who are then rendered as individuals displaced from their subjectivities; it is the onus of their friends, relatives, and society to reconnect these desubjectified individuals to their memory, most obviously seen in the case of Richard Grey in *The Glamour*, for to not do so would endanger society. These individuals, divorced from the powers of the state[2] which has historicised them, are radical elements and must be tamed, they are poststructuralist subjects in a structuralist society, and thereby endanger the social body. For Butler – and Freud and Lacan before her – gender and sex lay a foundation upon which the subject is built; within Priest's novels, gender similarly plays a vital rôle, but his use of gender is always heteronormative, stressing the heterosexual, which is a conservative move in relation to his more radical use of temporality and subjectivity, and, as such, points to the conservative function of heterosexuality. The use of sexuality, of sexual events and encounters, points to the *closing down* of the subject, the times when the subject becomes moored to history and, in Michel Foucault's words, allows the subject "to discover, in desire, the truth of their being" (Foucault 1990: 5). This "truth" is a socially and culturally situated one, however, and it is through this production of "truth" that the individual becomes a subject. Sexuality becomes the tool by which the individual is made a subject to culture; by engaging in sexual encounters and by partaking of the fleeting moments of sexual excitement and engagement, time works upon the body and makes subjects of us all. But, simultaneously, it is in the event of sex that we might begin to reposition the poststructural subject.

Temporality is always ideological. The Western division of past, present and future is eminently so, and as previously mentioned, has laid a faulty foundation upon which diverse arguments have been launched, all taking this linear progression as natural. Considering the advances made in the physics of time within the twentieth century, this is particularly disconcerting and points to the sheer tenacity of this "progressive" conception of historical time. The question of whether we can begin to think of post-relativistic temporal ideologies should be foremost in the debates regarding postmodernism and modernism as well as poststructuralism and structuralism. What is more properly postmodern than an attempt to subvert the very concept of historical time that modernist historians have laid before us, the very foundation of the grand narratives? The allure of "progressive" historical models is attested to by their taken-for-grantedness, their banality, and what is demanded is a deconstructive approach to these models, centred around the "event". The event is that which can be named, it is in the singular; history is that which must be told, while it contains events it is defined by its narrativity. Similarly, the event is that which can be shared: it has a name and is recognised as belonging to that name (Braudel 1980: 27).

History, however, comprises many names, and a succession of names, it is polyvocal and negotiated (White 1987: 45). The social identity of the subject strains this distinction: as subjects, individuals have names – not always unique: Richard Grey, Peter Sinclair, David Harkman, and so on – but they have histories. Not only are individuals subject to the narratives of others, but they are subject to their own narratives, breaking themselves from their status of an event (from a birth and a death), and placing themselves within the expanding realm of the historical, of the narrative. And it is here, in this relation between history and events, between names and language, that a radical politics of time, with the help of Priest's novels, might be furthered. Priest's characters are struggling between life and death, but not in any conventional sense that would rely upon biological status. Rather, these characters struggle on the biopolitical front, a conflict that has become the very essence of contemporary subjection (Agamben 1998). They have been rendered "dead" to the state through their inability to be incorporated within the fabric of society; whether they lie in virtual reality simulators, incapacitated in rehabilitation hospitals, or furrowed away in distant cottages. They no longer participate in the reproduction of everyday cultural life. They have become inert, trapped in non-productive fantasies. The state depends on rehabilitating these people, the burden of which falls upon the shoulders of their immediate social network – families, co-workers, and former lovers – who must provide narratives for the individual, producing them as a subject.

Narratives of the Subject

> History was the critical order that the present imposed on the past; it could not be created forwards! (DW 22: 140).

Photographs and film take a particular relevance throughout Priest's work, working as aporia for "real" memories; The Glamour's Richard Grey depends upon postcards to reconstruct his memory of the period of his life which amnesia has consumed, and A Dream of Wessex's Julia Stretton, as Priest writes, "had a minor superstition, that persisted from childhood, that if she looked at anyone thinking that it was the last time she would see him – and thus hold a mental photograph – then it would come to be so" (DW 1: 5). It may be more precise to say that vision plays a particular rôle in Priest's work, especially when it becomes confused, as in The Glamour, or subverted, as in The Prestige (1995). Because memory depends upon the senses, vision asserts its power over the substantiality, the fixity, of events, shaping them from subjective perspectives.

Photographs and film are always a bringing-into-the-present of the past, in a material, objective form. But scepticism about the validity, the Truthfulness, of these media is necessary. Because film and photographs are fixed, because they are apparently objective, they lack the ability to be negotiated: film and photographs are events unto themselves, and structure narratives. Similar to Peter Sinclair's autobiographies in *The Affirmation*, photographs become fantasy in and of themselves, they become postcards of idyllic memories, obscuring what is left out of the frame, they are histories that, through their narratives, deny their status as events. As Alice Stockton, in *The Quiet Woman*, writes of her project in recounting Eleanor Hamilton's life,

> Structure was like an ideograph. It formed a shape whose purpose was to contain or enclose an idea without expressing it overtly. [...] Her book was to *tell* the story of Eleanor's life, but it was *structured* around her death. Writing about life was a way of describing the death, because one was the ideograph that described the other. The structure contained not only the death but also its explanation (*QW* 27: 183-184, Priest's emphasis).

The problem with structures of any sort, textual, photographic or ideological, is that they provide explanations with disregard to the subjective perceptions of the individuals involved; ideographs – symbols or characters standing in for things – by their very nature produce silence. Similarly, ideographs allow only a surface understanding, like photographed images, like postcards, but, what all of Priest's characters have problems with are the events that happen outside of the ideograph – there are always events that fail to fit into the history that is attempting to be told, and it is these extraneous events that destabilise the ideograph. Life and death, a definite beginning and an absolute ending, are arbitrary constructs. If events, like identity and power, are always defined through processes of negotiation, even life and death are not absolute, objective historical moments, but rather can only ever be structures that enable a negotiation, that facilitate a telling.

While Priest's novels may be very postmodern, the characters who inhabit the novels are smitten with a predilection towards modernism; while the narratives often break down, create circuits, subvert themselves and the medium of the novel, the characters – Peter Sinclair, Richard Grey, Niall and so on – create narratives of their lives that make sense, that flow, that provide histories to contextualise the events of their very being. Critical in any narrative is the presupposition, dictated by the nature of the medium, that there is a future. The idea of technicity that Bernard Stiegler has put forward in *Technics and Time* (1994) involves the throwing forward of the self, of essential qualities that must later be inherited. In doing so, humanity creates a sense of lack and desire in which it produces a difference from its own origins where everything was close at hand (in the Heideggerian sense); everything becomes posited outside the self and must be individually attained. The production of narratives, of history, is, in Stiegler's terms, a technic-al process: in producing fictions of the self, of society, social life becomes defined by its relation to these narratives, it becomes always relational and mediated. But rather than a psychoanalytically inspired sense of lack that constantly motivates the subject, which is always a historical lack, something that has been perpetrated in the past and haunts the present, a technic-al lack is a lack in the future, it is an always productive lack (if it can be said to be a lack at all). It may be better to think of it as an inheritance that has yet to manifest itself, but which is always known, a Manifest Destiny for the subject. Throughout Priest's novels, characters tell stories of themselves, fictions and truths, which they then inhabit, mentally and spatially. *The Affirmation's* Peter Sinclair is the epitome of a fiction-producer who creates a productive lack, an inheritance for himself to "fall" into, and by examining the way in which he does so, similar processes from Priest's other novels can be made more evident.

The psychoanalytic project that began with Sigmund Freud and Josef Breuer in the late nineteenth century based itself on the idea that the subject is always historically created, that the problems that the subject encounters in the present are due to traumas in the past. Through the use of therapy, which involves bringing the past into the present, first under the influence of hypnosis, and then in a highly regimented free association session led by a trained expert, the past is confronted and conquered (and compare Hubble on this, elsewhere in this volume). The healthy psychoanalytic subject has de-integrated his or her trauma from everyday life through acknowledging its influence. Peter Sinclair, in writing his autobiography numerous times and in numerous guises, effectively becomes his own therapist, but rather than freeing himself from the past, he finds the present thoroughly infected by the fictions he has created for himself, he finds himself indebted to the technic-al world he has created. Rather than finding freedom from the past, a release from his own history, Sinclair finds himself trapped by the history-in-the-present, an inherited legacy that so thoroughly explains his life that he finds no escape from the truth that he has produced.

What Peter Sinclair struggles with is the production of truth, of an authoritative narrative of his life and the events that have transpired. In his search to achieve a higher fidelity of meaning, he progressively alters the mimetic representation of his "real" life to a more fantastic one. What Sinclair is unable to conceive of is the profundity of his daily life, what might be thought of as an "experience" of everyday life.[3] In order to manufacture an experience of his life, Sinclair narrativises it, he manufactures an authority. This places him in direct conflict with his family and former lover, who attempt to assert their own historical understandings of his identity. Sinclair's initial interest in reconstructing the narrative of his life is in an attempt to reconcile his personal catastrophes – the death of a family member, the loss of a job, the dissolution of a romantic relationship – with his everyday life, to reduce the shock of these moments to banalities. This is anti-experiential: "The production of shock always implies a gap in experience. To experience something means divesting it of novelty, neutralizing its shock potential" (Agamben 1993: 41). And it is only in this reduction to a state of everydayness that an event can become historical; the event, in naming, must be disempowered and divested of the potential of containing all meaning; a name is no explanation, an effect that only a narrative can offer. Sinclair's banal recreation of the historical narrative of his life conflicts with the everyday mundane knowledge of him that his friends and relatives have, and it is in this contesting of seemingly inconsequential information that histories are produced. And it is this banality that creates a technic that is always close at hand, always achievable; a banal technicity is the only technicity that inspires progressive movements, slowly dragging the subject forward, rather than providing abrupt leaps, radical transformations.

The protagonist of *The Quiet Woman*, Alice Stockton, is strangely similar to *The Affirmation*'s Peter Sinclair: like Sinclair, Stockton is a history-producer, a professional writer whose career has principally concerned the recounting of women's life histories, but who has founded her career "on the events of history without involving herself with the idea that history actually had to be made" (*QW* 15: 91). She decides, when her current project is foiled by the government censorship agency, to historicise the life of her writer neighbour, Eleanor Hamilton. In recounting her life to Stockton, Hamilton weaves herself into the narrative of *The Affirmation*, mentioning first that as a young woman she called herself "Seri" thinking "it was a name [...] young men might find attractive" (*QW* 5: 28). Eleanor-Seri later becomes involved with a "Peter Sinclair" during a stay in Greece, and while on their return home to England by ship they become lovers. The terminus of the relationship is historicised by Eleanor-Seri: "It was doomed never to last. He had not entirely recovered from the illness, and was preoccupied with his own complicated life at home" (*QW* 5: 29). It seems benign, and quite banal, but the very act of giving a child a name, universal in human culture, is the first mark of inscription, and while, as in some cultures, the name might change, what names always do is negotiate kinship and broader social ties for the society. Thus the amnesiac must be given back his or her name, first and foremost, for it is in this renaming that the individual can become, again, a subject – he or she can begin to understand and negotiate the social obligations and taboos associated with the given name. And every name has a history, or a denial of history: Biblical names, names that denote homelands through their linguistic meaning and heritage (Smiths, Steins, Wolfs, Millers), and "unique" names (Peter Sinclairs and Seris). Names carry with them the ability to territorialise the subject, to make of the individual a historical subject (juniors, and other legacies – the Kennedys, the Rockefellers, the royal families), and it is in this historicisation that the rooting takes place, not a rhizome in the sense of Gilles Deleuze and Félix Guattari,[4] but rather a genealogy.[5] By constructing such a grand narrative or metanarrative, weaved through diverse texts through the use of identical character names, Priest creates a rhizomatic relationship between characters, between realities, replicating, in a grander way, the same production of narratives, of intertwining histories, that Peter Sinclair and *The Quiet Woman*'s Gordon produce. But if *The Quiet Woman*'s Peter Sinclair is the same as in *The Affirmation*, this account of his mental illness is strikingly different, and aligns him closely with Eleanor-Seri's own son Gordon, who similarly suffers from bouts of narrative production.

Gordon describes his fantasy productions as an escape into conscious dreams, of fantasies counterpoised to everyday life wherein there was "seamless safety" and he retained the ability "to enter and leave at will, hold the dreamworld intact and alive in [his] mind" (*QW* 19: 115). Unlike Peter Sinclair in *The Affirmation*, Gordon's fantasy production is contextualised, given meaning through the traumas that have occurred to him. As a child, he is subject to the storytelling of his mother, which he finds endlessly droll; she tells stories of her everyday life and the more remarkable events that have occurred, offering them all as "explanations". Gordon later admits that he "stole the stories from her and made them [his] own" (*QW* 13: 82), and it is critical to read Gordon's fantasy-production as a reproduction of his mother's stories. Gordon, scarred by the death of his father and brother, recounts the rôle that photography played in the catastrophe that claimed their lives and altered the lives of his mother, Eleanor-Seri, and himself. His father, stranded atop a ferris wheel with his brother, documented their time there through photographs that Gordon, as an adult, finally develops: "The last [photograph] was a downward view of a ball of flame: a technically brilliant photograph, sharply defined, full of contrast, showing horrified faces and upraised arms beyond the explosion, the limbs of a fireman spreading wildly as he fell, the jagged splinters of a broken spar" (*QW* 7: 41). For both Gordon and Eleanor-Seri this photograph captures the pivotal moment in their lives, which, for Eleanor-Seri, is censored out and thereby allows her to have a serene continuity in her life; for Gordon, the moment is embraced, the single most detailed memory of his life, and it is from this point onward that he becomes, in his words, "sane and whole" (*QW* 7: 42). Any reader of *The Quiet Woman* realises that Gordon's perception of sanity is faulty in itself, and it is this difference between Gordon's perception of himself and the world that he inhabits and the perceptions of others that is the crux of *The Quiet Woman*'s narrative tension. Gordon decides to capture his mother's death photographically as well, lost in a fugue wherein a top secret stealth bomber crashes near the cemetery during his mother's burial, producing a photo of him, while the casket bearing his mother is lowered into the ground, "staring away to the side, [his] eyes stark with terror" not at his mother's death, but the imaginary explosion of the stealth bomber (*QW* 9: 57), an event that had actually occurred to his mother, and which she had related to him. For Gordon, the historical narrative of his life depends on the production, or reproduction, of events, of catastrophic moments, because the banal reality of his life fails to accord him the sense of subjection on which he depends. His mother's narrative rather than his own, supplemented with the fantasies that he produces, provide him with a more approximate sense of identity. Eleanor-Seri's implantation of her "explanations" are technic-al productions: she provides a line of flight for Gordon, an inheritance that he will, in time, fully inhabit, to the detriment of himself and those he comes into contact with.

The Affirmation and The Quiet Woman show the potential for the individual in producing historical narratives of themselves, whereas in A Dream of Wessex it is not simply the future of individuals, but of global society that becomes technic-al, that becomes future-historical. The purpose of the pseudo-scientific "Ridpath projector" is to allow the users of such to project themselves into a potential future. This future is extrapolated from their unconscious and conscious knowledge of the world, aided by the knowledge and experience of others, and, among other things, projects a world wherein the United States has become predominantly Muslim due to cultural and economic ties to the Middle East and England has become part of the Soviet socialist union. The task of those participating in the use of the Ridpath Projector is to discern what course of events transpired between their era and the future to allow for such a peaceful, if unexpected, turn of events; the future the participants project is a future that they want, and so the onus of creating that future in the real world is their burden. Unfortunately, the only participant who is able to discern the future-historical events that transpired to make the world what it will be, David Harkman, is trapped by his own desire to stay in the projected world of Wessex. Julia Stretton, a fellow Ridpath projector participant, takes it upon herself, when she begins to fall in love with Harkman, to extract him from the Projection unit, but they become mired in the plot of Stretton's former lover, and, eventually, wilfully trapped in their fantasy world. What is critical in Stretton and Harkman's relationship is their sexual contact, which Harkman describes critically:

> [A]s they'd made love Harkman had a sudden insight that her arrival in his bed was spontaneous, that she had always been there, and that the events leading up to the moment were there only in implanted memory. [...] Afterwards, the sex itself became a memory, the drained, relaxed hour that followed being in its turn the only reality (DW 12: 73).

It is this conflux of temporalities – spontaneities, events, moments, memories – that sexuality opens up in relation to history; it is in the strange temporality of sex that the subject at once becomes an event and can begin to create history. Because of this strange temporality of pleasure, it is of the utmost concern.[6]

Sex-Instants

> He possessed Julia in every conceivable way bar their permanently living together, but he did not experience her. He remembered her into existence (*DW* 20: 119).

It is in the event of the sexual that the individual is at once divorced from his or her status as a subject and becomes aware of such. It is in this moment that the history of the subject becomes manifest in its detachment from the individual, and when the moment is over, the status of the subject is re-instantiated. In her attempt to reconnect Richard Grey with his status as an invisible in *The Glamour*, Susan Kewley and he sneak into a middle class home in London, and after casual interferences with the inhabitants thereof, retreat to one of the bedrooms to have sex, aroused by their invisibility. It is in this sexual moment that Grey becomes acutely aware of his being, of the nature of himself and his rôle in society, but in order to fully become an invisible, he must engage in this sexual event. And it is after this sexual encounter, when one of the inhabitants of the house reveals herself to them as they gaze upon her, invisibly, that Grey becomes aware of his refusal of his status as an invisible, and, instead, establishes himself as a normal, productive member of society; hence the denouement of the novel, wherein he begins dating a "normal" woman, and takes a brief vacation in the south of France, reliving the fantasy he had earlier produced for himself, but this time, critically, he makes an event of the history, mailing Kewley a postcard eerily reminiscent of the earlier attempts to establish himself as a invisible. It is not simply the event of sexuality that inspires this recuperation of subjectivity, but the materiality of sexuality, the coupling moment, that forces the physicality of experience upon the subject, it is here that subjectivity begins, of a knowledge of the self in relation to others, to the pleasure and pain of others, of a "becoming".

Throughout their work, Deleuze and Guattari are interested in accounting for transformation, of theorising the process of becoming, which, in their thought, is always a becoming-[something]: a becoming-animal, a becoming-woman. This leads to an interest in rereading the work of Freud, who, with the Oedipal narrative of the child's sexualised relation with parents and castration anxieties, provided the principal narrative of becoming in trans-national Western culture. Deleuze and Guattari argue that the Oedipal narrative is wrong-headed, and ultimately only repressive in its limitations of a triangular configuration of subjectivity ("Mommy-Daddy-me"). In opposition to Freud, they argue for an "immanent" process of becoming, one in which the individual has the ability to transcend this triangular "family drama" and become something quite different. Becoming is a constant process in living, but is exacerbated at times to the point of a transformation; primarily, becoming is a "molecular" process – it happens microscopically, in gradual shifts, rather than a "molar", full-bodied transformation. Deleuze and Guattari, to stress this molecular/molar divide, argue that all becoming is initially a becoming-woman (Deleuze and Guattari 1987: 275), which "is not imitating this entity [woman] or even transforming oneself into it", that is not transvestism or transgenderism, because the category of "man" is too policed by the state, it is in the potentiality of woman that man, and other regulated entities, can find the space for movement, the space of becoming, and it is in sexual/love relationships, where interpersonal identification takes place, that this process is initially realised on a molecular level. Perceiving the molecular changes on the part of the individuals is impossible, but understanding that in sexual encounters participants are opening themselves up to new possibilities, to see that they are initiating potentialities that may radically alter their conceptions of themselves as subjects, is key to understanding, socially, this act of becoming.

Throughout Priest's novels, protagonists are routinely single or in relationships that have become stale and lack passion; narrative tension is found in the pursuit of new sex partners. The adventure of new sexual experiences is ultimately an attempt to become subject to new states, new social orders, and, in so doing, contesting old formations. *The Affirmation*'s Peter Sinclair invents Seri not only in the pursuit of a new sex partner, but to deterritorialise the old one. New partners, because of the nature of the subject as an event-history, become events in the history of other subjects, and assist in the production of historical narratives. Richard Grey's decision, at the end of *The Glamour*, to couple with Alexandra, a young researcher, is an attempt to historicise the "event" of his time with Susan Kewley. Only through moving on, by creating new events in a historical narrative, can an individual reterritorialise him- or herself; subjection requires a historical narrative, and when old narratives begin to preclude new lines of flight, radical shifts – new lovers – are required. But sometimes the imposition of subjectification can be destructive, can be intended to divest lines of flight of their potential.

The Quiet Woman, *A Dream of Wessex* and *The Glamour* each have either a rape or an attempted rape; the difference between rape and consensual sex, in relation to subjection, are a matter of degree, not kind. In each case, the rape's target is a woman who is breaking away from one order and entering another, or who has successfully broken away. In *The Glamour*, it is just as Susan Kewley and Richard Grey's relationship is allowing her to escape the crippling relationship she is in with Niall that Niall rapes Kewley while she lies in bed with Grey (G84 5: xiii: 209-211/G96 5: 13: 223-225). It is critical here that when Kewley and Grey were in the process of having sex themselves that Niall disrupted this, as his invisibility allows him to, and rapes Kewley while she lies with Grey: two social worlds are in collision, with Niall exerting his power over Kewley, radically re-subjectifying her, anchoring her to the order that he has created, reifying her rôle in his world. In *The Quiet Woman* it is Gordon's persistent fantasies of raping the versions of Alice that he imagines that allow him to subjectify himself (*QW* 22: 148-151; 31: 211-212). Especially in the latter of the fantasies, where he imagines her coming to him in his office, aware of his power over her and his social rôle, this process of self-subjection, of subjection through the production of fantasy, becomes particularly solvent. Gordon's ability – and need – to self-subjectify is quite similar to that of *The Affirmation*'s Peter Sinclair, although Sinclair is neither as violent nor dangerous to others as Gordon is. But in each case, it is because the real world lacks experience for them that they embark upon a process of narrative production, of historicisation, which, because of the strange temporality of sex and pleasure, finds structure in the incorporation of such. For Gordon, these rape fantasies are necessary fictions that he produces, they make sense of his status as a subject – they may be "events", but then Gordon is only able to imagine his life as a series of dramatic events; for Sinclair, however, it is the more mundane aspects of his daily life that he re-imagines, because, for him, it is the mundane that makes up history. The attempted rape scene in *A Dream of Wessex* is principally about bringing the past into the present. Whereas *The Glamour* is about competing subjections of the present, and *The Quiet Woman*'s rape scenes are about fantastic self-subjections, Paul Mason's assault on Julia Stretton in *A Dream of Wessex* is about re-subjectification. Mason is Stretton's former lover, from six years previously, and a manipulative one at that; Stretton's breaking away from Mason was a critical move in her life, and she sees her participation in the Ridpath project as a sign of her success at reinventing her life. Mason becomes involved in the project through Machiavellian moves in his career, largely to disrupt Stretton's new life. He corners her in her room and subjects her to sexual advances, in an attempt to reclaim her (*DW* 18: 108-110). Stretton's victory over Mason is only momentary though, as he begins to re-imagine the projected future, this time with Stretton as his compliant lover. Whereas the consensual sexual events allow men a becoming-women, these rapes and attempted rapes are moments of *becoming-men*, an aspect of transformation that Deleuze and Guattari, and their followers, have little stressed.

If becoming-woman allows the subject space to renegotiate his or her subjection, moments of becoming-man forecloses transformation. Becoming-man is the spirit of all hazing rituals, of rapes and coercion, of violence and pain; it is the social process of "making a man" of someone, of subjecting them to a new order, of producing a masculine subject. In the process of becoming-man, lines of flight are foreclosed, shut down, evacuated – the potentiality of the subject is rendered monological, producing a subject of the state. These rapes are principally moments of becoming-men for both the women and men involved: they all become aware of the eradication of possibility, of becoming subject to the state. If becoming-woman is a site of progressive movement away from the state, becoming-man is its regressive counterpart, and it is in this meeting of regression and progression that all sexual encounters must mediate a potentiality, a space in which the subjects involved can become aware of their desire, of their status as subjects. This is not to say that all sex is inherently violent or rape, but rather that rape is an extreme form of becoming-man, it is a radical attempt to recall a subject to the state. And it is in this mediation of becoming that the eradication of pleasure takes place; the moment of most potential becomes a non-event, a quotidian historical instant devoid of possibility. Rather than a creative event, sex becomes a procreative event, a production of technics, a throwing forward of the status quo, it becomes the "dead time", manufactured in the desire factory: "The experience of dead time abstracted from experience, which characterizes life in modern cities and factories, seems to give credence to the idea that the precise fleeting instant is the only human time" (Agamben 1993: 96). If the instant of pleasure can be realised, if it can be inhabited rather than simply allowing it to fleetingly pass away or being repressed, then the status of the subject, and the potentiality for new modes of subjection, can be manifested. It is in realising the potential of becoming-woman that we may begin a revolution in subjection, a revolution in time.

Inconclusives

> The original task of a genuine revolution [...] is never merely to "change the world", but also – and above all – to "change time" (Agamben 1993: 91).

What is particularly strange in the practice of producing theory in the contemporary academy is an avoidance of sex acts, of the actual physicality of sexual intercourse, as if the intellectual project of philosophy precludes discussing such banal characteristics of human daily life. When sex is discussed, it is "oppositional" or exceptional sex, gay and lesbian sexualities being in the first camp, paedophilia and other unlawful acts in the latter (Rubin 1984). Sex acts need not be solely the object of psychoanalytic study, but rather should be the purview of all academic discussion; how might an approach to sexuality through a historical materialist lens radically alter our understanding of intercourse, or through a poststructuralist approach? For all her theorising of the possibilities of sexuality disrupting the hegemonic gender constructs on contemporary Western life, Judith Butler avoids, seemingly at all costs, any discussion of the actual materiality of sexual intercourse. This may be due to the inability for language to properly describe pleasure; it may also be the fault of conservative ideologies limiting the discourse of what are appropriate academic topics. But it is in the non-apprehendability of pleasure, linguistically and discursively, that we may begin the project of a temporal revolution. And the work of Christopher Priest helps in providing examples of the way in which the dogmatic temporality of contemporary discourses of the subject may be challenged. Priest, more than any poststructural theorist, helps to broaden our conceptions of who we can be, how our positions as subjects are negotiable, and of how the state can be challenged.

Notes

1. By "minor" I refer to the work that Gilles Deleuze and Félix Guattari have conducted regarding the literature of Franz Kafka (Deleuze and Guattari 1986). Among the features of a minor literature is the way in which it is inherently and discretely political, which I believe, like Kafka before him, Priest is.

2. See also the work of Alain Badiou (2001, 2003). My understanding of the event is opposed to Badiou's in that he stresses the universality of the event, one event being able to create many subjects, whereas I would stress the particularity of any given event and how it produces individual subjects.

3. Agamben writes, "For experience has its necessary correlation not in knowledge but in authority – that is to say, the power of words and narration; and no one now seems to wield sufficient authority to guarantee the truth of an experience. [...] This does not mean that today there are no more experiences, but they are enacted outside the individual" (Agamben 1993: 14-15).

4. In Deleuze and Guattari's usage, a "rhizome" is a horizontal association between objects – think in this respect of the horizontal, or parallel, textuality of Priest's characters who appear and reappear with similar names, yet in wholly different realities. Cf. Deleuze and Guattari 1987, especially chapter one, "Introduction: Rhizome".

5. "Genealogy" is the process whereby a contemporary object – and this should be considered in the broadest sense – is situated in its historical particularity through recourse to detailed historical discursive analysis. Here I am drawing on the methodological work of Michel Foucault (1972, 1994, 1998).

6. Cf. Agamben's discussion of pleasure and its relation to history and time (1993: 104).

Reticence and Ostentation in Christopher Priest's Later Novels: *The Quiet Woman* and *The Prestige*

Nicholas Ruddick

> I have to confess that I am not a fan of my own fiction. Dissatisfaction surrounds it all. I know the ideas are sound, and the plots are intricate, and that each of my novels has at least one "good bit" that props up the rest, but once a novel has gone into print I cannot bear to look at it again. By then past dissatisfactions are being tackled internally, the process of reappraisal has already begun, hope rises once more (Priest 1990a: 101).

Prelude

Nineteen years ago, in the concluding note to *Christopher Priest* (1989),[1] I claimed that, while Priest's fiction was certainly good enough to justify a short study in the Starmont series, it was then too soon to be more definitive about a writer in mid-career (see Ruddick 1989: 81). Since then Priest has produced only four novels, but if I were now to venture a reappraisal of his oeuvre, I would begin by claiming that as he enters his seventh decade, he is one of the dozen most important living English novelists – even if the literary world still hasn't quite woken up to the fact, and even if he himself might be the last to admit it.

Priest, his own severest taskmaster, is also one of the harshest critics of what science fiction has become (see Butler elsewhere in this volume). Yet even if he is not always nice about science fiction, sf continues to be good for him. He shares the sensibility of the central radical literary sf tradition, the most notable ancestor of which is Mary Shelley's *Frankenstein* (1818) and the benchmarks of which remain the early scientific romances of H. G. Wells.[2] This tradition is sceptical, typically agnostic in its worldview, and temperamentally opposed to Tolkienian fantasy. Its canonical works express no enthusiasm for the spirit of technological boosterism that Jules Verne (rather against the grain of his own temperament) bequeathed to Hugo Gernsback and American sci-fi, and are unafraid to engage with the often horrific consequences of modernisation. However, since the notorious rupture between H. G. Wells and Henry James over the function of fiction, the British branch of this tradition has sometimes sought internal solidarity by cultivating a sense of resentful alienation from the mainstream literary establishment. The younger Priest, before he renounced all generic orthodoxies,[3] was guilty of such posturing; the mature novelist has moved on to a position from which he is able successfully, even triumphantly, to contrive a reconciliation between science-fictional and mainstream literary values.

For all his love of untrustworthy narrators and other forms of misdirection, for all his adept deployment of narrative strategies that emphasise *Unbestimmtheit* – a term also used by Thomas Van Parys in his chapter – Priest is at bottom a "profoundly moral writer" (Kincaid 1991: 44) – as an ambitious novelist should be. Of all tale-tellers it is the novelist, constructor of large-scale imaginary worlds, who is best equipped to explore the individual's relation to society and to the species. In a secular post-Darwinian civilisation, novelists as moralists are needed as much as ever, for little guidance is to be expected from the cooling corpse of theology or from obscurantist postmodern philosophy. Perhaps the most unequivocal evidence that Priest is the kind of moralist that we need – plain-spoken, self-critical, undogmatic, chastened but not paralysed by the ubiquity of human folly – is *The Book on the Edge of Forever* (1994). This pamphlet begins as a cry of outrage at one writer's betrayal of his fellows, then artfully transforms itself into a Swiftian exposé of the whole profession's susceptibility to self-deception and toadyism.

At Least Two Forms of Identification: *The Quiet Woman*

The Quiet Woman is the least visible of Priest's recent novels: it has never been published in the USA, while in the UK it garnered only half a dozen reviews in the mainstream press, lukewarm for the most part. Priest has been unusually dismissive of *The Quiet Woman*, claiming that it is "not a book I'm very interested in" and agreeing with Paul Kincaid that it is his weakest novel since *Indoctrinaire* (1970) (Kincaid 1999a: 5).[4] Those few critics who have read the novel with attention have noted that it returns to the overtly political themes of *Fugue for a Darkening Island* (1972) (see Kincaid 1991: 46-47); that it contains "some laceratingly deadpan satire" (Langford 1999: 10); and that it is a novel about writing, in that "all of the characters are writers, editors, and/or information managers" (Burelbach 2002: 334; see also Lashku 1990: 59). At the same time, provoked by an opening scene which details everything in the protagonist's kitchen but the sink, some critics (see, for example Keller 1990: 11) have seen *The Quiet Woman* as a further step by Priest away from science fiction towards respectable mainstream realism, and have felt either betrayed or vindicated according to their generic allegiance.

The Quiet Woman touches on matters very close to home for Priest. This is not because it is set in the Vale of Pewsey in Wiltshire where he was living in the 1980s, but because, more than any of his other novels to date, it directly raises a central question about the ambitious contemporary writer's relation to his profession. How can one retain serious literary aspirations in the face of the pusillanimity of publishers, the indifference of readers, the dull-witted cruelty of critics, and (perhaps the hardest blow to endure) one's own disappointment when a completed book fails to live up to its initiating vision? To try to answer this question, *The Quiet Woman* fictionalises its own conception and gestation. It is consequently a metafiction, though almost covertly so, as though it were possible to avoid through reticence the barely-concealed narcissism too often underlying the metafictional impulse.[5] The protagonist Alice Stockton and the antagonist Gordon Sinclair, embodiments of polar extremes in the novelist's psyche, are nevertheless two of the most convincing characters that Priest has drawn. We learn in the course of the novel how Alice, a low-profile writer specialising in the biographies of underestimated women such as herself, endures the transition between bidding a painful adieu to her last stillborn book and starting her next on its laborious road to daylight.

Alice's conceptive method is triggered by her instinctive identification with a new subject, after which she uses a partly instinctive technique of "talking" disparate elements of her project into a unified and coherent shape with the aid of a sympathetic listener (see *QW* 25: 174-178). Reversing the temporality of Alice's strategy, one can anatomise *The Quiet Woman* by unweaving its diverse threads. One element is a catastrophic event, while others derive from environmental and socio-political trends in Thatcherite England projected slightly forward into what it is convenient to call the near future, though the novel's temporal arena is more strictly a heightened alternative present circa 1990. A Chernobyl-like meltdown at a nuclear power station on the northern French coast has sent a radioactive spume into south-west England.[6] The accident, which silently and disturbingly irradiates Wessex, has intensified an existing trend towards the governmental management of environmental crises, not by a costly clean-up followed by a thorough review of flawed safeguards, but by spin-doctoring and suppression to ensure that those most directly affected learn least about the potentially dangerous consequences to themselves.

A second political trend identified in *The Quiet Woman*, one deriving from the intensified culture of governmental secrecy in post-catastrophic England, is towards either the privatisation of security agencies or their assimilation by supranational entities, with the result that their operations become inaccessible to the average citizen – indeed to any public scrutiny. A third trend, similarly derived, involves the surreptitious construction of databases containing the most intimate details of individuals' lives, enabling not only the surveillance and repression of political undesirables but also the active distortion of the historical record. A fourth concerns whistle-blowers in the media who, increasingly at personal risk in a paranoid climate of neo-Orwellian repression, must themselves become adept at information management if ugly facts are to be articulated in a way that will prod a reluctant public into activism.

Such trends are thought of as being political, but as they also directly affect the health and well-being of large numbers of people, each evidently raises a "moral issue" at the individual level (*QW* 18: 110). The personal implications of political trends can perhaps be dramatised most effectively in fiction through a sympathetic protagonist with whom readers can identify. In *Fugue*, Priest's linkage between the political and the personal was relatively straightforward: the dissolution of English society is reflected in the mental breakdown of Alan Whitman, and is dramatised by narrative fragmentation. In *The Quiet Woman*, which recapitulates the catastrophic, tragic scenario of *Fugue* as a sinister farce, Priest performs the perhaps more difficult task of offering corrective ethical guidance. Having belatedly come to awareness of the darkening condition of the part of Wessex in which she lives, Alice, who until the murder of her friend Eleanor has lived in an apolitical Wonderland, must learn how to intervene effectively in the political arena if she is to continue as a writer – or indeed survive at all.

While a sympathetic protagonist offers a potential linkage between the personal and the political, the novelist must activate the connection through plot – that is, through an artfully arranged series of character interactions. *The Quiet Woman* is indeed "astonishingly full of plot" (Clute 1995: 215), yet complex plotting for Priest has always been more than a means to evoke admiration for his considerable narrative skills. Peter Brooks has noted that plot is "perhaps best conceived as [...] a structuring operation elicited in the reader trying to make sense of those meanings that develop only through textual and temporal succession" (Brooks 1984: 37). But to construct a plot is also an heuristic process for the novelist himself, as Priest suggests to us through the analogy of Alice's approach to life-writing as self-exploration: "Everything Alice had written in the past had enlarged her in some way. [...] Writing was a way of learning" (*QW* 15: 92). When Priest belatedly gives us access to the data of Alice's life history (*QW* 28: 190-194), we realise that part of the plot has been to re-enact for the reader the novelist's long struggle to get to know his protagonist.

Priest sometimes uses complex plotting as a means of dramatising the difficulty of confronting disturbing knowledge. A good example emerges from the contrast between the story and plot in the first chapter of *The Quiet Woman*. In the story – the fictional events as they might be supposed to unfold chronologically – three apparently unconnected events occur: there is a meltdown at a nuclear reactor; then some time later the manuscript of Alice's latest book is impounded without explanation; then two weeks later her friend Eleanor Hamilton is found murdered. In the plot – the events in the artful order that the narrative unfolds them to us – we learn in the space of the novel's first five pages that the Home Office has suppressed Alice's manuscript (*QW* 1: 3), that there are an unusual number of dead birds in Alice's yard (*QW* 1: 3-4), and that Eleanor's body has been found (*QW* 1: 5). The quasi-proximity of these "reordered" events from the perspective of the reader, presented from a third-person narrative viewpoint limited to Alice's consciousness, suggests that the protagonist is, or has, the key to the events' as yet mysterious connectedness. The reader, noticing references to the cat's "symptoms" (QW 1: 6), slumping house prices in Wiltshire (QW 1: 7), and Alice's avoidance of tap water (QW 6: 34), can hardly fail to be affected by a narrative mood rendered more ominous by Alice's curious failure to acknowledge the all-too-visible omens. Why is the nuclear accident, which happened "first", not directly mentioned until chapter eight (see QW 8: 44)? Because, we eventually infer, Alice has pushed what she cannot face to the back of her mind. Lacking official information about or financial means to escape from the danger zone, and consumed with the impounding of her manuscript and then her friend's murder, she is perhaps understandably in a state of denial – which is exactly where the government prefers her to be.

By the end of chapter one of *The Quiet Woman* two main plot strands are already under way: Alice seeks to learn why her manuscript has been suppressed and how to recover it; and she has become involved in the mystery of who killed Eleanor and why. Alice's dawning awareness of the connectedness of these two mysteries will simultaneously see the re-emergence into her full consciousness of repressed material about the nuclear accident and its repercussions, followed by her acknowledgement that she must become more directly engaged in the political arena. This process is dramatised through a duplex subplot: Alice, putting her failed marriage behind her, hooks up romantically with the political journalist Tom Davie and, putting her failed manuscript behind her, commits herself to a biography of Eleanor the anti-nuclear activist.

The Affirmation (1981) dramatises Peter Sinclair's failure to achieve maturity as a failure of self-identification – a failure to locate, define, develop, and affirm an adult identity – represented by the "invisible" text of his autobiography. A similar theme is played out in *The Glamour* (1984, 1985, 1996), in which the central conceit (see "Interlude" below) of personal invisibility represents the failure sufficiently to assert one's identity. *The Quiet Woman* acknowledges its close thematic relation with *The Affirmation* by means of intertextual clues. Eleanor Hamilton "is" Seri Fulten (QW 5: 28), and Gordon Sinclair "is" her son by Peter Sinclair. (The function of these allusions is not only to remind readers of the (meta)fictionality of *The Quiet Woman*,[7] but also to suggest that the novelist himself also figures in the complex system of identifications that this work explores.) Viewed in terms of the central conceit of *The Glamour*, both Alice and Eleanor, while not exactly invisible, are "quiet women" whose unglamorous but highly significant relation to society at large is at first difficult to identify (see QW 2: 9; 14: 86; 27: 181). Indeed, if issues of identity were important in Priest's two preceding novels, then they are absolutely central to *The Quiet Woman*.

Etymologically, *identity* signifies sameness, and in particular that quality of individual personality which remains the same despite changing circumstances.

If having a personal identity makes one by implication unique, it consequently makes one different from everyone else, so that *identity* paradoxically embraces both sameness and difference. *To identify* is to discover, locate, and attribute identity to: the police identify Eleanor's corpse and we are invited to identify her killer. *To identify with* means to model oneself, sometimes unconsciously, upon someone else. Although one's identification with someone else may be delusional, the action of identifying Self with Other normally suggests a sympathetic capacity on the part of the identifier. At the risk of oversimplification, one might summarise the moral structure of *The Quiet Woman* as an opposition between two kinds of *identification with*. From the beginning of their friendship, Alice intuitively identifies with Eleanor, and the plot tracks Alice's gradual discovery that her sense of commonality can survive Eleanor's death as a source of self-transforming energy. Alice's identification with Eleanor is healthy because she always acknowledges the separateness and difference between herself and her friend. But Gordon Sinclair identifies Alice with his mother: that is to say, he imposes on Alice an unwarranted similarity to Eleanor in an attempt to efface Alice's uniqueness as Other and to make her *identical* to the object of his hatred. So, Gordon's fantasised sadomasochistic encounter with Alice (see QW 31: 212) is actually a confession that he has strangled his mother, distorted by his unhealthy identification of one woman with the other.

While Gordon is probably Priest's most dangerously untrustworthy character, his moral turpitude is, I think, plausibly accounted for in psychological terms.[8] Eleanor managed the trauma of her first husband's and son's death on the ferris wheel by repressing the memory and transforming its negative energy via sublimation into the creation of a successful series of children's books. But these books resulted from her exposing her younger son to verbal narratives containing adult material – her stories or "explanations" (QW 13: 80) – which as a child he was not emotionally capable of dealing with and which he came to detest (see QW 29: 200). These narratives became attached to his own psyche as a set of (false) memories. The mother's transmutation of her son *Gordon* into the fictional *Donnie* (see QW 25: 176) was psychotherapeutic for her, and when healed she gave up writing and remarried happily. But during the process of creative sublimation Eleanor resorted to the unhealthy sort of identification: of her surviving son with his lost – and from her perspective erased (see QW 7: 42) – father and brother. Her actions left Gordon with a hatred of stories and of the mother who imposed them upon him, while the lingering effect of his childhood absorption of his mother's "explanations" has left him as an adult barely capable of separating fantasy from reality. (In this at least he is truly Peter Sinclair's son.)

Gordon poses a severe test for the novelist: a sadist who strangles his own mother must be allowed to retain humanity. Priest evokes a measure of sympathy for Gordon primarily through granting him in eleven chapters a first-person voice, the narrative strategy most conducive to readerly *identification with*.[9] Moreover, through the recurrent "I" the novelist implicitly aligns himself with Gordon the "information manager", or, to drop the euphemism, Gordon the professional liar and fantasist. At the same time the novelist also aligns himself with Eleanor the "explainer",[10] one who transmutes antisocial and self-destructive psychic elements into fictions via a process that may be therapeutic for the self but can harm others too immature to distinguish between fiction and reality.

Of *The Quiet Woman*'s critics, only David Langford seems fully attuned to the satiric element that distinguishes this novel as Priest's most sustained articulation to date of his long-held anxieties, earlier sketched in *The Book on the Edge of Forever*, about the economic pressures tending to subvert the profession of authorship. In the novel's manuscript-suppression subplot, the satiric vehicle is copyright, the system intended to protect authors' financial interest in their works. In this England ruled by spin-doctors, image advisors, and gesture coaches, Crown Copyright, intended to reserve to the government copyright of publications by ministers, is now wielded as a blunt instrument of direct censorship and suppression by quasi-governmental "information management" agencies such as the one run by Gordon Sinclair. The seizure of Alice's manuscript would suggest that in a climate of state paranoia, Gordon will periodically flex his muscles just to keep the literary community cowed and submissive.

Moreover, Priest suggests, if writers cannot be intimidated, they can usually be bought. Significantly, it is Gordon who informs Alice about the intervention fund (see *QW* 23: 155) set up by idealistic Eurocrats to ensure that authors earn a reasonable living. Of course, such an initiative plays right into the hands of Gordon and his ilk. In return for yielding all copyright, authors are paid a flat fee, insultingly factored on the quantitative criterion of page length, so that their manuscript can be entered into the "European Repository of Knowledge" (*QW* 23: 155, etc.). However, far from providing universal access to texts, this grandiose abstraction serves as the mask for a huge warehouse in Luxembourg. To "disappear" a potentially subversive manuscript (and to a paranoid government, all manuscripts are potentially subversive) somewhere among the millions of others in this cultural catacomb is a far more effective method of suppressing it than censorship would be: it remains legally in the public domain while it has become in practice inaccessible.

Through Gordon's list of Alice's artistic deficiencies (see *QW* 29: 199-200) as pseudo-explanation why he has seized her manuscript, Priest may be suggesting that from a writer's perspective a suppressed manuscript is emotionally preferable to a damning review, or that the masochism of writers arouses the sadism of critics. He is certainly furthering the metafictional theme in the novel by anticipating the negative critical response to *The Quiet Woman*.[11] That Alice is subsequently prepared to collude in the disappearing of her own manuscript suggests that she acknowledges the accuracy of Gordon's scathing critique. However, her receipt of what amounts to indirect compensation for her persecution by Gordon is a kind of poetic justice, especially as she can use the money to support herself in a project worthier of her talents: a vindicatory biography of Eleanor the social activist. "Hope rises once more."

Interlude: Priest's Later Novels as Metaphysical Conceits

Priest's recent habit of giving his novels titles that consist of the definite article followed by an abstract noun – *The Affirmation*, *The Glamour*, *The Extremes* (1998), *The Separation* (2002) – contrasts with his more ostentatious denominative practice in his earlier fiction – *Indoctrinaire*, *Fugue for a Darkening Island*, *A Dream of Wessex* (1977). For these reticent titles, rather like those of certain seventeenth-century metaphysical lyrics, mark the presence in the texts of one complex, unifying, and stylistically striking *conceit*.[12] The shift reveals Priest's mature concern to enhance the aesthetic unity and thematic subtlety of his novels by attending to the details of fictional poetics.

The metaphysical conceit typically deploys the "multiple logical bases" inherent in one image, so that, for example, "a single but more tenuous logical link takes the place of two simpler logical relationships; the image embodying only one of the former will yet be the more logically complicated, and 'conceited'" (Tuve 1962: 264). In the metaphysical lyric, the title's definite article may have the function of indicating a special usage which overrides but does not entirely obliterate the abstract noun's common meaning, with the consequence that the poem's whole text is deliberately ironised and rendered duplicitous.[13] In John Donne's "The Canonization" (1633), for example, we find ourselves reading, not about a saint's posthumous elevation to sainthood and mystical resurrection for spiritual love, but about a pair of lovers prepared to "dye and rise the same" (Donne 1937: 14) (that is reach orgasm without any ill effects) as frequently as possible for carnal love.

In *The Affirmation*, Priest inverts Donne's strategy in "The Canonization". The novel's title seems at first to refer "conceitedly" and ironically to Peter Sinclair's increasingly futile attempt to immortalise himself, only for the text finally to offer itself as a genuine affirmation of the novelist's power to immortalise both his characters and himself through textualisation. In *The Glamour*, Priest's conceit is to yoke together two contrasting meanings of the eponymous noun. The common meaning of glamour is a quality of visually alluring charm; to be highly visible is a *sine qua non* of conventional glamour. But Priest generates for the purposes of his novel a counter-meaning,[14] namely the inability to assert one's identity in a way that allows others to register one's existence. Via the literalisation of metaphor – a technique characteristic of modern fantastic fiction – the novelist transforms a personality defect into a quasi-supernatural ability to become invisible at will. The profoundly "glamorous" Niall is paradoxically a character exhibiting very little glamour in the common sense of the word; Niall's extremely prominent rôle in the narrative is paradoxically likely to remain "unseen" by the reader until the last page of the novel.

In *The Quiet Woman*, in which the title refers with deliberate ambiguity to two characters whose social presence is, or was, at first glance unobtrusive and unassertive, the central conceit of "glamorous" invisibility that ironised every aspect of *The Glamour* is replaced by a conceit based on differing but related (rather than opposed) meanings of the word *identification*. For as we have seen, Priest in this novel explores ideas of figurative reincarnation and literal rejuvenation through one woman's close identification with another. In *The Prestige*, the title conceit, as we shall see, brings and holds together in a single conceptual frame the potentially chaotic doubling and redoubling that the novel's two main characters inflict upon their own identities. After *The Quiet Woman*, Priest continues to explore identity, but instead of using the conceit of invisibility to do so he turns to the conceit of bilocation, or the ability to be literally in two places at once.

"Car JE est un autre": *The Prestige*

To read *The Prestige* is continually to be encouraged to contemplate the analogy between the book that will eventually be laid aside and the material residue of a carefully plotted illusion. The novelist-magician, having invoked a "Pact of Acquiescent Sorcery" (*P* 2: 1: 37),[15] has indulged for more than four hundred pages a perverse passion to deceive us (see *P* 2: 1: 41). In turn we have indulged for the time that it takes us to read the novel a slightly different, slightly more perverse passion – an intense pleasure in being deceived. For the reader, perhaps the most valuable potential payoff of the interaction – to invoke the novel's main conceit, its *prestige* – is the glimpse of certain elusive truths about human nature (including the above passions), truths that can only be attained through that sustained encounter between mendacity and self-deception known as reading a good novel. Yet while *The Prestige* foregrounds the perverse complementarity of the narrative transaction between the author and reader of fiction, Priest's novel is far more than an elaboration of the peculiar psychological mechanism implied by the Coleridgean truism about "willing suspension of disbelief" (see Sawyer 1999: 218). By bringing two historical epochs, the Victorian *fin de siècle* and the late twentieth century, into a closely plotted relation to one another by means of a complex narrative framing system, Priest is able to explore simultaneously two major themes, each associated with a corpus of fictional texts that were in the late nineteenth century just reaching a point of generic divergence from one another. One corpus was Wellsian scientific romance, which would later be subsumed into the popular-cultural genre named science fiction; the other was the literature of the symbolist or proto-modernist movement, which would ultimately become subsumed into the high-cultural literary mainstream.

One of Priest's most remarkable achievements in *The Prestige* is to demonstrate how the century-old rift between sf and the mainstream might be healed to the advantage of literature.

The common modern meaning of prestige is "influence or reputation based on past achievement or success". But the *Oxford English Dictionary* notes that the word derives from Latin (singular) *praestigium*, a delusion or illusion, or (plural) *praestigiae*, "illusions, juggler's tricks". In English an early meaning of a *prestige* was "an illusion", while *prestiges* were "deceits, impostures, delusions, iugling or cousening tricks". As with *glamour*, then,[16] Priest invokes a semantic ancestry for prestige that tends to contradict the word's modern meaning, then he yokes these contradictory meanings together in an eponymous conceit. Moreover, although *prestige* is not etymologically connected to *prestidigitation* or *presto*, these words' associations with legerdemain (see P 2: 2: 46, Sawyer 1999: 218) are certainly also drawn into the conceit. So too are the connotations of *Priest*, the author as master of ceremonies and mediator between humanity and (illusory) supernature. As with *The Affirmation*, the title *The Prestige* refers directly to, even offers to summarise or define, the text that follows, in the latter case because, as with *The Glamour*, the narrative generates a specialised, probably nonce-meaning of the title noun. For according to Alfred Borden, an untrustworthy authority at the best of times, in magicians' jargon, "the prestige" is the material end-product of a magic trick, such as the rabbit that a conjuror pulls from his hat (P 2: 7: 73).[17]

The Prestige's five-part structure is comprised of a tripartite shorter external narrative set in the late twentieth century, Parts One and Five of which frame the much longer internal narrative, while Part Three divides it. This internal narrative, the main focus of the novel and about three-quarters of its total length, consists of two first-person memoirs each by a late-Victorian master illusionist, first the lower-class Alfred Borden, and second, the upper-class Rupert Angier. The chronological *story* of this part of the narrative ranges between 8 May 1856 (Alfred Borden's apparent birth) and 8 July 1904 (Rupert Angier's apparent funeral). The *plot* of this part of the narrative is impelled by the professional rivalry between the two illusionists, each of whom wants to find out the secret of how the other does his most characteristic trick. However, this rivalry is intensified far beyond all reason by their common desire for revenge for real and imaginary slights and by their common failure to forgive. If we imagine that we will easily be able to distinguish between protagonist and antagonist in this novel, we are soon disabused. It is not only that that the "same" events seem very different when related from two opposed perspectives, but it also transpires that Borden's first-person memoir, as it comes down to us, has apparently been "edited" by his deadly rival Angier (as Lord Colderdale) (P 1: 1: 7). Moreover, the text of Angier's diary has an equally doubtful provenance, and might well at some stage have been interfered with by Borden (see P 3: 1:

143; 3: 4: 165). Such initial problems of establishing narrative authority and trustworthiness are a mere foretaste of what is to follow.

The outcome of the feud between Borden and Angier is that each literally, but in a different way, "half-kills" the other (see Langford 1999: 12), with consequences that haunt their descendants for three more generations. Only in the late twentieth century does the laying of the feuding family ghosts become possible. The external narrative tracks the process of exorcism: two of the illusionists' great-grandchildren, Andrew Westley (whose birth name was Nicky Borden) and Lady Katherine (Kate) Angier, who in the 1990s have been driven together for reasons that they barely understand, begin to examine and confront their inheritance. Impelling the plot of the external narrative are the different (but, it is suggested, ultimately compatible) desires of Andrew and Kate. He, by temperament a sceptic and by profession a journalist with an interest in exposing fraudsters who claim such powers as the ability to bilocate, seeks to account rationally for his uncanny conviction that he has a twin brother, even though there is no historical record of one (see P 1: 1: 4-6). She seeks to purge herself of her guilt for having witnessed as a child the apparent murder by her father of the two-year-old Nicky Borden (see P 3: 3: 160; 3: 4: 162), a festering secret that she blames for her isolation, emotional inhibition, and social immobilisation (see P 3: 4: 166).

Westley's certainty that he has somewhere an identical twin – consequently, that his identity is shared at least metaphorically by someone who lives elsewhere – seems a faint but unmistakable echo of the obsessive drive of his ancestor Alfred Borden to perfect the "New Transported Man". In this illusion, Borden transports himself instantaneously from one part of the stage to another, a trick which, from the audience's perspective, is tantamount to performing the delightfully impossible action of manifesting oneself in two places at once. But why should an audience find bilocation, or at least its illusion, so appealing? Partly it may have to do with a dissatisfaction with the single Self's ability to assert itself sufficiently in mass society – we feel that we lack sufficient "prestige" – partly with an anxiety about the Self's mortal fragility – if only we could keep a copy of ourselves in case of a fatal accident to the original! Yet Westley's phantom twin is probably a better clue to the appeal of the "New Transported Man". As the Priestian "glamour" literalises a common personality defect (the inability to assert one's identity), so Westley's phantom twin embodies the almost universal craving in modernity for fusion with one Other who will complete what is lacking in the Self. However – Priest's conceit has an important moral dimension – this desired Other must not be too similar to the Self. For as the myth of Narcissus and the legends of the Doppelgänger both admonish, fusion with a duplicate Self rather than with a complementary Other is likely to lead to annihilation. Priest suggests in *The Prestige* that psychic self-alienation emerged in the later nineteenth century as a symptom of modernity and was passed on to later generations, sometimes expressing itself in extreme or critical form. Through the twin quests of Andrew Westley and Kate Angier, Priest proposes that the crisis of the deficient Self can best be alleviated through a fuller understanding of the inherited past and through a search for an Other who is a complement to, rather than a narcissistic replication of, the Self.

Both Alfred Borden and Rupert Angier act out, literalise, their late-Victorian audience's fantasies of completing the deficient Self via reduplication. (One might compare the motif of cloning in popular culture today.) In perfecting their respective illusions, however, both magicians in different ways bring disaster down upon themselves, thus suggesting that the fantasised goal of the duplicated (that is, literally bilocated) Self is a dangerous mirage. In the case of Alfred Borden, verbal clues early in his diary suggest that the Self represented by the first-person singular pronoun – for example, in such an entry as "I said nothing of this to me!" (*P* 2: 3: 50) – is not what it seems to be. "Alfred Borden" will gradually be revealed as a dual entity, a mask for a pair of identical twins who, in order to produce the illusion of the "New Transported Man", have concealed their separate identities from the world for so long that psychologically they have become two utterly co-dependent half-beings.

Unable to comprehend how "Borden" performs his illusion, his rival Rupert Angier, who is a singleton, must nevertheless find some way of outdoing him. Accordingly he resorts to the purchase of an artificial electrically-powered device, the Tesla apparatus, to construct his greatest illusion, "In a Flash", which also simulates bilocation. The Tesla apparatus has the ability to almost instantaneously project into the theatre an identical copy of the illusionist's body some distance away from his now defunct original body, which falls into a pit where it remains invisible to the audience who have been momentarily blinded by a flash of electricity. In fact, "In a Flash" is strictly not an illusion at all, but an effect of an advanced technology that, in accordance with Arthur C. Clarke's Third Law (see Clarke 1984: 147), will seem indistinguishable from magic to those who do not understand it. Moreover, in neither of the illusionists' tricks, then, is the *prestige* their real, whole self: "Borden" has literally two selves, figuratively two half-selves; the Angier who survives each performance of "In a Flash" is only the latest copy of a copy, the original having been long superseded. Consequently, the prestige (in its common sense) that the illusionists derive from their tricks is therefore in reality accrued neither by "Alfred Borden" nor "Rupert Angier" – though as neither of the denominated entities is authentic they should certainly accrue the inverted commas that signal a non-standard or ironic usage.

As a result of Borden's tampering with the Tesla apparatus at a crucial moment, Angier is literally reduced to what Borden already figuratively is and what Angier has already figuratively become: a half-self. For Angier's body is duplicated into two semi-existent entities, each "the prestige of the other" (*P* 4:

365), one barely more than a sickly corporeal shell, the other an insubstantial wraith. In a sense, Borden and Angier have always been one another's spiritual complement *in potentia* (see *P* 4: 359); as their common mistress Olive Wenscombe/Olivia Svenson puts it to Angier, "You and this Alfred Borden are like two lovers who can't get along together" (*P* 4: 257). But Borden and Angier never become fraternally fused – quite the opposite. While their rivalry drives each to ever more brilliant achievement in the manufacture of illusions, it is entirely destructive to their identities. Their unreconciled, ever more divergent, ever more incomplete selves, vainly craving the other, each follows a different trajectory to a similarly tragic but solitary dissolution. Their final sentences are ironically identical, each affirming only the terminal alienation of the Self: "I will go alone to the end" (*P* 2: 15: 134; 4: ix: 387).

One of Priest's aims in setting the internal narrative of *The Prestige* in the later Victorian period is surely to revisit the headwaters of the British tradition of literary science fiction, from which his own fiction has drawn much strength in the past. Specifically, he returns triumphantly to the heyday of the Wellsian scientific romance,[18] which he earlier visited with only moderate success in *The Space Machine* (1976). This epoch, in the aftermath of the Darwinian revolution, was characterised by theology's supersession by science: doubt replaced faith as the dominant cognitive mode at the level of metaphysics. It was also a time when spiritualists attempted to colonise the territory vacated by traditional belief (see *P* 2: 6: 63-69; 4: 202-205). The feud between Borden and Angier has its origin in a typically post-Darwinian ethical conflict, not about whether spirits of the dead are really present at a séance (both magicians are sceptics), but about whether it is right to pretend to contact them – in short, whether illusory faith or disillusionment better conduces to mental health.[19]

In the Victorian *fin de siècle* there was often an excessive confidence in the potential of science to perform miracles that would make those of the Bible seem pale by comparison. In this context, Wells's time machine was sufficiently plausible when used as a vehicle to explore, not the practicability of time travel, but the far larger and more critical issue of humanity's temporal place in nature in the wake of Charles Darwin and T. H. Huxley. By analogy Priest uses his then sufficiently plausible Tesla apparatus[20] as a means to explore, not the possibility of matter transmission, but the critical psychological ramifications of modern man's universal but impossible desire to be in two places at once. Wells in 1934 wrote astutely and rather dismissively about the demands of the genre that was just then becoming known as science fiction and which forty years earlier, under the rubric of scientific romance, he had had a large hand in shaping: "by the end of last century it had become difficult to squeeze even a momentary belief out of magic any longer. It occurred to me that [...] an ingenious use of scientific patter might with advantage be substituted" (Wells 1934: vii). The Tesla apparatus is pure Wellsian "jiggery-pokery" (vii); it functions with the help of what been termed spiritualised electricity, that is, electricity viewed at a historical moment when its power was starting to be tapped and its transformational potential glimpsed even though its material nature was not properly understood (see *P* 2: 9: 90-93; 4: 268).

A brief digression may clarify further Priest's current relation to Wellsian science fiction. Wells remains "the main man" (Langford 1995) for Priest, one of whose early ambitions was to prove himself a worthy follower of the grand-master of science fiction. However, Priest has recently noted that Wells was far more interested in science than he is, and (rather more controversially, though I think correctly) that Wells was essentially a "primitive" in the art of fiction (Kincaid 1999a: 7). Such statements suggest to me that the maturing Priest came to the conclusion that while Wells was a great science-fiction writer, even at his greatest, for example in *The Time Machine* (1895), *The Island of Doctor Moreau* (1896), and *The War of the Worlds* (1898), he was only a halfling as a novelist. Wells's foundational classics would probably never be bettered as science fiction, but while they incorporated plenty of science, they left out a lot of human life and art.[21] (In about 1900 Wells almost certainly came to a similar conclusion himself about the missing human life, or he would not then have turned to writing realistic novels.) For Priest, such deficiencies at the root of the science fiction genre congenitally weakened the work of all subsequent writers, no matter how ambitious, who remained within the genre's evolving constraints, for these constraints had come into being not for the benefit of the artist, but at the behest of the market.

A second major late nineteenth-century theme explored in *The Prestige* is one associated with writers who would retrospectively emerge as central figures in the proto-modernist literary mainstream. This theme, largely absent from Wellsian scientific romance, concerns the psychic fragmentation and self-alienation characterising the growth of the modern consciousness as Victorian certainties crumbled after the Darwinian revolution. The traditional idea of the body and soul combined harmoniously into a unitary self was quickly replaced by competing diagrams of the overlapping relationship between the corporeal and psychic Selves. From about 1895, Freudian psychoanalysis would begin to register its powerful claims that the human mind was split into discrete parts that were largely inscrutable to each other. Certain nineteenth-century writers foreshadowed the scientific exploration of the unconscious, sometimes using two characters to embody a divided and self-alienated psyche. Even as early as *Frankenstein*,[22] Mary Shelley by emphasising the Victor/Monster dualism[23] subverted the clear moral binarism of omnipotent Creator/weak Creature as sketched in Genesis and elaborated in John Milton's *Paradise Lost* (1667). Baleful doubles recur in Edgar Allan Poe and Fyodor Dostoevsky; the divided modern urban Self received its paradigmatic mythologisation in Robert Louis Stevenson's *Strange Case of Dr. Jekyll and Mr Hyde* (1886); while the hidden kinship between the civilised Self and the savage or demonic Other was explored by Joseph Conrad in *Heart of Darkness* (1898). Charles Baudelaire in "Au lecteur" (1855) extended the metaphor of uncomfortable psychic dualism to complicate the relationship between author and reader: "—*Hypocrite lecteur, —mon semblable, —mon frère!*" (Baudelaire 1961: 156);[24] while Rimbaud's "*Car JE est un autre*"[25] succinctly summarised the problem of modern self-alienation. Rimbaud's apothegm directly prefigures the strange pronominal configurations that litter the memoirs of "Alfred Borden" (see, for example, *P* 2: 3: 50; 2: 8: 82).

Priest's invocation of *Frankenstein* at significant moments in *The Prestige* strengthens his thematics via intertextual allusion while paying homage to one of his most important literary forebears. As *Frankenstein* is perhaps the most prominent common ancestor in English of both Wellsian scientific romance and the proto-modernist literary tradition, then Shelley's Gothic/Romantic novel offered to Priest the key to how these divergent varieties might be strengthened through attempted reconciliation rather than through enforced segregation. So, Kate Angier's father is named Victor (*P* 3: 2: 154); the scene in the "forbidden room" at Caldlow House involving Nicky Borden is pure Gothic (see *P* 3: 2: 147-156); while the Tesla apparatus by means of Shelleyan spiritualised electricity[26] turns Angier into a monster strictly neither alive nor dead (see *P* 4: 317). Finally, Priest alludes to the end of Shelley's novel when at the end of *The Prestige* Andrew and Kate discover the body of Nicky Borden in the catacomb of "prestiges" that have resulted from the use of the Tesla apparatus (see *P* 5: 2: 398). By this discovery, Westley finally rids himself of his phantom twin; this in turn leads to the banishment of the wraith of Rupert Angier, that slouches off into the dark, snowy landscape (*P* 5: 3: 404) like Frankenstein's monster (see Shelley 2001: 244; Kincaid 2000: 14). Now Andrew and Kate, disburdened of the oppressive weight of the past, are left to contemplate a future together in which each may complement the other's otherwise irremediably deficient self. "Hope rises once more."

Postlude: Reticence vs Ostentation

In *The Quiet Woman* Priest celebrates reticence, deadpan irony, and *ars celare artem*; he was rewarded by being largely ignored by readers and critics alike. In *The Prestige* he celebrates the art of the novelist as analogous to that of a master illusionist who aims to elicit gasps of bewildered awe from his audience; he was rewarded by almost universal acclaim from the critics and by two major fiction awards.[27] From its context in the Priestian oeuvre, one might speculate that *The Prestige* originated in the desire by a novelist, tired of having the low-profile literary career dissected in (and epitomised by) *The Quiet Woman*, to make a grand and wilful gesture. A few neo-Puritans, perhaps, may dismiss *The Prestige* from the start as mere attention-seeking literary showmanship. Perhaps some otherwise sympathetic readers, laying the finished *Prestige* down, may wonder whether the brilliant electrical effects have not blinded them to the emptiness of the container. Yet to most readers *The Prestige* is such an evidently outstanding achievement – even the self-critical author has declared himself "fondest" of it among all his works (Kincaid 1999a: 6)[28] – that it tends to overshadow everything in its proximity, and many will be tempted, with Priest himself, to relegate the dowdy *Quiet Woman* to a lowly rung in the oeuvre. This temptation should be resisted, for as I have tried to show, *The Quiet Woman* is also a major achievement, even if it is sometimes a little too reticent for its own good. Eventually, perhaps, the striking differences between these two works will be seen as evidence, not of the gulf between success and failure in Priest, but of his extraordinary range as a mature novelist, a range matched by few if any of his contemporaries.

Notes

1. The manuscript of this book was finished in 1986.
2. In an interview, Priest notes, "I see myself working within a clear and even conservative tradition created by Wells, Dick, Pohl, Sheckley, Aldiss, Ballard, Le Guin, Sladek, Wyndham" (Gevers 2002: 3). The tradition is clear enough, though it is hard to guess what he means by "conservative".
3. That is, "being trapped in genre expectations and genre thoughts"; see Kincaid 1999a: 7.
4. Perhaps repenting his public disparagement of an unloved child, Priest adds, "I know quite a lot of people who've said it's the best thing I've ever written" (Kincaid 1999a: 5).
5. For a good definition of metafiction, see Waugh 1984: 2, but note how Priest in *The Quiet Woman* avoids the deliberate self-consciousness that Waugh identifies as characteristic of the genre.
6. *The Quiet Woman* is thus linked (in a low-key manner) to that subgenre of British disaster fiction in which the sanctity of the home Island is invaded by a malign entity that is not as alien as it first seems to be. Priest's earlier contribution to this subgenre, *Fugue for a Darkening Island*, provides an interesting contrapuntal intertext to *The Quiet Woman*.
7. In this vein, one form of the name of Alice's friend Lizzie (who will ultimately be "deleted" from the narrative by Gordon) is the Nabokovian "L. Humbert" (QW 14: 84).
8. Kincaid disagrees (2000: 11-12). True, the ferris wheel incident and its consequences as described by Gordon probably never "really" happened because he is totally untrustworthy. But psychologically equivalent events surely did, for otherwise Gordon is a motiveless malignity and if he is then Priest cannot surely be a *profoundly* moral writer.
9. "Most people reading a novel told in the first person singular will reasonably

assume that it's truthfully or reliably reported, or that only one person is writing it, or that no one apart from the narrator has tampered with the text before it was printed" (Langford 1995).

10. Who in chapters five and eleven is also vouchsafed a first-person (epistolary) voice. Note that, by means of another piece of subtle plotting, the reader becomes privy to Eleanor's letter before Alice.

11. This authorial pre-emptive strike to my mind sounds the only false note in the novel, with its distinct echo of special pleading.

12. Cf. John Donne's "The Anniversary" and "The Ecstasy", George Herbert's "The Temper" and "The Elixir" (all 1633); it may be no coincidence that Andy Sawyer calls *The Glamour* and *The Affirmation* "metaphysical whodunits" (Sawyer 1999: 218).

13. *Irony* comes from the Greek εἰρωνεία [*eironeia*], dissimulation.

14. Via an archaic meaning of *glamour* as "fictitious beauty" with a connotation of delusiveness.

15. Like much in *The Prestige*, this Pact is ambiguous; it also refers to "Alfred Borden"'s arrangement to exist as a single identity (see *P* 2: 5: 58).

16. In definition 2 in the *OED*, *prestige* is glossed as "Blinding or dazzling influence; 'magic,' glamour [...]".

17. The highly trustworthy Kincaid notes unequivocally that the specific use of *prestige* in the novel is "a word of Priest's own devising" (2000: 209).

18. Rupert Angier's diary begins on 21 September 1866 (*P* 4: 177), H. G. Wells's date of birth.

19. The séance-breaking scene that initiates the Borden-Angier feud has a probable source in H. G. Wells's *Love and Mr Lewisham* (1900) (Wells 1993: 54-62).

20. The *fin-de-siècle* context of the internal narrative authorises the plausibility of the apparatus, a subtlety missed by John Gribbin who takes Priest to task for ignoring the implications of $E=mc^2$, "a sad reflection of the general state of scientific understanding" (Gribbin 1996: 52).

21. The absence of significant female characters in the scientific romances is perhaps the clearest evidence of the halfling status of great Wellsian science fiction.

22. In 1818 *Frankenstein* was read as a Faust-like warning "to shew how that the powers of man have been wisely limited" by God (Shelley 2001: 307); after Darwin, it became easier to read it as an exposé of how the imperfections of the Creature are an inevitable consequence of the flaws in the Creator.

23. Both Victor and the monster are identified at different times in the novel with Milton's Adam and Satan.

24 "Hypocritical reader – my fellow creature – my brother".

25. "For *I* is an other": in a letter to Paul Demeny, 15 May 1871 (Rimbaud 1962: 9).

26. See Shelley 2001: 84, 103, 357; see also *P* 4: 317; 4: 386.
27. *The Prestige* won the James Tait Black Memorial Prize for Fiction (1995) and the World Fantasy Award (1996). It also received nominations in 1996 for the BSFA Award and was short-listed for the Arthur C. Clarke Award.
28. Because it has so far come "closer [at 70%] than any of my novels to what I conceived" (Kincaid 1999a: 6). Priest later notes that "I can't think of another novel written by anybody that has such a uniformly good press" (Kincaid 1999a: 7), though John Fowles, the mainstream novelist with whom Priest has confessed an affinity (see Sawyer 1999: 219) hated it (Kincaid 1999a: 7).

An Unusual Suspect:
The Novelisation of *eXistenZ*

Thomas Van Parys

Nowadays it is a customary procedure to publish a novelisation to tie-in with the release of a film. David Cronenberg's *eXistenZ* (1999) was no exception. However, none other than Christopher Priest was engaged to perform the task. As part of the marketing strategy for a film, a novelisation is usually limited to an elaborate transcription of the screenplay. In that sense, it is merely a commercial exploitation of the film's success and actuality. In contrast to this rather mainstream novelisation, though, a noveliser may sometimes attempt to produce a more literary counterpart to the screenplay. Just as Cronenberg's *eXistenZ* was likely to become an intellectual cult film, given his track record (see Costello 2000 and Grant 2000), so it was thought appropriate to attract a renowned science-fiction author to write its novelisation. Priest seems the ideal choice. Not only has his oeuvre been widely celebrated, but also some of his works – *The Affirmation* (1981) in particular – thematically resemble *eXistenZ*. This chapter is concerned with whether or not Priest's novelisation lives up to expectations.[1]

To a certain extent, a critical search for traditionally defined "literariness" in this novel is beside the point. It can be argued that literary criteria do not hold for science fiction in general, since science fiction mainly expresses itself as a genre of ideas. Various highly regarded science-fiction novels hardly even compete with the literary style of "highbrow" fiction. As Farah Mendlesohn puts it, the "thought experiment, the 'what if?' (which Darko Suvin calls the novum), is crucial to all sf, and has led to the most popular alternative interpretation of 'sf': speculative fiction. It is here that sf most departs from contemporary literature, because in sf 'the idea' is the hero" (Mendlesohn 2003: 4). The film *eXistenZ*, for instance, deals, among other things, with the interchangeability of reality with virtual reality. In the novelisation, Ted Pikul, a main character, explicitly articulates this central issue:

> Anyway, what is reality without someone to observe or measure it? Reality in all its forms is being threatened now, more than ever. It is being eroded and it is washing away in the deforming storm of nonreality, which masquerades as reality and which will eventually replace it if we do not take the appropriate steps (*eX* 19: 190).

Mostly, science-fiction authors do not concentrate on elegant writing, but develop their story and its themes in detail, focusing on the object rather than the subject, for the purpose of entertaining as well as criticising. Adam Roberts remarks:

> At its best, science fiction provides the most supple and the most popular means of exploring questions of diversity and difference; it opens up new possibilities; it makes us think. Science fiction most effectively addresses the questions that have defined the age we live in: technology, gender, race, history. As a literature of ideas, where the emphasis is less on literary technique, SF has been able to trade in the concepts of philosophy, theory, history and politics in vivid and popular ways. [...] Science fiction is the dominant mode of imaginative writing today, a body of work that encourages readers to take nothing for granted, to challenge all their assumptions, to think through how things might be different. It is time and again, accordingly, a revolutionary mode of writing (Roberts 2000: 183).

In this respect, a science-fiction novel does not harbour literary ambitions, but manifests itself as paraliterary. Correspondingly, the following analysis should be partly put into perspective. Nevertheless, it is anything but irrelevant to subject this novelisation to standards of literariness, considering its unusual profile as an artistic text and Christopher Priest's reputation.

From Film to Literature: Perspectives on Novelisation

On the whole, novelisation can be defined as the adaptation from film to novel, although it is not considered as the inverse of the more common adaptation process from novel to film. Raphaëlle Moine argues that adaptation from text to screen does not presuppose a temporal relation other than the anteriority of the written text, whereas novelisation mostly involves a coinciding release of film and novel (Moine 2004: 88). On the basis of five parameters, Moine has distinguished the basic characteristics of a common novelisation: the book format, the textual form of expression, the narrative mode, the publication concurrent with the film, and the autonomy of the object, for, despite its cinematographic genesis, the novelisation can be read independently of the film. Traditionally, the phenomenon of novelisation fits in with the cinephile's urge to write about cinema and with the notion that a film is incomplete without an accompanying text (see de Baecque 2003). Novelisations have existed since the very beginning of cinema, but the genre gained notable popular attention in Hollywood's blockbuster era, when the studios started their "politics of conglomeration", releasing a novelisation simultaneously with the film (Moine 2004: 86). This procedure assured a certain yield: if the film was unsuccessful in theatres, the "book from the film" could perhaps bring in money. As a rule, a novelisation does not compete with the film in question: it is presented as a supplemental text which further explores and explains the film's main issues. Thus it does not aspire to be the film's "*other*", but its "*double*". It is a "*copy*", or "calque", that is an immediate transfer (Baetens 2004: 240). Novelisation has become a basic strategy to sell the same concept in another medium; its interest is mostly purely commercial and synergistic. This accounts for the general depreciation surrounding the genre. Christopher Priest justly comments on the impact of this prototypic type of novelisation on the science fiction market:

> Since [the mid-1960s], the images and ideas of SF have been comprehensively sold out to commercial interests, to TV and movies, to computer games and advertising, to soft-brained sagas and trilogies and series and sequels. Many of my contemporaries have given in to this pressure; many of the new writers obviously accept it as the norm. I've met young writers who have declared that selling *Star Wars* or *Star Trek* tie-ins is a way in to the writing of legitimate SF. The typical SF shelf in most bookshops is now crammed with these undemanding TV or film tie-ins, along with paranoid androids, heroic trilogies or larky fantasies. The serious kind of SF has become marginalised (Gevers 2002).

His pertinent criticism is similar to John Clute's. Clute argues that these spin-offs are "fatally indistinguishable from the media- and consumption-ridden world we live in, and incapable of *differing* from that world in any useful sense", since their focus is on the product they advertise (Clute 2003b: 65). Nonetheless, novelisations keep appealing to a wider public. In an interview with him on *eXistenZ*, Priest says:

> Novels based on films obviously have an appeal. I think people read them partly because they want to recapture some of the magic of having already seen the film, and a novel will help them re-imagine it, and partly because they are looking for an explanation of something they found obscure, or an expansion of scenes, or something like that (Van Parys, Jansen and Vanhoutte 2004).

In his triple definition, Jan Baetens designates novelisation as anti-adaptation, anti-remediation, and anti-ekphrasis[2] (Baetens 2004; Baetens and Lits 2004). Firstly, a novelisation is generally based on a screenplay. Both screenplay and novelisation use written language as medium to transfer their message. Thus, no intermedial transition and, consequently, no semiotic rupture take place, whereas exactly this rupture is the major adaptation problem. As novelisations are based on verbal pre-texts, they also avoid the difficulty of achieving the right balance between Brian McFarlane's concepts "transfer" and "adaptation proper" (see, especially, McFarlane 1996: 13). In broad terms, the former indicates the elements that can be transferred from one medium to the other, whilst the latter the ones that need replacing by equivalents. In this way, novelisation is merely a simple process of rewriting the screenplay by adding more detailed descriptions of setting and characters. Secondly, the genre of novelisation counters the theory and logic of "remediation". This model, as defended by Jay David Bolter and Richard Grusin (1999), explains the continual invention of new media in Western society as a pursuit of maximal realism. In other words, new media are conceived in order to represent the world more realistically. Novelisation, though, cannot be positioned within this explanatory hypothesis, since a return to the medium of the novel implies a decreasing degree of mimesis by comparison with film. Thirdly, although commercially dependent on its cinematographic peri-text,[3] the usual novelisation is anti-ekphrastic. For one thing, its narrative does not refer to the film itself. Oddly, instead of attempting to recreate the film's images with words, it also avoids descriptions as much as possible. Often a quire of black-and-white photographs, printed on cheap paper, is intended to compensate for this visual deficit. Thus, ambiguously, novelisations try to detach themselves from their visual origin, in order to foreground their validity as autonomous works, whilst remaining derived products.

Literariness, Horizons of Expectation and *Unbestimmtheit*
In spite of various elaborate attempts at genre definition, it is difficult to distinguish specific stylistic and textual features of novelisations, other than a notable lack of descriptions or overall clumsy writing. Hence it is equally problematic to discuss the literary merits of Christopher Priest's *eXistenZ*. First, of course, as René Wellek puts it, "we must face the problem of 'literariness,' the central issue of aesthetics, the nature of art and literature" (Wellek 1963: 293). The Russian Formalist Jurij Tynjanov approaches this notion dynamically. He states that the existence of a literary fact depends on its interrelationship with literary and extraliterary orders. Accordingly, what "in one epoch would be a literary fact would in another be a common matter of social communication, and vice versa, depending on the whole literary system in which the given fact appears" (Tynjanov 1971: 69). David Miall and Don Kuiken have provided an interesting take on the meaning of literariness. Their findings "suggest a three-component model of literariness involving foregrounded textual or narrative features, readers' defamiliarising or estranged responses to them, and the consequent modification of personal meanings":

> *literariness is constituted when stylistic or narrative variations strikingly defamiliarize conventionally understood referents and prompt reinterpretive transformations of a conventional concept or feeling.* [... W]e suggest that the key to literariness is the interaction of these component processes. [...] literature is unique because it initiates a distinctive form of psychological change (Miall and Kuiken 1999).

Remarkably, this definition bears peculiar resemblances to the concept of science fiction. For Darko Suvin and Robert Scholes the principle of sf was precisely a technique of defamiliarisation or estrangement, combined with a cognitive return to the readers' known world (Scholes 1975: 29 and 46). Suvin borrowed the term "novum" (from Ernst Bloch) for that discontinuous point of difference (Suvin 1979). Damien Broderick suggests that this novum is established and made cognitively recognisable through "*metaphoric strategies and*

metonymic tactics" (Broderick 1995: 155). Science fiction is in fact a symbolist genre, which connects "the exploration of the encounter with difference
to our experience of being-in-the-world" (Roberts 2000: 181). As Gwyneth
Jones has argued, science fiction does not require a suspension of disbelief, but
an active process of translation (Jones 1999: 6). In other words, the narrative
alienates the readers from their conventionally understood world, and prompts
through cognition a reinterpretation of that known environment. *eXistenZ*, for
instance, exposes the viewer's or reader's world as a "construction". It should
be noted, though, that, in science fiction, estrangement is almost always established by narrative variations, and seldom by stylistic features. Language is used
adequately and functionally, but in much science fiction a "*de-emphasis on 'fine
writing'*" prevails (Broderick 1995: 155), which is something the genre shares
with the bulk of novelisations. Furthermore, most science fiction does not take
advantage of its inherent possibilities. Roberts regrets:

> It is hard to deny that many SF texts are limited and narrow if judged by
> the aesthetic criteria sometimes applied to other literatures; that their
> characterisation often is thin, their style dull and unadventurous, their plots
> hackneyed. Moreover, the nova that differentiate the SF world from the
> recognisable world of realist fiction are more often than not drawn from a
> fairly narrow range of stock themes and situations (Roberts 2000: 14).

Additionally, science fiction will frequently be dismissed as lowbrow fiction by
definition. Although much has been achieved for the continuing emancipation
of science fiction from automatic dismissal, especially in this postmodernist
age, it is still perceived to be inferior to literature. Even "literary" science fiction is often read only on the level of the story. This can be mostly ascribed to
people's conditioned "horizon of expectation", a paradigm introduced by Hans
Robert Jauss (1982) to account for a particular culture's response to literature at
a certain moment. Readers will signal "literariness", provided that their attention is captured and held. If they do not expect striking or evocative narrative
variations, they will more likely ignore or discard alienating factors or ambivalent meanings. This still goes for both science fiction and novelisation.

Nevertheless, according to Miall and Kuiken, literary texts precisely pro-
voke readers to question the perspectives acquired from their culture, which
"points to the adaptive value of literature in reshaping our perspectives and
providing us with greater flexibility, especially by impelling us to reconsider our
system of convictions and values." Their defamiliarising stylistic and narrative
variations recall Wolfgang Iser's concept of *Unbestimmtheit*,[4] that is the unexpected gaps or blanks in a narrative which compel readers to construct their
own meaning and interpretation. Iser explains:

> Even in the simplest story there is bound to be some kind of blockage,
> if only for the fact that no tale can ever be told in its entirety. Indeed, it
> is only through inevitable omissions that a story will gain its dynamism.

Thus whenever the flow is interrupted and we are led off in unexpected directions, the opportunity is given to us to bring into play our own faculty for establishing connections – for filling in the gaps left by the text itself (Iser 1988: 216).

As discussed above, novelisations are often marketed as complementary texts. Moreover, many readers expect a novelisation to explain the cases of *Unbestimmtheit* in the film. Consequently, these novels are mostly devoid of gaps left for the readers to interpret. Yet many mainstream novelisations merely copy the film, causing disappointment to readers whose main motivations for reading the "book from the film" are additional explanations or explorations of the film's universe.[5] Nonetheless, novelisations are usually read after a viewing of the film, so that possible gaps are largely filled in with the film's images. In any case, this significant marker for literariness seldom occurs in novelisations.

Literariness in Christopher Priest's *eXistenZ*

On the one hand, Priest's *eXistenZ* thus suffers a dual disadvantage: it is both science fiction and novelisation. On the other hand, the text is profiled as artistic and literary. Originally, though, Priest published *eXistenZ* under the pseudonym of John Luther Novak, which he had also used for his novelisation of *Mona Lisa* (1986). He did this in order to avoid confusion with his own novel that had just been published, namely *The Extremes* (1998). Publishers outside Britain, appealing to the readers' horizon of expectation, asked Priest to use his real name, as the novelisation might in this way gain more prestige and attract another readership. Still, *eXistenZ* is, in certain respects, too attached to its marketing purpose as a "derived product". For instance, time after time Ted Pikul worries about the tangled mix of reality and fiction, or virtual game reality. Cronenberg's subject matter would lend itself well to more psychological, or especially philosophical digressions. The medium of the novel is particularly suitable for such elaborations. Instead, dialogues prevail and action predominates. This "missed opportunity" brings about a certain decrease in *Unbestimmtheit*; the reader could have been saddled with many more unanswered questions. The book *eXistenZ* does not pretend to be a literary novelisation, but chiefly tries to entertain.

Priest's task was not easy to perform. Nevertheless, not only did he transform the script into a readable and fluent story, the final result hints at "literariness", stylistically and narratively. Although, ironically, many novelisations eliminate the visual by avoiding descriptions as much as possible, *eXistenZ* depicts setting and characters with great care. The small amount of descriptions in novelisations can be explained in two ways. For one thing, it may mirror the minimal use of elaborate descriptions in screenplays, by contrast with the dialogue, which is written in full. For another, it may prevent discrepancies between novelisation and film in terms of visualisation, since novelisers usually have to base their adaptation on the script, instead of the actual film; certain locations and characters might thus still be undefined in the filming process. For example, Priest describes the place of the climactic scene as "a small area of level but broken rocky ground, where no trees were growing" (*eX* 25: 247), whereas in the film this is in fact a grassy spot.

A particular highlight in *eXistenZ* is Priest's simple but clever approach to the multiple shifts between reality and the embedded virtual realities. In each case he seizes the opportunity to change chapters too. One ends with the surroundings fading out:

> But Geller had flicked the nipple on the game-pod, and before Pikul could finish his answer the chalet began to melt away around them. The walls thinned out, light shone, light faded. Reality shifted (*eX* 11: 118).

Or: "The room began to dissolve away from them" (*eX* 17: 169). The next chapter begins with the forming of the new setting: "The Chinese restaurant quickly reformed around them, with light and noise and movement swimming into life" (*eX* 18: 171). Formally, Priest imitates the characters' experience by moving from generalities or specific details to more focused situations:

> They were standing. They were together. They were inside a building. They were inside a room inside a building. There were people around and many racks of things, but for a few seconds it was impossible to make sense of what they were seeing or even to work out where they might be (*eX* 12: 119).

Or:

> His fingers were twitching, as if his hands were still playing gently with Geller's soft and willing body, but the rest of his body was rigid and unmoving. Pikul found that he was sitting on a hard wooden bench. [...] Great noise burst in around him as the scene became more coherent (*eX* 14: 141).

Priest also uses the device of repetition effectively. For the last shift of reality layer, he reuses the description of the first setting of the story, which brings it full circle: "It had once been a simple country church, but was deconsecrated years ago. In recent times it had been used for dances, community meetings, elections, the occasional political rally" (*eX* 1: 5; 26: 259). Throughout the novel, Priest's word play remains stylistically precise:

> Possession of a bioport was clearly the entrance ticket to a whole range of sensual experiences, whose thrills could only be guessed at by those who had so far failed to get a bioport fitted. People like Ted Pikul, who had so far failed to get a bioport fitted (*eX* 1: 13).

The events in the novelisation are mostly internally focalised through Ted Pikul: e.g. "To Pikul's eye most of the interior did at least look the way he expected a ski-repair workshop might" (*eX* 9: 105). The reader is thus mainly limited to the inner thoughts of that character: "He was torn with indecision:

should he be the perfect gentleman and look away? Should he gently cover her? Or should he instead pretend not to notice, and let gravity and nature take their course?" (eX 6: 66). Because the narrative is bound to Pikul's point of view, Priest sometimes adjusts it so as to sustain this internal focalisation:

> Pikul wondered if he should continue to lie in the humiliating facedown position in the chair awhile longer, to ram home his point about having to suffer, then decided against it. Slowly he eased himself around. His eyes focused (eX 8: 89).

Or:

> Unable to see her without twisting his head, he sensed her moving around behind him (eX 11: 117).

Or:

> Pikul, still barely conscious, hardly able to take in anything other than the violent sensations of his own pain, [...] As his vision dimmed, he found that he could see down into the valley. [...] His mind was dying. The last words he heard before the ultimate blackness flooded in came from Geller (eX 25: 257).

The introduction of Pikul, who is not yet accustomed to Allegra Geller's game world, is a way of skirting the problem of our unfamiliarity with the novum of this sf text. In this way script and novelisation cleverly insert the required "info-dump" without making it too obvious. This technique involves a character lecturing "a captive audience about something they could be expected to know but which we do not" (Mendlesohn 2003: 5). Not everything, though, is focalised through Pikul. The short scene outdoors at the gas station is internally focalised through Geller:

> Geller walked as far as the Land Rover [...] She breathed the air deeply. For the first time since leaving the church, she was beginning to feel comparatively safe. Yes, the crazies were undoubtedly still out there somewhere looking for her, but it would take them a long time to narrow their search down to this particular filling station on this particular road (eX 7: 83-84).

Priest handles the transitions from one focaliser to the other very subtly. On a single occasion, the narrator takes over: "Unseen by Geller or Pikul: the restaurant dog had left his spot in the sunlight and was now cowering close to their table. [...] He began to gnaw at the gun, growling" (eX 18: 181). In the last chapter the events are externally focalised through a narrator-focaliser:

> They were interrupted by Ted Pikul and Allegra Geller, who had separated themselves from the main group. Pikul was leading the dog the security guards had been looking after for him while he was playing the game (eX 26: 274).

This discrepancy stresses the dissimilarity between Pikul's and Geller's "real" characters and their game personalities, which the reader assumed were real. The lack of internal focalisation also masks the status of this new layer in reality, increasing the reader's doubt whether it is the "real" reality, or still a game.

As a complex and critical science-fiction story, the novelisation of *eXistenZ* certainly draws attention to its narrative variations. It is likely that its readers' "reinterpretive effort modifies or transforms their conventional concepts or feelings" (Miall and Kuiken 1999). According to Miall and Kuiken, literary texts prompt readers to develop "an affective theme across striking or evocative passages," as they become "implicated in the existential concerns embodied in those passages". Arguably, this goes for *eXistenZ* too. Priest not only wields a refined style, paying much attention to word choice and sentence structure, but has also adapted Cronenberg's narrative as effectively as possible, despite a few "shortcomings". One drawback is that, overall, the novelisation is too explicit in terms of philosophical themes. Additionally, several inherent problems are brought to light when the novel is compared to the actual film, and when the filmic specificity of *eXistenZ* is taken into account.

A Comparison between Two Forms of *eXistenZ*

Christopher Priest's novelisation features a few, mostly minor, differences from the film. Although, according to Baetens, a novelisation is an anti-adaptation, the notions "transfer" and "adaptation proper" are not out of place in the case of *eXistenZ*. A screenwriter has a certain visual image of the film in mind. This does not necessarily need to be transposed in the film, but it is certainly a prominent, if not the most important, aspect of a screenplay. As David Cronenberg both wrote and directed *eXistenZ*, it is even more likely that the script is cinematographic rather than novelistic. In this respect, McFarlane's terminology is not invalid. A noveliser has to find a certain equilibrium between elements that can be transferred and elements which cannot. Likewise, Priest says:

> I read the script through to get some sense of what the eventual film might be like, thought about it for a bit, mentally decided which scenes would work best in a novel, and which ones would need to be revised slightly to make them work, then got down to it. [...] In general, what you try to do is produce a book that will run parallel to the film. It should try to have the same effect on the reader as the film will have on its audience. It should tell the same story, have the same characters, have the same general "feel". But a book requires many more words than a screenplay, so you have the opportunity to embellish a little: work in some back-story, fill out the background, describe the locations, and so on (Van Parys, Jansen and Vanhoutte 2004).

On the whole, the dialogues are extended in the novel. Most likely Priest deliberately added some lines, but it should be taken into account that a certain amount of filmed dialogue has not made it through the editing process. Of course, this goes for other differences as well. The novel includes two longer scenes not in the final film: one at the very beginning of the novel, which places Ted Pikul outside the church, where he is called up by the Antenna head office, and another in which the game "eXistenZ" is paused a second time, and Pikul and Geller are confronted with a "game residue".

A more striking change, however, is Pikul's explicit sexual motivation. In the film, Jennifer Jason Leigh's character persuades Jude Law's to play "eXistenZ" by promising him both freedom and sex. Cronenberg wanted to convey the seductive element in an artist: the game designer is trying to seduce the audience to buy and play the game, just as the actor seduces the audience to believe in his character (Cronenberg 1999). Laura Borràs adds:

> at all times throughout the film, this association of ideas is made between the game and pleasure, the desire for connection and sexual desire, as well as the process of stimulation in order to enter the game and the process of sexual stimulation, a game of seductions and promises to convince the other – an "other", which in this case, is the male, since the leisure nymphomaniac *par excellence* is Allegra Geller herself, the designer of the game system, who appears as a complete games addict, a hybrid halfway between nymphomania and drug-dependency (Borràs 2003).

Allegra Geller is a seducer or hypnotist, plus both director of, and actor in the game. As a conwoman, she is seductive in terms of both sex and freedom. Beyond sexuality, she offers Pikul the opportunity to escape from his narrow-minded existence. Thus, she promises him both sexual liberation and the overcoming of the problems he has with his own body. In the novel, however, the Pikul character is narrowed down, almost marginalised, as he is portrayed with very little innocence or integrity. His motives are questionable in comparison with Jude Law's righteous and naïve character; it is only the allure of sex with Geller that triggers his actions. For example:

> He was swirling with emotions and confusion. When she said games, did she mean ... ? He'd like to play with her, of course, but were they thinking about the same thing? (*eX* 6: 71).

And:

> She allowed him to return her kiss, and for a few moments Pikul thought she was about to give him a seriously messy time (*eX* 17: 168).

Priest comments:

> I felt that having a more overt sexual relationship between Jennifer Jason Leigh and Jude Law gave the story a bit more impact, so I made it more detailed. I was also drawing on experience. [...] The actual scenes are often improvised on the day between the actors and the director. The screenplay will confine itself to "they go to bed together and make love", and will only mention details if those details have a bearing on the characters or the plot. So from the point of view of the novelizer (who hasn't seen the

film, and only has a short paragraph to work with) all options are open. My own policy is to try to write such scenes so they are consistent with the characters, the story, what is going to happen next, and so on. It's literally impossible to second-guess the film, so you write the novel the best way you can (Van Parys, Jansen and Vanhoutte 2004).

At first, we might assume that this adaptation proper fits in with Pikul's deeper motivation to murder Geller in the end, since he is a "Realist" himself. However, that does not correspond with his inner thoughts. This problem is inherent to this particular novelisation. The narrator offers the readers a look into Pikul's mind through internal focalisation. As a Realist, Pikul should continually be acting in front of his companion, but his thoughts conflict with this plot. Instead of escorting Geller with intent to kill her, he is merely led by her sexual promises. Moreover, Pikul repeatedly idolises her:

> Clearly, she was nervous, but her modest smiles made her seem, to Pikul at least, a vision of all that was good, wise, intelligent, and beautiful in the world (*eX* 1: 11).

And:

> He couldn't figure her out, though. She wasn't leading him on: nothing in anything she said or did gave that impression. She was just ... good to be with (*eX* 6: 63-64).

In addition, he genuinely has no clue of what is happening to them both, and is in a constant state of panic, fearing for his life in "transCendenZ", and for his body in "eXistenZ". His inner mind is thus not in keeping with his real intentions. The *mise-en-abyme* structure complicates things even more, as from this perspective the narrator ignores another level of Pikul's consciousness. Of course, the problem should rather be attributed to the story itself; if Priest had not internally focalised Pikul, the novelisation would have been much less fluent and accessible. As a result, Pikul's character works perfectly visually, but is most liable to inconsistencies in the novelised narrative. Finally, this also serves as an example of the visuality of screenplays, as opposed to novelisations: screenwriters' primary concerns are not textual problems, but the final images.

Counteraction of Two Cultural Practices

Two points of divergence further pose problems for Priest's novelisation. Priest considers Cronenberg's conception of virtual reality as somewhat outdated (Vernet 2001). He states that Cronenberg's vision is a bit "eccentric, and not all that original" (Van Parys, Jansen and Vanhoutte 2004). He feels the mind is "not likely to be boggled too much by the Chinese restaurant". In the same vein, he criticises the political aspect of the story and the "corny ending". He explains that books from the 1960s like Philip K. Dick's *The Three Stigmata of Palmer Eldritch* (1964) already "contained ideas and situations that were many times more interesting and sophisticated". Likewise, John Clute observes that questioning the distinction between reality and virtual reality is typical of 1980s science fiction (Clute 2003b: 76). Priest himself has been working with "advanced concepts of virtual reality for at least the last twenty years, and most of those were a bit more ambitious than weirdo frog-parts". In particular, Priest mentions *The Extremes* (1998), which, he adds, Cronenberg could not have known about. Still, this discrepancy in view did not have any influence on Priest's efforts:

> For one thing, screenplays are endlessly rewritten, often to satisfy people in the film business who haven't the vaguest idea how screenplays are written. I could all too easily imagine that by the time the script reached me, it was the product of many compromises, revisions and substitutions. [...] I took his material and made the best book I could out of it (Van Parys, Jansen and Vanhoutte 2004).

Priest's first draft, though, was not approved: "someone in Mr Cronenberg's office (of course, it might have come from Mr Cronenberg himself) said that the novel wasn't dark or menacing enough, that it was too fast-paced, too light. They wanted it made more sombre" (Van Parys, Jansen and Vanhoutte 2004). Probably Cronenberg had nothing to do with that "rejection". Priest says:

> The irony of this, for me, was that one of the things I most liked about the script was its pace, its storytelling flair, and the witty and intriguing dialogue. [...] Cronenberg is an excellent writer. The Jude Law character, in particular, has a nice line in dry asides. The Willem Dafoe character is written in an over-the-top way, which Dafoe, incidentally, translated perfectly on the screen. [...] I mentally imagined the film as being something like a science fiction version of *The Big Lebowski*, kind of bittersweet, amusing, oddball. I wrote the book accordingly. [...] far from being dark and menacing, the movie was an amusing, interesting, well-made adventure film with a lot of witty dialogue and entertaining scenes. There was some fairly gruesome stuff [...] but even that seemed to us to be played not as horror but as black humour. Maybe it was a culture clash: our British sense of irony against North American literalism? (Van Parys, Jansen and Vanhoutte 2004).

Priest and his editor agreed that he would run through his manuscript one more time, and "look for every opportunity to introduce a sense of looming threat":

> I put in more negative adverbs: nervously, gloomily, darkly, terrifyingly, and so on. I made the weather worse. I kept the hours of daylight shorter. I described worrying noises. I interjected lines of dialogue and description. "I don't like this." "What the hell was that?" That sort of thing. I did what I could. It seemed to be enough, because after that, up to the present day, I have never heard another word from either Mr Cronenberg or his staff (Van Parys, Jansen and Vanhoutte 2004).

Both these issues should have been resolved in a discussion between director and noveliser, but no form of communication has come about. Although *eXistenZ* was released by independent companies Serendipity and Alliance Atlantis, thus without assistance from the Hollywood hype-machine, it is likely, though not certain, that it was the film's producers who blundered, or, to recycle Priest's paraphrase, "people in the film business who haven't the vaguest idea" (Van Parys, Jansen and Vanhoutte 2004) how novelisations are written. In that way, they have thwarted their original idea of assigning the novelisation of this artistic film to a literary author, by contrast with the usual noveliser.

Raymond Williams has argued that every medium is established by the interaction of four forces: the apparatus, the psychological, physical or emotional experience, the public, and the producers (Williams 1990). This concept has been denominated as the "cultural practice", or "cultural form", of a medium. Viewing the novelisation of *eXistenZ* in such a framework explains why it partly fails to come up to literary expectations. Firstly, it is clear that the technological infrastructure of the novel does not have any limitations in this respect. Secondly, though, the overall "experience" of the novelisation may be partly responsible. A novelisation is generally bound to disappear rapidly from the market, because its life span is largely dependent on the film's circulation and attraction as a novelty. Consequently, novelisations are subject to the experience of the respective films; Cronenberg's *eXistenZ* spent little time in movie theatres, and was a box-office failure, although it was critically acclaimed. Thirdly, the horizon of expectation of the mass public clashes with the producers' intention of hiring a literary noveliser. A novel at the same time science fiction and novelisation, both disdained genres, is not likely to be treated as the film's "other". Fourthly, the producing force, apart from the actual writer of course, blocks Priest's original reading of the screenplay. His novels, from *The Space Machine* (1976) onwards, have often had metafictional connotations or contained characteristics of the pastiche. He has repeatedly pushed at the limits of science fiction, contributing to the genre's ongoing discussion. In that sense, he can be considered a postmodern science fiction author. Precisely Priest's thematic input and personal interpretation, based on his deeper insight into the matter, could have constituted an important artistic factor in the novelisation of *eXistenZ*. Yet, by toning down the parodic nature of Priest's novel, the person from Cronenberg's office partially shifts the novelisation from the film's "other" to its "double". In conclusion, Priest was counteracted by three of the four poles. This discussion also sheds light on the dominance of the film's practice over the novel's. The "experience" of the novelisation depends on the reception and actuality of the film, and its readership is largely a subset of the film's hard core audience. Furthermore, neither Priest nor his editor had the final say over the novelisation; the producers of the film, on the other hand, did. This repression of the novelisation's manifestation as a cultural practice limits its pursuit of an unconstrained identity. However, a certain dependence on the film intrinsically holds for every prototypic novelisation, and should not necessarily be deemed negative. Novelisers should take advantage of the genre's vague definitions and ongoing search for recognition, and experiment with its various potentialities. Still, in this case, the film's influence has probably not been for the good; the novelisation of *eXistenZ*, as a cultural form, is not fully-fledged.

Specificity in David Cronenberg's *eXistenZ*

eXistenZ perfectly fits within the "Cronenberg project". David Cronenberg's works "manipulate the imagery of medicine, trauma, sexual desire, the surgical and the organic, to conduct an ongoing interrogation of human embodiment and identity" (Bould 2003: 93). Over the years he has become an acclaimed director, an auteur; yet many critics are still repulsed by the sexuality and violence in his films, features emphasised by his distinct sense of visuality. This section will argue that the filmic specificity of *eXistenZ* makes the screenplay less fit for novelisation. Priest brings up this issue as well:

> at the time the novel is being written, the author only has a screenplay to work with. It's probably not even a final version, a shooting script. You have no real idea which actors will be in it, or where the film will be shot. You have no knowledge of the music, the pace, what the special effects will look like, the way the lighting will be used, the overall style (Van Parys, Jansen and Vanhoutte 2004).

In other words, the noveliser can only guess at the scriptwriter's imaginary images of the film.

The film's specificity is foregrounded through a combination of auditive and visual aspects. The auditive manifests itself in the significance of language and Howard Shore's score: both are used functionally. Traditionally, many essentialist theoreticians defended the idea that sound was some sort of parasite, and that film lost its specificity with the addition of the soundtrack, as sound allegedly narrowed down the images and their philosophy. While images are open to multiple interpretations, sound would direct the viewer more to one specific emotion or interpretation. However, the soundscape in *eXistenZ* adds to the meaning instead of reducing it. Firstly, the players' speech differs from conventional discourse in the virtual reality games. For one thing, the system largely controls dialogues in order to advance the game. "Free will is obviously not a factor in this little game world of yours", Pikul says (*eX* 18: 178). Game characters, as well as game players, have words put into their mouths against their will, and are switched to "memory-save mode" when another player utters a useless line. As a consequence, players frequently repeat and rephrase sentences in conversations. For another thing, many players have strong accents, for example Gas's country accent, or Kiri Vinokur's pronounced East European accent. Thus language turns out to give the game players something to hold on to when they try to discern reality from virtual reality. The characters' repetition of lines and the presence of accents play a revealing rôle. Borràs remarks:

> it is the words, or more exactly, the dialogues, that let us know whether we are in reality or in a game. The images [...] are fantasy, fictions, while it is language that provides a context of truth, of reality. The same words that have served since time immemorial to create fiction, are here the only anchor to reality (Borràs 2003).

Secondly, the construction of Shore's score to *eXistenZ* reflects the film's *mise-en-abyme* structure. Howard Shore is a long-time collaborator of Cronenberg. Recently, he has stepped in the limelight by scoring Peter Jackson's *The Lord of the Rings* (2001-2003), but previously he had already composed small masterpieces such as *The Silence of the Lambs* (1991) and Tim Burton's *Ed Wood* (1994). Shore is a quite intellectual, unconventional and, although many only associate him with thriller and horror music, a versatile film composer. His music for *eXistenZ* mirrors both the texture of Cronenberg's film and the film's various layers of reality at the same time. Shore comments:

> The score is all about perception and perspective of sound. [...] If you listen to a symphony orchestra, there's a context to how the sound reaches you because of the way the orchestra is seated. The brass are in a certain position, so you hear certain things in a certain perspective. [...] we've developed this perspective of what we accept as being correct for the way music is supposed to sound. The movie explores that idea on another level – not in music, but in reality, what's real and what's virtual – and the attempt was to do something similar to that musically. What I did through the recording was to create certain sounds and certain perspectives that you wouldn't normally hear. Things that play very soft in musical terms might be very close to your ear and might in effect be very loud. Things that are very loud might be placed further back in perspective, and sound very quiet. The perspectives are being constantly altered depending on the scene in the film. The score uses a lot of elements of sound. It's a large orchestra, but it's been recorded in a unique way. It also uses other layers of sound. There are live electronic instruments like the theremin and a sextet of electric guitars. There is also an electronic soundscape [...] that we then combined with the acoustic recordings. It's a very layered, very textured score, and the studio was used as a creative tool to create it (Broxton 1999).

In "eXistenZ by Antenna" and "Anti-eXistenZialists", for instance, Shore creates the effect of multiple sound layers on top of each other by means of a continuous bass sound on which different motifs are stacked by other instruments. In "MetaFlesh Game-Pods", among other cues, he puts instruments into the foreground which are normally more drowned; the strings, for example, rise above the brass section. The score thus echoes the film formally, in its structure, as well as thematically, in its mood and humour. Cronenberg acknowledges Shore's merits:

> Il fait partie des premières personnes à qui je demande de lire mes scénarios. Sa musique est celle du murmure et de la répétition, elle nous parvient par vagues. Son rythme est parfaitement en phase avec mon cinéma, essentiel à sa réussite (Joyard and Tesson 1999).

> [He has become one of the first people that I ask to read my scripts. His music is of whispers and repetitions, it comes to us in waves. His rhythm is perfectly in tune with my cinema, essential to its success.]

These auditive elements can hardly be transferred to the novelisation. It can describe the characters' pronunciation, but lacks Shore's contribution altogether.

Visually speaking, Cronenberg's *eXistenZ* has a very specific texture and outlook, which makes the film, and the script for that matter, particularly difficult to novelise. It is basically a visual nightmare: virtual reality functions as a dream, with nightmares within nightmares. In accordance with Freudian dream psychology, the game players' dreams can become real via their unconsciousness, which also determines the course of the game.[6] In the title sequence, reminiscent of Saul Bass's work, Cronenberg creates "a dream-like atmosphere", evoking the film's biocentric theme through different layers of colours, animal tissues and cell structures. Other losses in the novelisation are the visual references to the game universe. As part of the game pact, many objects in the film are parodically labelled, such as the "Motel", the "Chinese Restaurant" and the "Country Gas Station". In addition, the sets, decor and the players' clothes are simplified, just as in computer game design details are avoided to save memory and to make the characters' movements more believable three-dimensionally. Cronenberg also integrated subtle differences in the characters' appearance in the diverse layers of (virtual) reality. For example, when Pikul and Geller enter "eXistenZ", their hair styling and clothing are different. Similarly, the church set for "transCendenZ" at the end is basically the same as the one for "eXistenZ" at the beginning, but with subtle changes: different paint and banners suggest an alternate "alternate present". Finally, some shots in the film have an estranging effect during a first viewing, but make sense to the viewers when they realise that "eXistenZ" is a game within a game, for example Geller's touching of a wall at the gas station and Pikul's clasping of a seat in Vinokur's cabin. These scenes refer to the idea of examining the authenticity of the created world; in other words, the players of "transCendenZ" experience a sense of wonder about how real everything is. In conclusion, the medium of the novel is not quite apt to convey the script's narrative and the film's specificity, neither through transfer nor through adaptation proper. The novelisation's ineffective attempt at visuality ironically emphasises its lack of that quality. The novel is unable to "detach itself from its visual origin", as, for instance, a significant amount of descriptions continually but incompletely evoke the film's final images.

A "Different" Novelisation?

Christopher Priest began as a distinctive science-fiction author, but by the late 1970s broadened his literary path and published work that was less determined by the norms of the science-fiction genre (see Butler's chapter for his attitudes to the genre). He has combined science fiction with fictional innovations to elevate the genre from its degraded level. Like Cronenberg, he has put science fiction and so-called highbrow texts into perspective, generating hybrids of these genres. Not many people will have "expected" this when, in 1999, they saw the novelisation of *eXistenZ* lying among stock mass-distribution paperbacks on supermarket shelves. However, in line with the artistic profile of the text, the novelisation was offered to an eminent science-fiction author. This establishes *eXistenZ* as possessing an unusual suspect of "literariness". The novel's aspiration to the literary, unmistakably present, is balanced by its readability and accessibility, without falling into the commercial trap. In that way, this "uncommon" novelisation more or less manages to be the film's "double" and "other" at the same time. Thus, not only has Priest refreshed the nature of science fiction time and again, but he has also made a worthy contribution to the genre of novelisation.

Notes

1. I would like to thank Lien Jansen and Elisabeth Vanhoutte for their help on the research paper which provided the basis for this essay, and Jan Baetens for his input and feedback.
2. "Ekphrasis" generally means the detailed description of an existing or fictive work of art in poetry or prose. The term "anti-ekphrasis", then, signifies that in a commercial novelisation the text itself usually ignores its connection to the film.
3. This term derives from Gérard Genette's notion of the paratext, the textual layers which give a book meaning. It consists of the epitext – binding, paper, typography, typeface and so on – and the peritext – interviews, essays, media responses and so on. See Genette 1991.
4. A similar term is used by Nicholas Ruddick in his chapter.
5. A perfect illustration of this explanatory function is the novelisation of *The Sixth Sense*, which contains a coda with answers to frequently asked questions about the film.
6. This paragraph is partially indebted to Cronenberg's "Director's Commentary" (on Cronenberg 1999).

The Other War: Christopher Priest's *The Separation*

Victoria Stewart

The Second World War continues to be a compelling topic for both historians and authors of literary works. In recent years, writers across genres have displayed a particular interest in the often problematic interface between history and memory exposed by the conflict and its aftermath. In history, writers such as Antony Beevor (in *Stalingrad* (1998) and *Berlin: The Downfall 1945* (2002)) have revivified the use of individual testimony as a means of forging a connection between historical events and the ordinary people affected by them. In literature, meanwhile, authors have interrogated the relationship between history and memory, often through the use of narrative techniques which, rather than simply giving priority to personal testimony and, therefore, to memory, problematise the ways in which memory either works or fails to work. Novels including Ian McEwan's *Atonement* (2001) and Michael Frayn's *Spies* (2002) expose the difficulty of simply displacing the authoritative voice of the historian with the voice of the individual "on the ground". The replacement of one explanatory metanarrative – history – with another – memory – can efface the extent to which it is in the interaction of the two that experience resides. Like Frayn and McEwan, Christopher Priest, in *The Separation* (2002), chooses to complicate this interaction through the use of a protagonist whose memory is far from reliable. This has startling results on a narrative dealing with an alternate outcome to the Second World War. As Liz Williams has suggested, the novel is not only about the "contingency of history" but also about the "contingency of identity" (Williams 2003: 104), and these are not always clearly separable from each other.

In what follows, I will be showing how Priest uses a variety of "found texts" to create a narrative in which neither history nor identity are certain. Drawing on connections with other texts dealing with the Second World War, by both Priest and other writers, I will show why the tropes of amnesia and anamnesis (forgetting, and the remembering of what was forgotten) are particularly suited to this type of narrative. I will also suggest that part of the impact of *The Separation* stems from its production of uncanny effects, that is, its play with notions of un/familiarity and its disconcerting use of repetition. In Sigmund Freud's classic analysis of the uncanny in his essay of 1919, the double is identified as a particular locus of uncanny effects in literature. Although the double can function for the child or the primitive mind as "an assurance of immortality", at later stages it "becomes the uncanny harbinger of death" (Freud 1990: 357). In his use of doubles, appropriately a recurrent theme in his writings, Priest exploits the fact that the reassuring can, often through persistence or return, take on uncanny qualities. In *The Separation*, the impact of this trope is increased by the fact that Priest's references to the doubles of historical figures have a grounding in the cultural mythology of war. The implications of this doubling, therefore, resonate beyond the boundaries of the narrative, and Priest's doubles have both political and psychic impact.

Fiction and the Archive

Priest chooses to structure his alternate history through the construction of an alternate archive. The use of "found" documents in conjunction with the exploration of memory is a technique that Suzanne Keen sees as characteristic of a culture "[l]acking consensus about the appropriate uses of the past [...] but acutely aware of a past demanding reinterpretation and inviting exploration" (Keen 2001: 96). Keen explores a range of novels which take this approach – notably A. S. Byatt's *Possession* (1990), a reconsideration of popular conceptions about the Victorian period – although she misses the opportunity to discuss Priest's *The Prestige* (1995), which also uses this technique to powerful effect. Constructing and presenting "fake" documents is a means of questioning the authority (and even authenticity) of historical accounts, and has been considered a quintessentially postmodern narrative method. Linda Hutcheon coined the influential term "historiographic metafiction" for such novels, in which a "theoretical self-awareness of history and fiction as human constructs [...] is made the grounds for rethinking and reworking the forms and contents of the past" (Hutcheon 1988: 5). She stresses that such texts question not only historical processes, but also subjectivity: narrators are often sceptical about both historical events and their own powers of recall. However, as Keen argues, many "fictions of the archive" in fact attempt to assert, "[i]n the face of postmodern scepticism" (Keen 2001: 3), that questions about the past can, albeit provisionally, be answered. Many are firmly rooted in the techniques of literary realism and their metafictional aspects, those which raise doubt about the status of any attempt to represent the world realistically, are implicit, rather than being foregrounded as they would be in less realistic postmodern texts. Despite being rooted in an alternate world – one in which the Second World War ends in 1941 – *The Separation* is also rooted in realism, and if anything this serves to make its effects even more disconcerting.

Priest's focus on the Second World War chimes in, as I have suggested, with a continuing cultural interest in this period, but it also has biographical roots. Like Ian McEwan – also named, in 1983, as one of the book industry's Best Young British Novelists – Priest grew up with an awareness of the aftermath of the war. McEwan has noted that his interest in writing about Dunkirk in *Atonement* stemmed in part from him having a relative who saw action in the campaign;[1] Priest, meanwhile, has described the impact on his childhood self of growing up amid the post-war ruins of Manchester:

> Every childhood trip into town took us through the bombed inner suburbs, with their acres of rubble [...] Gradually, the authorities cleared away the mess [...] but I continued to be haunted by vivid imaginings of what might have gone on during those traumatic winter nights of 1941 (Priest 2003b: 31, and see also the interview in this volume).

Stuart Gratton in *The Separation* is also affected by the "traces of the war" in the form of the ruins of Manchester which remain "unrepaired for many years" (S 1: 4: 14) and are one factor behind his decision to become an historian. The idea of the war leaving both physical and psychic residues also echoes Gordon Sinclair's description of the city in *The Quiet Woman* (1990):

> The country was enduring the aftermath for most of the time I was growing up. For instance, much of the centre of Manchester had been destroyed by German bombs, and for many years my unconscious assumption about how any big city must look was that it consisted of acres of wasteland and rubble (*QW* 19: 113).

But here, having used realistic techniques to establish the atmosphere of post-war England, Priest introduces the counterfactual in the form of the Guard Volunteers, a para-military group established during the war to "free the police from defence and air raid duties" (*QW* 24: 162). The persistence of this force after the end of the war, its uniform providing Sinclair with "anonymity and a feeling of power" (*QW* 24: 163), has implications that are also relevant to *The Separation*. The violence of war cannot simply be ring-fenced within a discrete historical period or set of events. Just as the ruins of the city remain as a per-sisting reminder of what has passed, so in *The Quiet Woman* the violence of wartime cannot simply be effaced or forgotten.

Such sentiments have a corollary in the work of the playwright Howard Brenton, who was born in 1942, and who shares with Priest an interest in the cultural and historical status of both Winston Churchill and Rudolf Hess. In his dystopia *The Churchill Play* (1974; rev. 1984), Brenton develops arguments put forward by Angus Calder in his influential study *The People's War* (1969), suggesting that the successful conduct of the war effort required an emulation of the type of organisational structures that were in place in Nazi Germany: "[I]n fighting fascism, the country started slipping *towards* fascism" (Boon 1990: 115). Brenton also implies that the violence that was apparently neces-sary in wartime could not simply vanish after the war, although he is clearer about the consequences of this than he is about possible alternate courses of action that could have been taken.

Whilst Priest's portrayal of Churchill in *The Separation* will bear comparison with Brenton's in *The Churchill Play*, it is worth distinguishing briefly between Priest's narrative structure in *The Separation* and those employed by other recent British "alternate world" fictions in which different outcomes to the Second World War are considered.[2] To take an example discussed by Suzanne Keen, Robert Harris's *Fatherland* (1992) uses the generic characteristics of the thriller, but its action is set in an alternate 1964, with the Nazis having won the war. The "archive" aspect of the novel centres around the discovery by detective Xavier March of an account of the Wannsee conference, at which the fate of European Jewry was sealed. In Harris's Germany, nothing is known of the Holocaust; the Nazi desire to eradicate the events from history has been fulfilled – almost. Spurred on by American journalist Charlotte Maguire, March embarks on a search through the archives in the hope that the Nazi insistence on bureaucratic efficiency will mean that the relevant documents have been preserved, which indeed they have. Harris recreates missing sections of the minutes of the conference, and March learns the truth, albeit at the cost of his life. Less skilfully done and more crudely polemical, although still a useful point of reference, is Stephen Fry's *Making History* (1996), in which a young history student learns of a machine which could enable him to go back in time and ensure that Hitler is never born. Having decided to change the course of history, the protagonist wakes up in an alternate world which is not at all to his liking: America has world dominance and some of the worst excesses of totalitarianism have not been avoided. He eventually decides to turn history back, although by sleight of hand he is able to retrieve his lover from the alternate present.

Fry's novel establishes the present using realistic techniques and then has its protagonist move from it into an alternative; Harris carefully establishes the causes of his alternate 1960s, making playful references to events, such as the formation of The Beatles, which, strangely, manage to happen even in the event of a Nazi victory.[3] Whilst Priest, like Harris, imagines a threatened and insular USA, he uses a different narrative technique, one which has highly disconcerting effects on the reader. The novel opens using third-person narration to describe Stuart Gratton's book-signing and his encounter with Angela Chipperton; then, through a description of Gratton's own historical research, it is established that the war has ended in 1941, with the success of Rudolf Hess's peace mission to England. In the second section of the book, however, the reader is confronted with a switch to first-person narration, and eventually discerns that this is the manuscript given to Stuart by Angela. It reveals that, for Angela's father Jack Sawyer, the war ended in a way that will be familiar to the reader: Nazi Germany is defeated in 1945. I will return to the particular ways in which the processes of disordered memory are used to structure Jack's narrative; for the moment, it is worth stressing the vertiginous effect that the introduction of this familiar account of the war has on the reader. The compass points of Stuart's version of the war are established through a summary of his book, *The Last Day of the War*. The reader is given descriptions of how both recognisable historical figures, such as Joseph Goebbels and Guy Gibson, and more minor, perhaps invented, players, including Kurt Hofmann, a test pilot, spent the last day of the war, and what became of them afterwards. The description of Gratton's book acts to establish, for the reader, the "official" version of events: in *Fatherland*, a description of the contents of Xavier March's daily paper acts in a similar way (Harris 1993: 39-40). The reader might expect Jack's narrative to support or verify Stuart's account, but to be reintroduced to the familiar, after having absorbed the details of the alternate version of the war produces doubts about the status of both Stuart's history and Jack's testimony. The recognisable Second World War here re-emerges in an uncanny fashion, having been rendered unfamiliar by the section of the narrative that precedes it. It soon becomes evident, however, that Priest is not simply staging an encounter between Jack's version of the war and Stuart's, or between "official" history and the less easily verifiable memoir. The use of the Sawyer twins' progress through the war, at times parallel, at times intersecting, undercuts the trustworthiness of both history and the memoir. Official documents, which are introduced later in the narrative in the form of material extracted from various archives by Sam Levy, one of Jack's aircrew, tend to obfuscate rather than clarify. Equally, letters from Birgit, Joe Sawyer's wife, seem, impossibly, to support both twins' versions of events. Thus, where other fictions of the archive or alternate world narratives grant us fixed co-ordinates, here the use of twins creates what Liz Williams has described as a double helix structure, "in which the same points are revisited from different perspectives, only to split apart and twist away" (Williams 2003: 103). There are similarities here with Priest's use of different accounts of the same events in *The Prestige* (1995); there, too, an uncanny element is crucial, coming to the fore in the climax of the novel when Andrew Westley's suspicions about being a twin are confirmed.

Remembering War

Entangling Jack's memoir and Joe's notebooks and diary entries in this double helix means that Priest avoids simply instating memory, in the place of history, as the best means of accessing the past. As I have noted, the foregrounding of the processes of memory is a tactic employed by a number of other writers in connection with the Second World War. In a novel such as Michael Frayn's *Spies*, however, despite his self-doubt, uncertainty and scepticism about the powers of memory, the narrator eventually manages to produce (or re-produce) a version of the events of his wartime childhood that has coherence. The activity of remembering has restorative qualities, and going back over old ground, literally as well as figuratively, allows gaps to be filled and many, if not all, questions answered.

Perhaps more akin to Priest's rather less comforting account of the processes of memory is Chris Paling's *After the Raid* (1995). Here, Gregory Swift, who is traumatised following the death of his wife in an air-raid, can never be sure whether what he is inhabiting is dream, hallucination or reality, and the reader shares this uncertainty. Paling's protagonist repeatedly falls asleep at the end of one chapter and awakes at the start of the next not into consciousness but into another dream. Regaining the co-ordinates of reality becomes an increasingly fraught and difficult process for both Swift and the reader. This Chinese-box structure has similar effects to Joe Sawyer's disordered memory processes; before I move on to examine these, however, it is worth considering further the reasons why disordered memories of the Second World War should have interested so many recent writers.

I have already indicated that for Priest and others of his generation, the war left tangible scars on surrounding cityscapes but was also impressed at the level of family history. Yet writers such as Paling, Frayn and McEwan also appear to echo, sometimes consciously, sometimes not, the concerns of a number of novelists writing while the Second World War was in progress. Paling's novel bears the stylistic fingerprints of Henry Green, who, particularly in *Caught* (1943) and *Back* (1946), attempted to represent the memory processes of those traumatised either by combat or by other forms of involvement in the war effort. Patrick Hamilton in *Hangover Square* (1941) and Graham Greene in *The Ministry of Fear* (1943) use the form of the thriller but complicate this by featuring protagonists who have damaged memories. In Hamilton's case, George Harvey Bone suffers from dissociation, and, during his attacks, expresses the desire to inflict violence on his flighty girlfriend. He begins to spend more and more time in a murderous state of mind and eventually carries out his plan, just as the outbreak of war is announced. For about a third of Greene's novel, Arthur Rowe is suffering from amnesia brought about by an air-raid, a state which allows him to forget his pre-war mercy killing of his wife. He is happier not knowing the truth, but ultimately has to return to wartime reality.

Even James Hilton's *Random Harvest* (1941), a novel now less familiar than its romanticised 1943 screen adaptation, uses memory loss as a means of analysing the rights and wrongs of going to war again. "Smithy", a shell-shocked First World War veteran, unable to remember his life before the war, has pacifist convictions and abhors the idea of a further conflict. Regaining his memory, and forgetting his life as "Smithy", Charles Rainier takes up his rôle as head of the family firm and, through his business concerns, contributes indirectly to preparations for the coming war. Paula, the wife he married during his amnesiac state, helps him to regain his lost years, but although the lovers are reunited, in other key respects, Hilton's narrative is inconclusive. Smithy could have continued to work to prevent the war, but it seems unlikely that Charles Rainier will be able to renege on his contribution. In showing the two alternatives – Smithy's pacifism and Rainier's business-mindedness – consecutively, Hilton accedes to the historical logic unavoidable at the time he was writing: the war has broken out, and there is no means of resorting to an alternative.

In using the uncertainties of memory as a structural device, then, Priest is both sharing the concerns of other contemporary writers, and echoing a number of works produced during wartime. Considering memory allows an exploration not just of how the past is made sense of retrospectively but also how the extreme experiences of wartime could affect subjectivity. Nor is it incidental that the narratives attributed to each of the twins display quite distinct experiences not only of the war, but of memory itself.

Jack's narrative is marked from the outset as a war memoir: "I was a serving officer with RAF Bomber Command from the beginning of the Second World War" (*S* 2: 1: 29). Yet, before embarking on an account of the war proper, Jack makes an apparent diversion via his account of the Berlin Olympics. Having asserted that, during his time at university, he had no "premonition" (*S* 2: 1: 29) that war might break out, he nevertheless has to begin his "story of what happened to [him] during the war" (*S* 2: 1: 30) with a description of his and Joe's participation in the Berlin Olympics. Jack therefore attests to what might appear to be a truism – that events which at the time seemed to be merely contingent turned out, with hindsight, to be closely implicated in each other. Rather than simply beginning in 1936 and proceeding forward chronologically to the present of writing, Jack's memoir has a second time-line which interrupts his account of the Olympics with a description of the aftermath of his accident in 1941. In the light of what has been learned from Stuart Gratton's narrative, 1941 is a key date, and the fact that Jack, in hospital, has to work backwards to recover his memories of the lead-up to the crash, serves to delay, temporarily, the revelation that Jack is describing a different war. Jack's narrative clearly and explicitly marks the switches between 1936 and 1941: "Five years later, in the early summer of 1941, I was in hospital in rural Warwickshire [...] Five years later I was in hospital in rural Warwickshire, working backwards to memory [...] Five years later I was in a convalescent hospital in the Vale of Evesham, working backwards to my memories of the crash and before" (*S* 2: 5: 40; 2: 7: 46; 2: 9: 58). These reiterated temporal markers give Jack the status of a controlling narrator. They also seem, initially at least, to separate the earlier from the later events of the narration, but as the two strands move into proximity with each other, the reader is invited to think the events together and to make connections which were inaccessible to Jack at the time.

Jack frequently asserts that understanding could only happen retrospectively: "Only afterwards would we be able to look back and begin to comprehend what had happened, what had changed" (*S* 2: 17: 135). Such comments appear to stress that Jack's rôle in foiling the "Hess" peace plan is an unwitting one; he cannot know that his honest assertion that the man he meets at Mychett is an impostor will lead to a further four years of war. Jack is not simply a belligerent foil to his pacifist twin. He acknowledges that, despite the claims of propaganda, the RAF's bombing campaigns are as damaging to civilian targets as those of the Luftwaffe (S 2: 16: 119), but this insight comes at the cost of satisfying his desire to be "fully engaged with the enemy" (S 2: 21: 159). Intercutting incidents from before and from after the crash means that Jack's initial enthusiasm for the war can be juxtaposed with his later feelings of guilt and uncertainty. The crash in 1941 is therefore marked as, simultaneously, a personal and historical turning point. However, the backwards moving and forwards moving narratives converge on Joe's death, and it is the impact of this, together with his guilty feelings about his affair with Birgit that lead to Jack re-immersing himself in his RAF duties: "For me, the war was the only distraction I had from my private troubles. [...] I realized the danger in which I had inadvertently been placing my crew. [... H]alf the time I had been flying with them my mind had been on Birgit" (S 2: 22: 164). At the climax of the novel, Joe echoes this belief that there is a choice to be made between private life and public duty, but in the description of Jack's response to Joe's death, there are indications that it is not always easy to keep the private and public sealed off from each other. Joe's death is a private loss, but he is also a casualty of the war: "wars are filled with deaths" (S 2: 22: 164). Part of the force of Priest's narrative is to re-individuate anonymous "deaths". Joe's might be one among many, but it matters.

Jack's narrative also provides the opportunity for the complication of the trope of the double. At the outset of the memoir, when Jack reveals that he is a twin, Stuart Gratton's confusion about the RAF man who was also a pacifist becomes explicable. But the use of twins is not merely a means for Priest to provide alternate accounts of the war; the introduction of the doubles of Churchill and Hess implies a doubleness and duplicity at the core of even the "official" version of history. Jack soon ascertains that Churchill has a double who goes on morale boosting visits to civilians in the East End: "At every point his message was the same, endlessly repeated, with only minor variations" (S 2: 16: 130). His cigar and hat are waved to the crowd, and Priest implies that these items, standing, metonymically, for the man himself, serve in and of themselves to signify "Churchill" to the expectant crowd. A similar idea is expressed in *The Churchill Play*, where Churchill, described in a stage direction as "*in an overcoat, with Homburg and walking stick*", appears to the residents of Peckham "[l]ike he'd come down from a cinema screen, out of a film show" (Brenton 1986: 169). In both texts, the Churchill "function" is what matters, rather than the man himself, who proves, behind closed doors, to be a far less benign figure than the one presented to the public.

If a double of Churchill will suffice for public relations purposes, however, it is clear that a double of Hess cannot take the place of the original. In suggesting Hess had a double, Priest draws on the same theories that underpin Brenton's play *H.I.D. (Hess is Dead)* (1989):[4] Hess's eccentric behaviour after his flight of 1941 is interpreted not as madness but as evidence that it was not Hess himself but a double who landed in Scotland. Implicitly, in Jack's version of events, the wrong Me-110 is shot down on the way to Scotland, and Jack's own report on "Hess" puts paid to an early peace. To have doubles in both the Allied and Nazi camps seems to be a means of implying, as do Jack's reflections on the damage wrought by bombing campaigns, that duplicitous tactics were used by both sides in the conflict, a suggestion which undermines any notion of the moral superiority of the Allied cause. A potential difficulty with this line of argument is not its overstatement of the invidiousness of the apparently benign Churchill but its understatement of the iniquity of the Nazi regime, particularly the Holocaust. However, Priest is not blind to this danger. The world in which Stuart Gratton lives is not a peaceful and idyllic one. The Jews have their homeland, but this has only been achieved at the expense of the Malagasy people. Joe himself experiences moral qualms and suspicions about Hess, particularly when Hess offers him a job in Germany, acknowledging that "[w]ith the Nazi regime still in power [...] Birgit would never return to Berlin" (S 5: 22: xxv: 433).

The section of the text in which Joe's notebooks are included takes the form of the dossier sent by Sam Levy, a member of Jack's crew, to Stuart. One of the documents, included late on, is a letter containing a psychologist's diagnosis of Joe's condition. He is said to be suffering from "lucid paramnesia [...] he feels he is predicting events that do not in the event turn out to be true" (S 5: 21: 415). Whilst this diagnosis gives a gloss of scientific plausibility to the experiences Joe has been describing, it also foregrounds the inadequacy of the language of science as a means of explaining or accounting for the nature and impact of his "delusions". Whilst the psychologist provides an identifiable cause for this memory disorder – concussion suffered after his accident – there is much in the preceding narrative that the letter cannot explain away. These are the characteristics that set Priest's narrative apart from other texts dealing with disordered or simply unreliable memories, such as *Spies*, the points at which realism encounters improbability, or enters the "slipstream". A similar effect is produced in *The Glamour* (1984, 1985, 1996); Richard Grey is diagnosed with "retrograde amnesia" (G84 2: iv: 27/G96 2: 4: 24) but this medical terminology is not sufficient to explain what he later experiences. An important aspect of Joe's narrative, in this respect, is the excessive nature of his "imaginings", in terms of both their temporal scale and their detail. Priest also provides documentary support for incidents such as Joe's visit to Jack at the RAF base, an encounter apparently verified by Sam Levy, only to imply, through the logic of

Joe's narrative, that what is being verified is something that, if it has happened, has not happened yet.

Jack, following his crash, has to retrieve his memory piecemeal, making leaps further back in time until he has constructed a complete, or near-complete, version of events. Joe, on the other hand, is not thinking back but remembering forwards; the incidents in his notebook are described in the past tense, but Joe is then repeatedly thrown back to the start again. Joe's disorder is as much to do with imagination as with memory, or rather, it involves an uncanny confusion of the two, an echo of a similar confusion at the heart of *The Affirmation* (1981). The content of these imagined memories is partly a wish-fulfilment narrative, in which Joe is able to play a crucial rôle in peace negotiations. But as he himself acknowledges, his relationship with his brother is integral to his disorder. Towards the end of the narrative, when, during the peace conference he fears that he may again be experiencing an attack of *déjà vu*, Joe reflects: "Almost all my episodes of lucid imaginings directly or indirectly involved my brother and led to a confrontation, which in turn led to an abrupt return to real life" (S 5: 22: xxv: 436). The wish-fulfilment aspects of his imaginings are tempered by painful incidents that he would not wish for. What this ultimately serves to stress is the complex relationship, in wartime, between personal relationships and public rôles.

Joe's first "slip" occurs when he believes he has returned home after his crash, and thinks that he sees his brother there: "He was in uniform, in RAF uniform" (S 5: 11: ii: 308). The emphasis on Jack's uniform becomes significant in the next slip, when Joe finds an RAF uniform hidden on a shelf in the wardrobe at his and Birgit's house. The effect of trying on the "unfamiliar clothes" is a dramatic one: "I tilted my head up, as if scanning the skies. I saluted myself. Engines seemed to roar enthrallingly around me; distant explosions echoed" (S 5: 11: vi: 317). Simply wearing the uniform seems to conjure for the pacifist Joe the potential excitement of war; more disconcertingly, after believing that he sees his brother on the landing behind him, he is then mistaken for Jack by Birgit. Dressing up out of apparently benign curiosity takes on a sinister twist; it is also notable that the only clear descriptions provided of the brothers' physical appearance focus on their clothes. Jack has described, earlier, how he was asked by Birgit to dress in civilian clothes and pretend to be his brother in order to fool the neighbours; but the reverse procedure, enacted here by Joe is shown as dangerous, disorientating and frightening. In Jack's version of events, it is the death of Joe, and by extension, the eradication of his pacifist beliefs, that means the war will continue: but Jack is not sacrificed to the peace effort in Joe's version, even though Joe's mission to prevent his brother from flying does not work. The incident with the uniform illustrates the deadly seductive qualities of combat. Pacifism is more difficult to promulgate or conceptualise because it is predicated on an absence of these things.

Birgit, Joe's wife, is clearly not incidental to the network of connections between the brothers. If Joe is initially marginalised by reason of his pacifism, Birgit is doubly so, by both her sex and her nationality. In fact, whilst her neighbours in England are suspicious of her because she is German, she herself realises that her Jewishness complicates further such issues of allegiance:

> [I thought I was German, because that's how we thought of ourselves, a German family. An ordinary German family. I was a German first who was born a Jew, but still a German]. Then I found that I was *only* a Jew, not a German at all. So I came to England to escape being German, to escape being Jewish. But here I am not British, not even Jewish, but German again! (S 2: 21: 154-155).

To emphasise her distress and indeed her confusion Priest has Birgit slip between German (represented by the enclosure of words in square brackets) and English. Her comments here serve to complicate further ideas about duality so prominent, and so contested, in the novel. Like Joe's discomforting desire to try on his brother's uniform, and like Jack's casual masquerade as Birgit's husband, Birgit's comments indicate that identity is never simply about the outward expression of an interior state of mind. Birgit has been subject to multiple instances of labelling or interpellation. Having been (self) identified as German, her family is then labelled as Jewish. On her escape to England, having rejected her German identity, she finds that this is re-imposed. Therefore, whilst the twins are discrete individuals who follow quite different paths, only to have those paths intersect in disconcerting ways, Birgit finds her subjectivity rendered unstable by external political and social factors. Not only this, but when Birgit is given a voice in the narrative, in the few letters that are included in Sam Levy's dossier, she almost exclusively identifies herself as Joe's wife, rather than being able to assert her own individuality. The female, here, is a unique individual, in a way that the male protagonists – Joe, Jack, Churchill, Hess – are not, but this does not mean that she has any advantage when it comes to taking action on her own behalf; she is simply doubly reliant, needing both Joe and Jack to assist her. This is not to say, however, that being one of twins is necessarily advantageous. Jack's description of the Olympics stresses apart from when rowing, the brothers can only function as a unit through reaching compromises which are satisfactory to neither of them (S 2: 4: 40; 2: 11: 75).[5]

Birgit seems to have to bear a heavy burden in that, as one of the few female protagonists in the novel, she not only emblematises the uncertainties of wartime national identity, but also serves as a reminder of the experience of those on the home front. Joe's shock when he realises how traumatic it must be for her to be hiding under the stairs at night during air-raids is one incident which throws Birgit's war into relief. Birgit's experiences serve to further problematise the division between combatant and non-combatant. The very notion of the "Home Front" implies that the war was being taken into the domestic sphere and Birgit's anxieties foreground this. Besides this, if Joe and Jack are principally exercised with their attempts to negotiate between the present and the past, Birgit's pregnancy is a means of looking to the future. To have Stuart and/or Angela born on the day war ends (or not) might seem an overly symbolic gesture on Priest's part, but it serves to emphasise again the complex relationship between history and memory. Stuart's interest in the end of the war is spurred in part at least by the accident of his own birthday: a personal fact spurs an historical investigation which itself could prove to have significant personal ramifications. Here, too, the pattern of doubling in the novel is given a different twist. On the one hand, Birgit and her child are themselves a dyad, a divisible but always to be intimately associated pairing of two. On the other hand, Priest chooses to break the pattern by having Birgit give birth to a girl in Jack's version of events, and a boy in Joe's. The apparently impossible meeting between Stuart and Angela at the start of the novel signals the beginning of Stuart's investigation, and therefore, the unravelling of the complex pattern of symmetries between Jack's and Joe's lives. However, his fruitless search for Angela's home, the address she gives him proving to be a building that has been "demolished about ten years earlier" (S 3: 3: 212), shows that ultimately the pattern has, and has to have been, broken. Stuart might initially have "a fleeting illusory sense" (S 1: 1: 5) that he has seen her before, but, unlike Andrew Westley in *The Prestige*, he is not about to discover a lost twin. The trajectories of Angela and Stuart's realities can graze against each other but will never be united.

Conclusion

Priest's establishment of Stuart Gratton's reality as the reader's benchmark timeframe at the start of the novel implies that, ultimately, Joe will be able to actually experience the events that reader has only seen him imagining. At the end of the novel, however we are left in suspense. Joe, lying injured in the ambulance again, is faced with a dilemma: if he loses consciousness, he will never see realised his vision of peace; but this peace can only come at a heavy cost:

> [A]head of me lay that life that was obscurely rejecting me: my alienated brother, the marriage that was failing, the son who has been born and named in my absence, the intrusion of other, all of it the product of my own neglect (S 5: 24: xxxi: 463).

Although, on one level, we know both what he has decided, and the consequences of this decision, it is this uncertainty which stays with the reader after the end of the narrative. It seems inconceivable that the life or death of an individual could change the course of history; perhaps Joe is supremely arrogant in believing this to be the case. What is clear, in Joe's acknowledgement that his immersion in history has been at the expense of his personal relationships, is that memory and history are not related to each other simply as the part is related to the whole. Although the idea of history as the sum of individual experiences and memories is an attractive one, one which gives significance to the experiences of every single one of us, it also belies the extent to which even memory itself is a collective and often political process. We might believe we have a memory of seeing Churchill on a visit to the East End, but the actuality could be something quite other. Priest, therefore, also seems to resist the temptation to instate memory in place of history as an alternate grand narrative, reversing the hierarchy which would place memory at the service of history. In Priest's analysis, memory and history do not exist in a symbiotic relationship but are connected in complex, unpredictable and often disturbing ways.

Notes

1. McEwan mentioned this connection during a reading from *Atonement* in October 2001 in Bristol. See also McEwan 2002: 40-41.

2. In *The Churchill Play*, the outcome of the war has not been changed, only the consequences of this: Britain is envisaged as a state under martial law, with internment camps for political prisoners, a scenario which bears similarities to Derek Raymond's *A State of Denmark* (1970). Other notable British examples of fictions in which the war ends differently include Sarban's *The Sound of his Horn* (1952) and Len Deighton's *SS-GB* (1978).

3. Nicola King has noted that Harris appears to suggest "an equivalence between 'totalitarian' states of the left and right" (King 1995: 211) in the novel and interprets Harris's description of teenagers listening clandestinely to The Beatles as a reference to life in the former GDR.

4. Brenton cites Hugh Thomas's controversial historical work *Hess: A Tale of Two Murders* (1988) as the source of these theories.

5. Priest follows the historical record in awarding gold to Germany and silver to Denmark in the rowing event at the Berlin Olympics in which the twins participate. The twins displace Podesta and Curatella, the Argentinian pair who took the bronze. The times given for the medal positions in *The Separation* are historically accurate.

Beyond Competing for Beer Money: The Criticism of Christopher Priest

Andrew M. Butler

Introduction

There is a moment in an autobiographical article by Christopher Priest when he confesses: "I can never re-read my work with any pleasure, and as a matter of rule I always regret any non-fiction from the moment it appears in print" (Priest 1978a: 56). In this chapter I will explore a range of his criticism and non-fiction, particularly those pieces in which he examines science fiction and reveals his attitudes towards the genre – although when asked directly by Paul Kincaid about this subject, he responded: "Oh you can never clear up that one" (Kincaid 1999a: 5). Nevertheless, that is what I will attempt to do.

Priest's non-fiction has appeared in a number of venues: in fanzines such as Peter Weston's *Zenith* and *Speculation* and Bruce Gillespie's *SF Commentary*, in the British Science Fiction Association magazines *Vector*, *Focus* and *Matrix*, and in the academic journal *Foundation* – where he was reviews editor 1974-1977. He has published his own fanzines, such as *Deadloss*, a later incarnation of which, *The Last Deadloss Visions* (1987, 1987, 1988), was a piece of investigative journalism on the non-appearance of Harlan Ellison's anthology *The Last Dangerous Visions*. As *The Book on the Edge of Forever* (1994), this was nominated for a Hugo Award. His fannish writing also includes pieces in science-fiction convention programme books and membership of at least one Amateur Press Association (APA). He has written or contributed to books such as *Seize the Moment: The Autobiography of Helen Sharman*, Robert Holdstock's *Encyclopedia of Science Fiction* (1978) and Patrick Parrinder's *Science Fiction: A Critical Guide* (1979). Much of the material appeared in ephemeral publications, unheard of by copyright libraries, and some of his first articles were published under pseudonyms, housenames or anonymously, including some pieces which appeared in *Vector*. I run the risk that anything I say will be contradicted by an article, review, letter or fanzine I have not been able to track down or have not even heard of. For example, as a freelance writer he spent at least eighteen months producing "filler work for the popular general-interest journals" (Priest 1970a: 15).

Much of his non-fiction has a polemical tone, sometimes relating to current political issues within the real and science-fiction worlds. Some of the external concerns have significance to his fiction writing, including the nuclear threat described in "Crouching in Cheadle" (Priest 1983a) which fed into *The Quiet Woman* (1990) and *The Separation* (2002), and his near-miss with the Hungerford massacre, examined in "A Retreat from Reality" (Priest 1999a and 1999b), which was part of the inspiration for *The Extremes* (1998). In his writing about science fiction it becomes clear that not only is Christopher Priest frequently disappointed by reading his own work, but also that he is disappointed by much, if not most, other science fiction. The few exceptions have included Brian Aldiss, J. G. Ballard, Philip K. Dick, Ursula Le Guin, Dan Morland (a pseudonym of Reginald Hill, better known for his Dalziel and Pascoe novels), Frederik Pohl, Keith Roberts, Robert Sheckley, Bob Shaw and John Wyndham, although his enthusiasm can ebb and flow. Even his taste for Wyndham varies, as is demonstrated in his description of a sense of disillusionment at a genre he had embraced in the early 1960s, it is clear that he rapidly became bored or jaded: "How could I have ever interpreted [Wyndham's] THE KRAKEN WAKES as being part of some kind of philosophy? How did I ever blow my mind on *Analog*? Why did my first encounter with *Vector* excite me so?" (Priest 1970c: 40).

In his account of British science fiction in Patrick Parrinder's *Science Fiction: A Critical Guide*, Priest seems at first glance to be less kind to Wyndham than he was in the late 1960s: "Wyndham is the master of the middle-class catastrophe; his characters are of the bourgeoisie, and his books lament the collapse of law and order, the failure of communications, the looting of shopping precincts and the absence of the daily newspaper" (Priest 1979f: 194), an opinion which concurs with critical orthodoxy that Wyndham's disasters are less disturbing because of their alleged cosiness (cf. Aldiss 1973: 293-294 but contrast Wymer 1992). Priest's comment that "His books are comedies of English manners" (Priest 1979f: 194) perhaps does not seem any more positive. But when Priest's opinion was cited by L. J. Hurst in an article in *Vector* (Hurst 1986), Robert Steele objected (Steele 1986). Priest responded, not in order to vilify Wyndham, but rather to defend Wyndham's reputation and Priest's own championing of it: "I loved his books when I was young, and when I re-read them a few years ago I thought they were a lot better than I had secretly dreaded I might find them [...] They were a bit chatty [...] but still exerted a great power" (Priest 1986/1987: 5).

Roberts and Wyndham possibly appealed to him for the same reason: their use of the catastrophe narrative: "There is something about a catastrophe novel that has an irresistible attraction for me [...] I think what holds me is the overriding image of a few chance-picked survivors eking out an existence from the decaying remains of a civilisation" (Priest 1967: 30). He compares Roberts's *The Furies* (1966) to novels by Wyndham, and suggests: "There will be few more entertaining or enjoyable novels published this year" (Priest 1967: 30). He was even more complimentary about Roberts's *Pavane* (1968) which he declared to be "a magnificent, miraculous novel" (Priest 1968: 15). Priest goes on to note: "This book has the appeal of magic, being simple yet complex. It is melodious and discordant. It is fantasy, and philosophy. And at a time when sf groans and creaks, it is very, very welcome" (Priest 1968: 21).

Selling Out: The Science-Fiction Tradition

For Priest, science fiction is primarily a publishing or marketing niche, indeed he argues that it has "no actual existence except as a publishers' category" (Priest 1979f: 187). This category has both positive and negative effects – although even the positive can have a downside. The community of science fiction is clearly one within which Priest has lived, to a greater or lesser extent, since the early 1960s, and he accepts that the science-fiction community understands his work more than portions of the non-sf community. The "bush telegraph" of the sf community also allows a degree of publicity about individual works and authors which is perhaps less apparent in other genre or literary fiction. At the same time, the welcoming side of the science-fiction community can lead to the championing of lesser talents: "writers without any track record are encouraged to think of themselves as important or influential figures" (Priest 1978a: 52). This can in time damage their abilities because they are lauded before they have fully learned their craft.

In an article aimed at aspiring writers, "Writing a Novel? Do!", Priest asks the question "is a novel something that has to be *sold*, or is it something that has to be *written?*" (Priest 1979d: 10). The first alternative, of *selling*, requires the author to accept the demands of economics and the market, with compromises made simply to get into print according to particular generic formulae. To support the second proposition suggests artistic intention and artistic integrity, and that the book is to be written to allow an author to communicate a particular "message", whether aesthetic or political. Elsewhere, in the 1979 "News for High-Octane Water-Lilies", he poses the question: "Do you want to sell, or do you want to be a writer?" (Priest 1979a: 5). Slightly earlier, he was perhaps slightly less hardline in his demand: "I suppose the ideal lies somewhere between the two: fiction that *looks* like it has been written with an audience in mind, but which is deeply personal to the author" (Priest 1978b: 48). It is this rejection of the market that has been central to much of Priest's thinking about science fiction.

The downside of marketed, generic science fiction includes writers attempting to mimic what has been published before in order to get published in turn, leading to a uniformity in style, theme or subject matter. Priest recalls a panel at the convention Skycon, where he got into an argument with Jim Baen, then at Ace Books and now the owner of Baen Books. Priest had argued for the writer producing what interested him or her, whereas Baen demanded that the author should write for the market; Priest said that Baen claims "the very fact that a writer is being paid means he *must* put market considerations first" (Priest 1980c: 8).

Science fiction as a distinctly commodified market has its origins in the magazines published by Hugo Gernsback, most obviously the run of *Amazing Stories* which began in 1926. Gernsback wanted to publish "the Jules Verne, H. G. Wells and Edgar Allan Poe type of story – a charming romance intermingled with scientific fact and prophetic vision" (Gernsback 1926: 3), and indeed reprinted many of Wells's scientific romances, as stories or serialised novels. He also printed stories which imitated Wells, Poe and Verne. Priest is clearly not impressed by this, declaring that "Hugo Gernsback was a menace" (Priest 1980c: 9), and, moving on to denigrate one of the other significant editors with the field, "John W. Campbell is irrelevant".[1] In rejecting Gernsback and Campbell he rejects the whole science fiction pulp tradition, and the generic straitjacket imposed by proscriptive magazine editors who are not sufficiently interested in the inspiration of an individual writer.

Priest sees the work of Wells and his Gernsbackian-Campbellian imitators as being different: "Wells wrote science fiction as a primitive, he was interested in the science" (Kincaid 1999a: 7). It was a scientific education that gripped Wells, and inspired him to write fiction from his gut or from the bottom of his heart. Those who simply wish to emulate the Wellsian scientific romance, and come at it from the angle of the market, are writing "from the top of the head" (Kincaid 1999a: 7).

Gernsbackian-Campbellian science fiction – what John Clute has referred to as First sf or agenda sf – put a stranglehold on the genre well into the 1960s, if not beyond. Despite – or perhaps because of – Gernsback's position as a Luxembourgean immigrant into the United States, the default ideological position of (genre) science fiction was analogous to American ideology. Priest notes: "Modern science fiction is a primarily American phenomenon and much of the genre is written either by Americans or by authors who adopt the American idiom" (Priest 1979f: 187).[2] The result of this is an orthodoxy which is difficult to challenge and which Priest wishes to reject:

> It shouldn't be that, books should not be an orthodoxy, but science fiction has rules. People say, you can't do that in science fiction. This is sf, this isn't sf. All the time you're getting orthodoxy, the politically correct thing. All my life, ever since I've been old enough to think for myself, whenever I feel an orthodoxy coming on I want to break it (Kincaid 1999a: 6).

Perhaps the clearest example of what Priest identifies as an orthodoxy in action lies in a letter to a Science Fiction Writers of America magazine. In it an author – unnamed by Priest – says, "There's only one way to write science fiction. Whenever I get to a scene I think, how would Isaac [Asimov] write this?" (Kincaid 1999a: 7). Priest is clearly horrified.

Priest occasionally sees his own novels as traditional science fiction – "[*Inverted World* (1974)] is the one novel that comes closest to most people's idea of 'trad' science fiction" (Priest 1990a: 96). More recently he has argued that "*The Extremes* is as close as you're going to get to a trad sf novel" (Kincaid 1999a: 7). Whilst it is possible to see a thread running though most of Priest's novels – the collision of two or more worlds or world views, a sense of misdirection, an attitude to violence – each of the books is very different and there appear to be attempts to reinvent what he is writing between each novel. *The Separation* is a very different novel from *The Extremes*, and both are different from *The Prestige* (1995) and so on. As Lee Montgomerie has argued, "Christopher Priest refuses to be predictable" (Montgomerie 1978: 68).

As each new writer imitates that which has gone before, science fiction risks becoming more and more ossified and in-bred – Priest argued that "science fiction, *as the form has now become*, is in a shagged out state" (Priest 1990a: 100). This parallels John Clute's argument, advanced in some of his reviews around that period and emphasised in his 1995 collection *Look at the Evidence*, that generic or Agenda sf had died, probably as far back as 1958, because it had failed "to marry out" (Clute 1995: 356) or "miscegenate" (Clute 1995: 354). Under the market conditions of Gernsback, the genre had been a slave trade (Priest and Watson 1976: 62), now it had solidified into a ghetto, supposedly distinct from a mainstream. Priest would rather this apartheid be ended:

> I am all in favour of so-called science fiction rejoining the so-called mainstream (Priest 1980c: 9).

> [I]t is vital at last to get rid of the "science fiction" label from the books we publish, integrate with the generality of fiction publishing, take our chances in the wider world without the protection of a health warning (Priest 1990a: 100).

Certainly he wants to apply the same standards to science fiction as are applied to other fiction: "science fiction novels (particularly) should be able to survive the same standards of criticism that apply to other books" (Priest 1981c: 48). But despite this wish for science fiction to take its chances as fiction, Priest has not insisted on his publishers relabelling his own novels, telling Paul Kincaid that "I've never, ever said to a publisher you mustn't put science fiction on the cover" (Kincaid 1999a: 7). Since *The Affirmation* (1981), though, many British editions of his novels have not been labelled science fiction, although earlier books have been reprinted as science-fiction classics or under Simon and Schuster's science-fiction imprint Earthlight.[3]

Stanislaw Lem, the Polish science-fiction writer and critic, had long been critical of American science fiction, labelling it in the title of one article "A Hopeless Case – With Exceptions".[4] In an article in the February 1975 *Frankfurter Allgemeine Zeitung*, translated in the August 1975 issue of *Atlas World Press Review* as "Looking Down on Science Fiction: A Novelist's Choice for the

World's Worst Writing", Lem describes American science fiction as "a literary form that claims to be a mythology of technological civilisation while in fact it is simply bad writing tacked together with wooden dialogue" (Lem 1977: 127). Lem refers with scorn to a statement from Poul Anderson in one of the *SFWA Bulletins* that Robert A. Heinlein had noted that science-fiction writers were competing for their readers' beer money. Lem insists that: "marketing prospects or official approval or similar concerns have no place intruding in that narrow gap between the author's eyes and the blank page. That the muse cannot be pursued over a bottle of beer goes without saying. In short, honest literature can never conform to external pressures or exigencies" (Lem 1977: 128). In other words, the author's individual voice should come before market economics. The article was reprinted in the *SFWA Forum* 41, a quasi-confidential publication, and a number of SFWA members wrote in to complain. Lem had been an honorary member of the organisation, but this honour was rescinded "on a technicality" (Le Guin 1977: 100) and Lem was expelled from the organisation. Le Guin objected to this in *Science Fiction Studies*, writing that when the SFWA "uses the tactics of the Soviet Writers Union, I think there is cause for concern, and reasons for shame" (Le Guin 1977: 100).

The controversy rumbled on through the pages of *Science Fiction Studies*, as some of the parties went public; Pamela Sargent and George Zebrowski set out a chronology of events, Jack Dann and Gregory Benford regretted what happened and Andrew Offutt, the then SFWA president, put his side of the affair: Lem had wrongly been made an honorary member when he could have paid to join, and that at least two paid members had resigned as a result of Lem's comments as printed in the *SFWA Forum*. James Gunn later wrote to *Science Fiction Studies*, criticising Lem's polemic by noting "the long tradition of writing for money [...] or for patrons, or for dramatic or literary judges" (Gunn 1977: 315)[5] and that whilst kicking Lem out of the SWFA did not look good, "Lem has not been deprived of life, freedom, money, or reputation. His work will continue to be published [...] as long as his publishers are happy with it [...] The SFWA action will not cost Lem a single sale" (Gunn 1977: 314).

Christopher Priest had joined the SFWA in the early 1970s, on the invitation of Anne McCaffrey, but came to see the organisation as "a malign influence on science fiction" (Priest 1990b: 4). Priest found the pages of SFWA publications to be "filled with foolishness, greed, vanity, self-importance, arrogance" and, while admitting to liking many American science-fiction writers in person, he found them in print to be "obsessed with money, status, awards. They are conservative, xenophobic, narrow-minded, stubborn and certain of everything. As a writers' organisation SFWA represents the triumph of egotism and self-interest over common sense" (Priest 1990b: 4-5).

In this context, it is hardly surprising that Priest took Lem's side in the furore over whether science fiction was competition for beer money or should be an artistic endeavour. Like Lem, he attempted to change things from within, in particular attempting to undermine the Nebula Award by ticking the "No Award" box (Priest 1980a: 9). He felt that corruption had entered into the award because there were so many books being nominated that it was impossible for any writer to read more than a handful of them and make an informed choice as to what the genuine best book of the year was. The low number of actual voters meant that any attempt by an individual writer or publisher to campaign on behalf of a particular book could swing the totals and "fix" the result (Priest 1980a: 9-14).

Priest felt that the SFWA was "concentrating on [...] the sort of success attached to making a lot of money rather than the sort of success attached to writing well" (Priest 1980a: 6). The SFWA – as the name of the organisation might suggest – was very much geared to the American market, so the professional qualifications necessary to join it meant that "The sale of a 100,000-word novel to, say, Sanrio in Japan, or Calmann-Lévy in France, or Victor Gollancz in Britain does not count [whilst ...] a 600-word vignette [in] *Isaac Asimov's SF Magazine* does" (Priest 1980a: 7). The SFWA's decision to revoke Lem's honorary membership struck Priest as an act of "revenge" (Priest 1980a: 8) for Lem's criticisms of American writers.

In ignoring Lem's criticisms and refusing to admit how bad excluding him made them look, the SFWA was endorsing the market place's consensus. Whilst the SFWA had successfully challenged Ace over royalty payments and rejected Pocket Books's new contracts, the organisation was "mistaking the short-term gain for the long-term strategy" (Priest 1980a: 14), and was failing the future of science fiction as an artistic medium. According to Priest: "It condones the shame of the Nebula, it punishes the heretic, it applauds the quick buck" (Priest 1980a: 14). Priest could not in good consciousness stay in the organisation and so he let his membership lapse in 1979, going public with his concerns in the article "Outside the Whale" which appeared in *Vector* and was also reprinted in *SF Commentary* and *Science Fiction Review* in 1980. Lem's banishment, meanwhile, was one more sign that "science fiction is no longer a place where serious writers are welcome" (Priest 1981d: 55).

Escape from Escapism?: The New Wave(s)

The orthodox genre of science fiction also has an orthodox history, which is one that Priest has told, and I confess that I have told as well: of the influence and gathering together of Gernsback in 1926, the Golden Age of Campbell post-1937, the increased literacy of Gold's magazines post-1950... It is a narrative of progression and linear improvement – or perhaps of continual coups and new orthodoxies. In his skewering of Lester del Rey's *Science Fiction 1926-1976: The History of a Subculture* (1979), Priest suggests that he "characterizes the 'development' of science fiction as a series of revolutions, out of each of which emerged a 'better' or purer form of science fiction" (Priest 1981a: 57). The revolution too far for del Rey is the most important one for Priest: the moment of the New Wave.

Priest began reading science fiction just before the Wave first broke, and had a sense of the finiteness of the genre: "SF was something that could be *completed*" (Priest 1970c: 41). He felt that every science-fiction film could be watched, every science-fiction story or novel could be read. Each title could be ticked off the list, and each one was pretty much like the last. There were a few towering geniuses, naïvely embraced: "Simak, Asimov, Heinlein, Wyndham" (Priest 1970c: 42), but suddenly new authors with new novels intruded: "Ballard? Zelazny? Disch? Moorcock?" (Priest 1970c: 42). With the arguable exception of Zelazny, these writers together formed "the single most important development of the science fiction genre" (Priest 1978f: 164): the New Wave. At the same time, Priest makes various attempts to distinguish himself from the wave and absolute support: he "wasn't the true-blue new-waver [... he] pretended to be" (Priest 1969b: 35). More than a decade later he wrote: "I happen to be at odds with what remains of the New Wave movement; writers like Michael Moorcock and M. John Harrison dislike my own fiction and disagree with my views. I find this healthy and bracing" (Priest 1981a: 58). In the interview published in this volume, he continues to demonstrate an ambivalent attitude towards the genre, and the New Wave.

Genre science fiction had become middle-aged, bourgeois and in-bred, and this orthodoxy was to be challenged from both sides of the Atlantic. In Britain there were two science-fiction magazines published by Nova Publications and edited by John Carnell: *New Worlds*, established in 1946, and *Science Fantasy*, established in Summer 1950. The economics of the British market was unsuited for supporting two magazines, and in the early 1960s they began to decline in sales and quality. According to Priest "1963 was a rather bad year for NEW WORLDS [... which] settled into a rut that was to be broken only occasionally" (Priest 1964: 19). In 1963 both magazines were sold to Roberts & Vinter, and Michael Moorcock, a young writer with editorial experience, was given his choice of the two to edit. Despite having a grounding in fantasy, he picked *New Worlds*, and Kyril Bonfiglioli took the vacated chair of *Science Fantasy* until 1966. During that time the latter was retitled first *Impulse* and then *SF Impulse*, and it featured first or early professional appearances by Thomas Disch, Keith Roberts – including stories which formed *Pavane* – Brian Stableford, Josephine Saxton and Christopher Priest. Keith Roberts and Harry Harrison replaced Bonfiglioli for the final few issues, before the magazine was merged with *New Worlds* in 1967.

Meanwhile Michael Moorcock was beginning to shape his magazine into a more radical periodical,[6] although this may not have been immediately clear as Moorcock (and presumably Bonfiglioli) worked through the inventory of stories already accepted by Carnell. In 1965 Priest wrote: "There is very little to distinguish between the fiction of the two magazines" (Priest 1965: 9). To Priest's eyes the material in *New Worlds* looked like it had been rejected by American magazines, whereas that in *Science Fantasy* felt like "early Aldiss stories" (Priest 1965: 9) – although it may be worth noting that Priest wrote that Aldiss was "the leading stylist at present working in science fiction" (Priest 1966a: 36). Of the new writers, Priest celebrated Thom Keyes, Langdon Jones and Keith Roberts: "Roberts is the most obviously talented, yet in the long run I expect Thom Key[e]s and Lang Jones to outstrip him in both popularity and competence" (Priest 1965: 11).[7] In contrast, Priest was unimpressed by the two-part "Equinox" by Ballard, a serial version of *The Crystal World* (1966) which appeared in *New Worlds*: "tedious and wearying [...] pretentious" (Priest 1965: 11). Priest suggests Moorcock tempted Ballard and Aldiss back from the US market to join his project, but Ballard had already published his polemical guest editorial in 1962, calling for the exploration of inner space (Ballard 1962a). Moorcock offered "encouragement, enthusiasm, polemic and – most important of all – mutual loyalty" (Priest 1978f: 166) to his writers, and was not, according to Priest, a doctrinaire editor, in the way that Campbell had been.

But the New Wave was not purely a British phenomenon, and Priest did not neglect the American side when he came to write his entry on the New Wave for the Holdstock *Encyclopedia* (1978). Even at the heart of the science-fiction orthodoxy, things were changing. At genre science fiction's birth place, *Amazing Stories* (retitled *Amazing Science Fiction Stories*), Cele Goldsmith was assistant editor from 1956 and then, from December 1958 to June 1965, editor. She was also editing *Fantastic*, where in 1962 she published Thomas Disch's first story, "The Double Timer", and Ursula Le Guin's "April in Paris"; she was also to publish Roger Zelazny, Harlan Ellison, Norman Spinrad and Philip K. Dick. But Goldsmith did not make a noise with her editorials which might startle the old horses. Priest also notes Frederik Pohl's policy at *IF*, which he edited 1961-1969, of publishing new writers in each issue – although a new writer does not necessarily mean a fresh talent when the pressure is to be steeped in the genre. Priest acidly comments that one of these new writers, Larry Niven (with the story "The Coldest Place" (1964)), was an author "so deeply entrenched in the traditional idiom that not even the glibbest debater could argue that he was of the New Wave" (Priest 1978f: 168). Elsewhere in America, *The Magazine of Fantasy and Science Fiction* (Autumn 1949-) was "a sort of New Wave of its own" (Priest 1978f: 168) and the paperback imprint Ace published novels by Samuel Delany and Ursula Le Guin. Damon Knight's *Orbit* (1966-1980) series of anthologies had a very New-Wave tinge to it, including stories by Disch, Roberts, Gene Wolfe, Le Guin, Aldiss and many others. Harlan Ellison edited *Dangerous Visions* (1967), a collection of taboo-breaking science fiction which could not have been published in the traditional magazines – but it should be noted that the American new wave was much more about pushing back the boundaries of what could be represented in commercial science fiction in terms of sex, violence, drugs and swearing rather than in shifting the ideology of the field.

Given that the revolution in American science fiction predates Moorcock's tenure at *New Worlds*, and given some of Ace's publishing choices – they had long been publishing Philip K. Dick, of course – it might be worth questioning how much hegemony the orthodoxy had. It certainly unsettles a straightforward linear narrative of progression – especially when it is remembered that *Amazing Science Fiction Stories* and *Fantastic* largely moved to reprints of traditional science fiction after they were sold in mid-1965 to Sol Cohen's Ultimate Publishing Co. But it was Moorcock who was generating most of the publicity – along with Judith Merril, an American writer who became a significant anthologist.

Merril came to England to speak to British science-fiction writers who were associated with the New Wave, and began to draw the disparate threads together, producing an anthology *England Swings SF* (1968). According to Priest she "was imposing form to what, until then, had been formless" (Priest 1978f: 169). Whereas once the New Wave had broken the mould of the genre, it could now be codified and copied, and fell into a new orthodoxy. With the Arts Council grant to *New Worlds* in July 1967 the magazine could afford to be more experimental but for Priest it acquired "an aura of intellectual snobbishness and complacency" (Priest 1978f: 171). Perhaps the writers were beginning to confuse obscurity with meaning, and opacity with depth: "obscure and difficult writing can too easily be used to disguise a poverty of imagination or skill" (Priest 1978f: 173).

This new orthodoxy and new poverty led into the 1970s, a period often ignored within science-fiction criticism, first as being in the shadow of the New Wave, and then as being the dead period which cyberpunk disrupted. This is to neglect the emergence of writers from outside the New Wave as significant novelists – Michael Coney, Richard Cowper, D. G. Compton, Robert Holdstock, Ursula Le Guin, Marge Piercy and Joanna Russ among others, including Christopher Priest himself. Nevertheless Priest felt that "It was utterly, utterly mediocre, almost everything published in the '70s by the new writers emerging then was sophisticated in some ways and elegant and worked and wrought, but it was dead-headed and dead-hearted, and it's now mostly forgotten, thank God" (Kincaid 1999a: 7). There were exceptions; clearly Bob Shaw stood out from the others, and an established writer such as Ballard produced in *Crash* (1973) "one of the best novels of any kind of the 1970s" (Priest 1979f: 198; cf. 1978e: 6).

For Priest, the legacy of the New Wave was the possibility of writers escaping the orthodox tone of science fiction: "Its greatest contribution was the public proclamation of the individual writer's voice" (Priest 1979f: 199). Two years later he added: "The New Wave, if it was anything, was a state of mind, a revolutionary attitude [...] it was an exploration of the ways in which the idiom might be enlarged, brought more in tune with the minds of the kind of people known to be reading it" (Priest 1981a: 58).

Speaking Out: The Author's Voice

This is the point at which we can return to Priest's division between the "novel [as] something that has to be *sold*, or [...] something that has to be *written*" (Priest 1979d: 10). A hack writer like John Russell Fearn simply churns out product to pay the rent: "low-quality work in large quantities for low-paying markets" (Priest 1969a: 13).[8] Typically such writers would sell the copyright to a given story and not be able to exploit that material for royalties or overseas sales; however by rewriting it, expanding it, converting it to another genre or changing the names, the canny hack could make their material do extra work for them. There was little space in such a treadmill of work for creativity and originality. Often they had to work within tight limitations; there was a magazine which demanded "stories which *must* contain two sex-scenes, which *must* have reference to crime or violence, and which *must* be exactly two thousand five hundred words long" (Priest 1970a: 16).

In the modernist-like attempt to make it new, New Wave science fiction was attempting to do something that had not been done before within science fiction, and that was to champion style and the voice of the individual writer. This is not something that comes easily, and needs to be worked at: "Finding one's own voice is hard, and often frustrating. But in the long term it is the only thing that counts, that brings satisfaction, that brings a readership" (Priest 1979a: 5). What precisely is this voice? Christopher Priest explored this question in an article "The Authentic Voice" published in 1981. "Are we talking about another word for prose style" he asks, "Or is it just a different kind of plot? Or is it, perhaps, one of those things established writers say to mystify what they do, or to conceal the fact that they don't quite know how they do it?" (Priest 1981b: 4). It might be that the voice is something which is detected by a sensitive reader, having been exposed to a number of works by the same author, rather than something which has been a conscious act on the part of the author.

We do risk here falling into subjective division between the literary genius and the genre hack. In the former case what emerges is the artist consistently pursuing his or her obsessions in different guises across a number of works, such as for example Philip K. Dick's exploration of the two themes of "what is real?" and "what is human?", or Wyndham with his "cosy" catastrophes. On the other hand, the hack is simply retreading the old ground, rubber-stamping another version of the same old quest or adventure. In an attack on Clifford D. Simak's pastoral, essentially decent, down-to-earth, novels, Priest identified "a writer mimicking himself [...] soulless writing, imaginatively sterile" (Priest 1981b: 5). There is a double bind here – it would be difficult to explore the same obsession over a body of work without a degree of repetition, and equally it is across a corpus that a distinctive voice may be divine. The authentic voice has to be variants on the same voice, without falling into the self-parody of which Priest accuses Simak. It seems perilously like one critic's "artistic unity" is another critic's "formulaic rubbish", and that in the end it is a subjective label.

The need for an individual voice is at odds with the demands of genre, which through editorial dictation can impose specific formula, and which as a market offers a limited range of products to customers who operate under the illusion that they are making a free choice. The market offers a mixture of the consoling, unchallenging, familiar material which is much like the reader has purchased before and is bound to like again, and allegedly novel material which will appear to fulfil new needs. Obviously every writer who wants to be read has to operate within the market, but there are degrees to which an individual talent may be prostituted. Priest recounts an anecdote from a Milford writers' conference, in which Brian Aldiss asked an author whether he wanted to develop his own voice or to tailor a story to a market, sacrificing their uniqueness in the process. Priest goes on to suggest:

> A writer who has found a market but who lacks a voice makes an empty, comforting sound; he says what is expected of him, he sings other men's words, he sounds familiar and reassuring. But a writer with a singular voice is one who surprises, who unsettles his audience, who does not immediately satisfy the expectations of him, but is one who in the end will develop his own unique following (Priest 1981b: 5).

If science fiction is really a genre about novelty, then it should be one which constantly unsettles or estranges its readership rather than consoling it with the same old tropes. The writer may pursue the same obsessions, but each time returns to them from a fresh perspective or in a new situation, perhaps even writing dialectically where the expectations of a previous fiction are turned upon their heads.

Aldiss and Priest's support for the authorial voice seems to be at odds with the approach to the genre of many American science-fiction writers. James Gunn, for example, argued that "I would say that the first problem is to free beginning writers from the notion that writing is self-expression" (Gunn 1978: 57). The anonymous author cited above by Priest who slavishly followed Asimov's model (Kincaid 1999a: 7) is ventriloquising the no-longer unique voice of an earlier writer.

Moving to the fringe of science fiction, it is perhaps telling that Priest approves a series of British writers who have written fiction cognate with the genre: H. G. Wells, Olaf Stapledon, George Orwell and Aldous Huxley. This is not an identification they would all be likely to accept, as Priest notes: "Stapledon, apparently, was in contact with Eric Frank Russell, who sent him some pulp magazines. Stapledon said take these horrible things away from me. He had no interest in that kind of stuff" (Kincaid 1999a: 7). This does not mean that a writer who produces a science-fiction-like novel outside of the genre should automatically be applauded. Priest notes in a review of Anthony Burgess's *1985* (1979) that "Burgess has become one of those novelists whose work is sometimes claimed for science fiction, in an attempt to dignify the whole genre" (Priest 1979c: 55), but is actually rather damning of the fiction part of the book and accuses the author of being out of touch with real people. Priest has also noted the hostility within the genre on the entry of literary writers: "It's simple paranoia, and it amounts to the fear that if we let the literary types at science fiction, then the results will be about plump girls living in bedsitters and recovering from abortions" (Priest 1977a: 15). Since the only existence that science fiction has for Priest is as a marketing niche, such inside/outside distinctions are purely imagined. In a 1981 letter to *Vector*, Priest suggested that "Most people in the SF world have a genuine liking for the work of what we call *good writers*... but at the same time they will also be able to enjoy what George Orwell once called *good bad writers*" (Priest 1981c: 47). The only distinction is between good and bad writers, or at least between good and bad examples of writing.

It is thus important that "a science fiction novel should be a novel first and science fiction second" (Priest 1980c: 6). At the same time – paradoxically – there *is* a criterion for assessing science fiction: "the test of good science fiction is, or should be, an examination of the idea rather than the notion" (Priest and Watson 1976: 56). For Priest the notion is the extrapolation at the heart of each science-fiction story; this is connected to what Darko Suvin, borrowing from Ernst Bloch, called the *novum*, the network of words, images, sounds or signifiers which communicate a sense of novelty and the defamiliarised to the audience. The idea is what the author is attempting to express through the deployment or representation of that notion. For Suvin the novum inculcates a sense of Brechtian estrangement – the *Verfremdungseffekt* – which, tempered by cognitive logic, leads to an assault on the alienation (*Entfremdung*) of the individual audience member or reader as worker/consumer (see Suvin 1979). There is the idea which is being communicated, the vehicle by which it is being communicated – which would include style at the level of the sentence and the narrative form – and the purpose underlying that connection.

For Darko Suvin, this purpose is explicitly or implicitly political: contemporary industrial humanity is alienated by their relation to the means of production, and science fiction can either demonstrate that alienation in operation (dystopia) or offer an alternative to that system (*eutopia*). In parallel Priest perceives science fiction – to the extent that it is anything more than a market niche's commodity – as a political art-form: not "of the Right or Left [...] but one which deals with the essence of politics: with people, with controls, with revolution from those controls, with planning, with mistakes, with personal initiative and public folly" (Priest 1971: 33). Whilst remaining ambivalent about propaganda, Priest privileges those books with some kind of a political agenda, or at least which explore political ideas: this enables him to say that Moorcock's "THE BLACK CORRIDOR does have a political tub to thump, and so in this sense it has a greater claim to being 'literature' than, I feel, TIGER! TIGER!" (Priest 1972: 50), despite being more poorly written. It should be clear that this does not need to be party political, but a writer should be "at the very least, a moral" figure (Priest 1971: 34) – again, not necessarily embracing a specific creed, but to have a coherent and thought-through world view. The notion should be an appropriate means of illustrating this idea.

This distinction between notion and idea made by Priest might be seen best in application to four novels of the same period with related notions. Three of them were reviewed or discussed by Christopher Priest – Larry Niven's *Ringworld* (1970), Arthur C. Clarke's *Rendezvous with Rama* (1973) and Bob Shaw's *Orbitsville* (1975) – the other, *Inverted World* (1974), was of course written by Christopher Priest.

Niven's Ringworld is a huge alien artefact, a vast cylindrical shape around a star which can be occupied on its interior surface. The novel features discovery and exploration by a group of humans and aliens of this big dumb object. Priest concedes that "is a startling notion. However a brilliant notion does not by itself create a novel, nor even an science fiction *idea*" (Priest and Watson 1976: 58). What interests Priest is what the novel says, but "What *is* said is hardly worth saying at all" (Priest and Watson 1976: 58) – Priest summarises it as "man's spirit of curiosity and adventure is irrepressible" (Priest and Watson 1976: 58).

Rendezvous with Rama features the exploration of a huge, mysterious alien spaceship which is passing through the solar system. This, for Priest, is "intrinsically unimaginative" (Priest and Watson 1976: 63). When he reviewed the novel two years earlier, he found it plotless and argued that "the level of characterization is that of a boy's adventure magazine" (Priest 1974a: 93). He does not revise this opinion in his brief history of British science fiction: "Clarke is an over-rated writer – his work is redolent of a naive romanticism, made palatable by homely similes, and simple, logical plotting" (Priest 1979f: 196). In both of these novels the discovery of something new is deemed to be enough to interest the reader – but for Priest it is just lazy plotting and thinking to merely depend upon readerly estrangement at the supposed novelty.

Orbitsville is much more to Priest's taste, but then he seems well disposed towards Shaw's work, and the man himself, Shaw being one of the remarkable men of his guest of honour talk, "Meetings with Remarkable Men" (1980b). He noted in an approving review of *Tomorrow Lies in Ambush* (1973) that Shaw "pays attention to plot, as well as to story" (Priest 1973d: 78). As E. M. Forster notes in his *Aspects of the Novel* (1927), story is just the unfolding of events in a linear order, whereas plot introduces causality and consequences – this happened because that had, and therefore... This approval of Shaw's work seems to survive through Priest's career. In his letter to Vector defending Wyndham's work, he took the opportunity to support Shaw: "To tell the truth, he's more or less the only trad science fiction writer whose work I still unashamedly enjoy" (Priest 1986/1987: 5). In *Orbitsville* the eponymous big dumb object is a Dyson sphere, a hollow planet which contains a star and an unbelievably vast surface area to colonise. The novel begins with the spaceship captain Vince Garamond waiting for an audience with Elizabeth Lindstrom before he can depart from Earth. Whilst she is delayed, her son accidentally dies in his care. Garamond departs in a hurry, pausing only to pick up his own family. Lindstrom pursues him in search of revenge, but is uncomfortably consoled by Garamond's discovery of this valuable real estate. Tom Shippey felt that "A theme like Orbitsville, perhaps, demands a series, not a novel" (Shippey 1974: 90). Indeed sequels were to follow, but as Bob Ford argued, these were "dilutions" of the theme (Ford 1997: 10). Priest argues that "[*Orbitsville*] is *about* something more than invented incident" (Priest 1979f: 201). According to Priest, *Orbitsville* is not just a representation of the exploring spirit of man, but within the novel Orbitsville "acts as a sort of cosmic sponge to soak up and dispose the outward drives of super-technological civilisations" (Priest and Watson 1976: 59). Orbitsville is as much the antagonist in the novel as Lindstrom, but the focus is on Garamond's actions: "In Niven's book the protagonist is the artefact itself [...] In Shaw's book the protagonist is a man" (Priest 1979f: 200).

I have noted that Christopher Priest sees *Inverted World* as one of his few traditional science fiction novels, and at first sight its representation of a hyperboloid environment makes it his nearest equivalent to the big dumb object novel. Priest is not content with this one notion, and undercuts our responses to it by the middle of the book, as Nick Hubble, Paul Kincaid and Graham Sleight discuss elsewhere in this volume. As Peter Nicholls says: "It is only in the last fifth of the book that we get the final bonus – that the novel is about something" (Nicholls 1975: 186), although that "only" may appear to be damning with faint praise. But it contains a science-fictional idea as well as a science-fictional notion.

Conclusion

Science fiction operates within a market economy and when it expresses ideas it is doing this despite more than because of market forces. The market does not set out to gratify our needs, because then we might not consume more products. It wants more of the same – what worked before may work again, what is new can be portrayed as an updating of an earlier product which has already been marketed. The market oscillates between offering us something we know we will like and find consoling because we have consumed something similar, and offering us something (apparently) new because we have jaded palettes and it has to stand out from the mass of almost identical products. Christopher Priest confronts the tyranny of the market and its suppression of the stylish, authentic voice which has something to say. He argues for a resistance to the ghettoisation of works of fiction as that bracketing enables a limitation of what may be expressed.

This act of resistance inevitably needs to be read back into his own works of fiction, which should perhaps be regarded as subversions of the science-fiction orthodoxies: *Indoctrinaire* as too surreal for science fiction, *Fugue for a Darkening Island* as a non-cosy catastrophe, *Inverted World* as spin on the big dumb object or the Hal Clement extreme physical environment, *The Space Machine* as a dialogue with H. G. Wells... This continues with *A Dream of Wessex* as "a satire on the sort of sf where you extrapolate a few social trends to depict a possible future society", *The Affirmation* began "life as a meditation on the familiar science fiction idea of human immortality", *The Glamour* took on the theme of invisibility, *The Quiet Woman* was political satire, and *The Prestige* "began, perhaps surprisingly, with an idea that goes back to the pulp roots of science fiction: matter transmission or matter duplication", *The Extremes* has a rather more sinister take on virtual reality than the average cyberpunk novel, and *The Separation* was "an attempt to write a novel of alternate history in a new way" (Priest 2001: 13). Priest's refusal to repeat himself and his often complete re-evaluation and critique of his own work must inevitably slow down his production as a writer; if he is a writer who needs to say something, he can only write when he has something to say. Because of his championing of the individual, because his books become challenging acts of communication, we should be ready to listen, and to respond, to interact.

Notes

1. Cf. Aldiss and Wingrove (1986)'s judgments in chapters eight and nine.
2. This is not to say that Priest dislikes all American writers and likes all British writers – Delany, Dick, Disch, Le Guin, Pohl, Sheckley and Zelazny seem generally to be approved of as writers. Priest rather backhandedly compliments British science fiction by saying "a mediocre American science-fiction novel is usually poor in an uninteresting way, and a mediocre British science-fiction novel is poor in an interesting way" (Priest 1979f: 201).
3. *The Separation*, like *The Prestige* and *The Extremes* before it, were published under a Simon and Schuster imprint. Simon and Schuster did run an sf imprint, Earthlight, which reprinted some of Priest's works under the capable editorial hands of first John Jarrold and then Darren Nash. However this

division has been abolished and the books are not now designated as science fiction. This is in line with most British publishers in the twenty-first century. *The Separation*, Priest's first novel to be a paperback original, has since been reprinted in hardback by Gollancz, still without a specific generic label – although the history of mergers and acquisitions means that Gollancz now survives only as an imprint for science fiction and fantasy.

4. One of the exceptions was Philip K. Dick, elsewhere referred to by Lem in another title as "A Visionary Among the Charlatans".

5. This attitude exists on both sides of the Atlantic, of course. Priest recalls E. C. Tubb asserting that "the *only* justification for writing was the money earned, and that to attempt to justify it with anything else was to descend to the pretentious" (Priest 1970a: 15).

6. Critical history has perhaps been unkind to John [E. J.] Carnell, who had more experimental tastes than he is credited for, and some of the Carnell writers continued under Moorcock.

7. Keyes is the author of two science-fiction novels, *The Battle of Disneyland* (1974) and *The Second Coming* (1979), as well as an episode, "The Tabor", of *Space: 1999*. Jones was most associated with *New Worlds*, and went on to edit the definitive British New Wave anthology, *The New SF* (1969). He also edited the definitive edition of *Titus Alone* (1970).

8. M. John Harrison defended Fearn's reputation from his detractors, saying: "I used to get a big kick out of Fearn. [... G]ranted, he was never the most accomplished of writers but, if I remember correctly, at least he never adulterated his escapism with fifth-form political allegory, or attempted to sell a minor flair for story-telling as a public service" (Harrison 1970: 43).

Blank Pages: Islands and Identity in the Fiction of Christopher Priest

Paul Kincaid

Peter Sinclair had reached the age of 212 pages. As with many other protagonists in the novels of Christopher Priest, from Alan Whitman to J. L. Sawyer, his knowledge of who and what he is is compromised, open to doubts and hesitations. We discover during the course of *The Affirmation* (1981), for instance, that Sinclair is not even sure whether he is 29 or 31. His confidence in his own identity is invested in the manuscript to which he clings obsessively throughout all that happens to him. In this manuscript he has poured out the story of his life, displaced into an imaginary landscape which may be London or may be the Dream Archipelago. In putting himself within this other place Sinclair has, as he says, "imagined myself into existence" (A 3: 15), "[m]y manuscript had to become a metaphor for myself" (A 3: 23). So fully is the manuscript linked to his identity that the revelation, late in the novel, that the pages are all blank is a devastating revelation of what is going on in Sinclair's mind. In the end, "blank pages lay scattered across the floor, like islands of plain truth, auguring what was to come" (A 24: 212).

There are islands of plain truth scattered throughout Priest's work. Sometimes these are genuine, sea-girt islands – Wessex, Muriseay – sometimes they are set within a more metaphorical ocean – the Planalto, Earth City. They are not solitary places, Priest has shown no interest in writing about a Robinson Crusoe or a Pincher Martin, a lone figure whose humanity is the key to whether he masters or is mastered by his environment. Invariably, Priest's islands are socially, politically and morally complex places, though they are also, equally invariably, places that are equated with the identity of his characters, their nature essential in any understanding of how a protagonist writes the story of who and what he is.

And the story usually is written. It is not just *The Affirmation* in which books play an inextricable part. The written word, in one form or another, reveals or undermines the world in *Inverted World* (1974) and *A Dream of Wessex* (1977) as much as it does in *The Quiet Woman* (1990), *The Prestige* (1996) and *The Separation* (2002). Nor should we forget the importance of a novel called *The Affirmation* in Priest's story "The Negation" (1978, revised 1999). The world of Priest's novels is created and understood through the written word, so that the book is one of the three key images that echo and recur throughout his work. The second is the double, whether it is Edward's brief glimpse of a second Amelia that sets the events of *The Space Machine* (1976) in motion, Peter Sinclair bifurcating in *The Affirmation*, the secret of *The Prestige*, or the twins whose separation splits the world in *The Separation*. The third is the focus of the exploration undertaken in this chapter: the island. However, it is impossible to examine any one of these tropes in isolation; to consider the island in Priest's work inevitably involves books and doubles, because all three pertain to his investigation of identity. In that other novel called *The Affirmation* a journey "through the exotic landscape of the Dream Archipelago [... is] also a voyage of self-exploration" (*DA* 42).

In accompanying "the endless island-hopping of the restless characters [...] forever seeking a sense of identity" (*DA* 32), our journey must begin with the scientific project, the "Concentration" of *Indoctrinaire* (1970, revised 1979), the "observatory" of "Real-Time World" (1971), the "establishment" of *Inverted World*. These are notable for their "absolute impregnability" (*I* 1: 1: 11), but it is their very impregnability that cuts the inhabitants off from consensus reality. The less they know about the world around them – "*We never get to know about the weather down here*" (*I* 1: 2: 20; italics original), as Wentik comments in a letter to his wife – the less they know about themselves. When, in both "Real-Time World" and *Inverted World*, the local reality becomes distorted, the residents interpret it as a distortion in the world outside them. They are adrift in a sea of ignorance, not realising that the ignorance is their own. Throughout his career, Priest has found ways to cut his characters off from consensus reality. Even in the post-Dream Archipelago stories, where islands as literal settings tend to disappear from his work, there is a sense that his characters are isolated from reality by invisibility (in *The Glamour* (1984, 1985, 1996)), by virtual reality (in *The Extremes* (1998)), by alternate realities (in *The Separation*) – but it is still the same impulse. *Indoctrinaire*, his first novel, may explore the idea less subtly than in his later works, but that does not alter the fact that some of the issues of identity and insularity first raised there resound throughout his entire oeuvre.

Indoctrinaire is the closest Priest has come to a Robinson Crusoe type of island story. Taken from the Concentration by the enigmatic agents, Astourde and Musgrove, Wentik finds himself in the Planalto, "a part of the world where you can see in one direction but not the other. A place you can walk into, but not out of" (*I* 1: 3: 26). It is an island of time: stepping out of the Brazilian jungle into the circle of grassland that is the Planalto, the men travel two hundred years into the future. The setting alone is enough to give Wentik "a hopeless sensation of separation from reality" (*I* 1: 7: 64), but he finds himself further isolated by his sanity as Astourde and Musgrove, themselves becoming increasingly irrational, subject him to bizarre imprisonment and interrogation. When he does eventually reach the future Sao Paulo, Wentik learns that it was a "Disturbance Gas", an off-shoot of his own research, that was responsible for their madness. His entirely peaceful research was used for deadly military purposes. "It was all part of the permanent gulf between theory and practice, between the cold clinical light of a research-bench and the blinding heat of an interrogation-room" (*I* 2: 18: 162). The gulf, in other words, between the island of the Concentration and the mainland of Wentik's family (whom we never see), between asocial insularity and social context, between madness and sanity.

Though there is always some such gulf to be found in Priest's work, and social connection is always applauded, the island is not always associated with disconnection. It is, however, always associated with identity. Here, for instance, when Wentik itemises all the people he knew and loved who would be lost in the war, he concludes: "But even more than this, a whole set of memories and impressions and images which go to make up an identity. For Wentik to accept the destruction of all this would be to condone the removal of a part of himself" (I 3: 21: 195). It is significant, therefore, that having travelled back in time but still not able to rescue his family from the war, Wentik chooses to cast himself away on the island of the Planalto at the end of the novel. He has become a Robinson Crusoe, or perhaps more appropriately a Pincher Martin, because the social context that makes him who he is has already been taken away from him. The island does not isolate him, it is his isolation that leaves him washed up on the island.

All that occurs in *Indoctrinaire*, the war, the bizarre imprisonment in the Planalto, is a direct consequence of the malevolent insularity of the Concentration. But in Priest's first novel we hardly have a chance to see how this disconnection from the world distorts perceptions of the world. In two subsequent works, however, the story "Real-Time World" and the novel *Inverted World*, this distortion would be brought into sharp focus. This is because, in both instances, our attention is almost exclusively fixed upon the closed, insular world of the blandly-named "observatory" or "establishment".

In many ways, "Real-Time World", notably the Tolneuve Theory around which it revolves, encapsulates everything that islands represent in Priest's work at this stage: "people raised in a high-stimulus environment become a product of their society, and could not keep their orientation without some knowledge of what is outside their sphere" (*RTW* 139). From *Indoctrinaire* all the way to *A Dream of Wessex*, Priest's fiction is filled with people who lose their orientation, their sanity, their sense of identity, through losing their context, their connection with consensus reality. The story is, in fact, an experiment in just such loss of orientation, an experiment that is summarised thus: "what, *precisely* what, would be the effect on a community deprived of news? Or in another sense: does an awareness of current events really matter?" (*RTW* 138).

The form of the experiment involves complex layers of deception. The story is that the scientists are manning an observatory on another planet, though, as in the Planalto, they are enisled by time more than by space due to an effect known as "elocation":

> Elocation had about as much relation to time-travel as a flight of stairs has to space-travel [...] All the elocation field can do is to push the observatory back in time by about one nanosecond (*RTW* 141).

In other words, they are cut off from their reality in every way possible. Their only access to the world outside this hermetically sealed observatory is through a series of personal news sheets which are doled out, once every twenty-eight days, by the narrator, Dan Winter. It is Winter's job to observe the experiment, plotting the way rumours about what is actually happening on Earth spread through the community. After a while, "[t]he rumours lost any basis in reality, became fantastic, wild, demented" (*RTW* 144), but then speculation turned towards reality again, "incredibly, the rumours began to anticipate fact" (*RTW* 145). As he follows this bell-curve, Winter believes that he alone knows the truth: that they are not on some distant planet but in the Joliot-Curie crater on the Moon, which is visible from earth only once every twenty-eight days, hence the four-week pattern in receiving news from outside. But as the scientists' understanding of their world returns towards consensus reality, they realise that they are not on some distant planet, nor on the Moon, but are still on Earth. They simply walk out. Only the narrator, Winter, enmired in his own distorted view of reality and unable to imagine that they are not on the Moon, remains. He cannot walk out because in his reality that would mean dying instantly in a vacuum, so he stays in a social and intellectual vacuum of his own making.

It is not the island of the observatory that physically cuts its inhabitants off from the world; it is the consensus view of the scientists. When their view of the world changes, when their social, political and intellectual context allows a connection with outside reality the scientists are able to move freely between the worlds. Only the narrator, socially at odds with the other scientists, is unable to share their consensus reality and therefore alone is left a castaway.

"Real-Time World" is probably the best of Priest's early stories because of its psychological and moral complexity, but it would soon be overshadowed by another work that employed exactly the same scenario. In *Inverted World* Priest would once again examine the social insularity of his characters by placing them upon the island of a scientific establishment that is technologically cut-off from outside reality, and again it would be the willingness of the characters to connect with that outside world and share in its consensus that would dictate whether they can escape the dying island of their imaginations for the world of our reality.

Practically the first thing we learn about Earth City, after Helward Mann's startling and famous opening declaration – "I had reached the age of six hundred and fifty miles" (*IW* 1: 1: 15) – is about its confinement and regulation. Helward's mother, for instance, had left the city soon after his birth and all he had known while growing up were "the confining walls of the crèche" (IW 1: 1: 15), but now there are rituals to go through as he enters the highly regulated adult world of the guilds. This emotional isolation is combined with a deliberate intellectual and cultural insularity. Like the scientists in "Real-Time World", for instance, the inhabitants of Earth City understand that they are not on the planet Earth, but knowledge of the planet they are on is withheld from them.

> We knew, or thought we knew, much about everyday life on Earth planet, but we were told that this was not what we would find on this world. A child's natural curiosity immediately demanded to know the alternative, but on this the teachers had kept their silence (IW 1: 6: 53).

Although Helward's future wife, Victoria, will rail against the frustrating limitations of this insularity –

> the system which runs my life is itself dominated by what goes on outside the city. As I can never take part in that I can never do anything to determine my own life (IW 1: 6: 58)

– nothing is done to understand the world. The guilds, who alone have contact with anyone or anything outside the city, are constrained by their rituals to tell no-one of what they see, even the spiked shape of the sun. More than that, they behave towards the people they encounter with a disdain bordering on disgust that is typical of the reaction of islanders to others in all Priest's work from *Fugue for a Darkening Island* (1972) to the Dream Archipelago stories. Reason enough for this disdain is shown in the novel's bravura central section in which Helward journeys "south" and experiences all the distortions of the inverted world. But it is after he returns, in the war with the "tooks" (as the local inhabitants are called, a name clearly cognate with the "gooks" of Vietnam; see also Hubble in this volume) that we learn something of the social and political consequences of this isolation.

We have already learned, when Helward discovers the old plan of Earth City, that it had once had several languages, and realise that it has become homogenised. We know, also, that the population is shrinking, and especially that fewer girls are being born. So we have an impression already of a society becoming smaller and narrower, more and more cut off. Now Helward himself, seeing parallels between what he has been taught and what he has experienced, recognises Earth City as the inheritor of an uncomfortable truth about Earth planet, where "[c]ivilisation [...] was equated with selfishness and greed; those people who lived in a civilised state exploited those who did not" (IW 3: 4: 168). Earth City is repeating that pattern: the guilds see themselves as civilised and therefore exploit – economically in terms of their labour but also sexually by taking and using their women – the tooks whom they see as non-civilised, their physical isolation is a graphic representation of their emotional and moral isolation, their selfish and self-chosen insularity.

All of this is possible only as long as the City and its inhabitants remain detached from the world through which they travel. As Helward puts it:

> Survival on this world was a matter of initiative: on the grand scale, by hauling the city northwards away from that zone of amazing distortion behind us, and on the personal scale by deriving for oneself a pattern of life that was self-determined (*IW* 3: 4: 169).

But already that self-determination, that "evident discipline, the sense of purpose, and a real and vital understanding of their own identity" (*IW* 4: 8: 232), is starting to break down. The guilds, with their secret oaths and their sense of being special, are comparable with the sort of fascistic organisation that crops up elsewhere in Priest's work, in *Fugue for a Darkening Island* and in *The Quiet Woman* for instance. But these can survive only as long as all their members are united in the same dream, and as long as they remain inviolate from the influences of an outside world. But on Earth City the sense of unity is already slipping. After attending a meeting of the Navigators, the city government, for instance, Helward concludes that "perhaps more guildsmen should attend the Navigators' meetings" (*IW* 3: 7: 188), suggesting a declining commitment to the group even among the supposedly élite. And when the attack by the tooks opens part of the city to the sky so that even the restricted ordinary inhabitants can see the strange sun, it awakens a wave of protest and rebellion, led by Helward's former wife, Victoria, who has already expressed her dissatisfactions with the restrictions of city life.

Nevertheless, Helward himself is totally committed to the enclosed world of the city, his experiences in the outside world have convinced him that the disciplined rituals of the guilds are the only possible response to "the hostile world that daily threatens our survival" (*IW* 3: 6: 182). And because his own response to the world is determined so totally by the group, his reaction when Elizabeth finally reveals that Earth City is still on Earth, that their distorted view of reality is a physical and psychological effect of the machinery that powers the city, is simply "despair" (*IW* 4: 7: 228). So much so, in fact, that he refuses to accept the real world as we perceive it. Our final glimpse of him has him thrashing in the Atlantic Ocean, convinced it is just a river that the city can cross. Like Winter in "Real-Time World", he cannot leave his island because he can see only death outside it. Later, when Peter Sinclair crosses desperately between Jethra and London, unable to accept the non-reality of either, we see it as the breakdown of his own identity. And so it is now, Helward Mann cannot leave Earth City though it might mean death through the horrible distortions he has already witnessed, because to do so would be the even more terrible abandonment of his identity.

After *Inverted World*, Priest shifted from artificial islands to what we might as well call real islands, real in the sense that they are bodies of land surrounded by water, although all are to some degree imaginary. As they emerge from the dreams of their inhabitants, so they are tied even more closely to the wished-for identities of his characters. But before we consider the related creations of Wessex and the Dream Archipelago, it is worth turning back briefly to one other sea-girt island, Britain, as it appears in *Fugue for a Darkening Island*. In the early seventies the British catastrophe novel as established by writers such as John Wyndham and John Christopher (to both of whom Priest has acknowledged a debt; see also Sawyer in this volume on this) was enjoying a late flourish. The previous year M. John Harrison had published *The Committed Men* (1971), and shortly afterwards Richard Cowper would produce *The Twilight of Briareus* (1974), and *Fugue* seems to fit neatly within this pattern: helpless men move in a complex dance through a shattered landscape in which their helplessness, their inability to act, is part of the catastrophe.

In a way that would become characteristic of Priest's work, he begins the novel by undermining our confidence in the identity of the narrator. The two opening paragraphs of the novel provide echoing descriptions of our narrator, Alan Whitman, but with strange and significant differences: "I have white skin [...] I have no political ambitions" (*FDI* 9) the first tells us; "My skin is smudged with dirt [...] I do not think I have political ambitions" (*FDI* 9) we learn from the second. In a novel that deliberately eschews a straightforward chronological narrative we soon realise that this is our hero as the story opens and as it closes, so we see from the start how he is changed and how he stays the same. But at the same time the effect is to make us doubt, to establish from the start that this is no coherent and reliable figure. We will see the same undermining of identity right at the start of *The Affirmation*, and even *Inverted World*'s "I had reached the age of six hundred and fifty miles" (*IW* 1: 1: 11) tells us not to take Helward Mann's identity in our own terms. So we have a shattered political climate reflected in a shattered narrative structure which in turn presages a shattering in the identity of our narrator. That our narrator is a comfortably middle class everyman, or at least an every-Englishman, only asks us to accept the shattering of his identity as the shattering of our own.

Again, as in *Inverted World*, we have an inviolable island whose grip on its own inward-turning reality is dislodged by an intrusion from a greater outside world, by the forced acceptance of a new consensus reality. The inward-turning nature of British reality prior to the "Afrim" (African immigrant) invasion is represented by the largely off-stage rise of an extreme right-wing government. The lesson we will learn from the fascistic inventions of Gordon in *The Quiet Woman* is that fascism is equated by Priest with dislocation from reality, and so it is here. Whitman, drifting into an unsatisfactory marriage and an unsatisfactory career, has lost his way even before the first of the Afrims arrive, and so has his country. The war that follows, glimpsed only tangentially, appears to be a conventional one of national forces battling invaders, but is marked by disruption to national unity with individual streets barricaded and towns fortified. It is an abandonment of the moral values that might in other terms be considered a part of the national identity: "a small and vociferous section of the community [...] adhered to its moral principles, but more and more ordinary people were coming into direct conflict with the Afrims as the armed insurgence went on" (*FDI* 52). The whole country, in other words, is broken down into individuals fighting for their personal survival. The presence of United Nations personnel staffing refugee camps suggests that the rest of the world has not reacted so violently to the influx of African refugees, but there is very little awareness of the rest of the world in this England.

Although the chronology of the novel is deliberately out of sequence, there is a clear dynamic towards greater isolation. Whitman successively loses his work, his home and his family; he leaves the refugee band when it starts to arm itself, but also rejects the seaside town which has managed to preserve old values; in the end he is left standing alone over the bodies of his wife and daughter. Like Wentik, he is cast away upon an island of his own making, for the failure that has destroyed his country is a direct consequence of his own failure. The fascist government that is the root cause of the disruption – "Everywhere [Afrims] caused social upheaval; but in Britain, where a neo-racist government had come to power on an economic-reform ticket, they did much more" (*FDI* 83) – has achieved power through an abdication of their social and cultural obligations by people like Whitman. His lack of commitment is described as "insularity" (*FDI* 54), of his marriage he says: "While we were living at our house we were able to disregard both the fact that our relationship was hypocritical and that the political situation of that period had an effect on us" (*FDI* 57), and even when his father dies "I tried unsuccessfully to feel more than a few minutes of regret" (*FDI* 65). When he describes one of the women with whom he has an affair as existing "in a kind of personal vacuum ... living in but not belonging to our society" (*FDI* 124) we recognise that the description applies to him and to all around him. Each man is an island, and having abandoned society they have abandoned all that contributes towards their security and their identity.

In these early works, from *Indoctrinaire* through to *Inverted World*, insularity is seen in broad terms as an avoidance of social or political commitment. *The Space Machine* acts as a sort of *entr'acte*. Though not really an island novel, his central characters, Edward and Amelia might be seen as castaways upon Mars, where they are forced to engage politically with the revolutionary Martians while Edward learns to engage psychologically with the more sexually and socially liberated Amelia. From this point onwards, psychological and sexual engagement, and the issues of individual identity implicit in this, become a significant part of the political commitment that is a continuing theme in Priest's work. Concomitant with this new focus was a new maturity in Priest's writing, first evident in stories that sprang directly out of the writing of *The Space Ma-*

chine, "An Infinite Summer" (1976) and "Palely Loitering" (1978), but which was more fully expressed in his next novel, *A Dream of Wessex*.

One shift in attitude is immediately apparent. The near-future England in which the novel opens is undergoing a political upheaval reminiscent of *Fugue for a Darkening Island*. In the very first sentence we learn that "[t]he Tartan Army had planted a bomb at Heathrow" (*DW* 1: 1) and travel about the country is disrupted by army checkpoints. But where Whitman in *Fugue* was expected to engage politically to hold together his disintegrating society, Julia Stretton in *Wessex* is allowed to escape into the personal and psychological commitment represented by the future island. Similarly in *The Glamour* there are terrorist disruptions to the body politic, and in that novel our viewpoint character, Grey, is appropriately a news cameraman, an observer of rather than a participant in the political scene, who escapes into invisibility.

The bomb at the start of *Wessex* is only a part of a world turned upside down. We also learn, for instance, that "now in July there had been reports of snow-flurries along the Yorkshire coast" (*DW* 1: 1). In part, of course, this acts as a contrast with the endless summer of Wessex, though it also speaks of a disorder greater than any individual, no matter how politically engaged, could hope to change. Though, of course, Julia's imaginative engagement within Wessex will eventually mend disorder of a similar scale.

Wessex Island is a projection from the minds of the volunteers of the Wessex Project, it is literally a concretisation of their identities, and because we see it mostly through Julia's eyes it is primarily an expression of her identity. It is a place of contradictions: politically, for instance, Britain is now a repressive communist state while America is part of the austere Moslem world; yet Wessex Island is an international holiday destination popular with American tourists and a place of open-air cafés, casinos and casual nudity. In part, we can gather from this that old-style party politics are really irrelevant to the social healing represented by Wessex; in part, it simply emphasises that the island is a place apart.

Both Julia and, by inference, the island with which she is associated, "seemed degenerate and wanton, giving off an air of anarchy and irresponsibility" (*DW* 3: 20). Much the same is discovered by Peter Sinclair when he reaches Muriseay: "The whole city was a new kind of sensation: a feeling of careless indifference to many things I took for granted [...] a teeming, shouting and colliding city, uneven and untidy, yet charged with life" (*A* 7: 57). Both of these impressions of the island echo something John Fowles says in his island novel of psycho-sexual exploration, *The Magus* (1965, rev. edn 1977): "It was Greece again, the Alexandrian Greece of Cavafy; there were only degrees of aesthetic pleasure; of beauty in decadence. Morality was a North European lie" (Fowles 1978: 249). The Greek Islands, where Britain's post-war generation shook off their repressions, were an ideal more than a real, a fantasy of liberation. And both Wessex and the Dream Archipelago are representations of the Greek Islands in their warmth, their aesthetic pleasures, their decadence. The specific identification of the Dream Archipelago with the Greek Islands comes later, in *The Quiet Woman*, when we learn that the old writer, Eleanor, is also Seri Fulton, the name of the woman who personifies the Dream Archipelago in *The Affirmation*, and that returning from Greece at the outset of war she had an affair with a man named Peter, we presume Peter Sinclair. Here, then, is an ideal setting for sexual liberty, for freedom and fulfilment, a place where Julia's sexual happiness and the curious sexual experiments of the Dream Archipelago stories rightly seem to belong. But at the same time, it must be protected from the repressions that are being escaped. Hence, as a place apart, an island of desire, Wessex must remain inviolate, shut off to most visitors, a Grail whose achievement is itself a measure of some grace. So it is that, despite David Harkman's "instinctive knowledge that Wessex was a spiritual and emotional home" (*DW* 4: 23), it had seemed "a part of the world as unreachable from London as the Presidential Palace in Riyadh" (*DW* 4: 22). The Dream Archipelago, similarly, would be a place where access is restricted, where only the fortunate can enter, and which, like the Planalto, can be entered but not left.

Thus enclosed, protected as much as isolated by the sea that surrounds it, Wessex "had a hypnotic quality of peace and security, an ordered languor; it was a restful, secure place [...] Wessex, tourist island in an imagined future, became the ultimate escapist fantasy, a bolt-hole from reality" (*DW* 13: 78). To the participants, Wessex comes to seem real, and the world they have fled is shadowy:

> Although they were sometimes accused of running away from the real world, the fact was that once they had lived in Wessex the participants became distanced from real life, and there was no need to hide from something insubstantial (*DW* 16: 95).

Into this protected world intrudes Paul Mason, Julia's manipulative and destructive former lover. Paul is portrayed as intrusive from the first moment we see him. When Julia runs into him at Wessex House "it was like the breach of a sanctuary" (*DW* 1: 1) and "he had the ability to invade her life" (*DW* 1: 2). If Priest's books, politically, are about engagement, then in Julia and David we have people who engage with their world, even if it is a world they have created from their own imaginations; but in Paul we have someone who does not engage, but who tries to make the world, any world, over in his own image. Like Niall in *The Glamour* who sees invisibility as a means of denying the morality of the world (to the extent that he can engage in an invisible rape of Susan), so Paul sees Wessex as a way of twisting the world (and Julia in particular) to his own moral rules. For Julia and David, Wessex is not a perfect place: David is caught up in a dull, grey bureaucracy in Dorchester; Julia is locked in a loveless sexual relationship. Nevertheless, it is a place they can make better through their own personal engagement, such that on their first encounter David feels "a need to stay with her, a need to talk and make some kind of contact" (*DW* 7: 41). Paul, on the other hand, stands for "the destruction of her pride, of her sense of identity, of her self-respect" (*DW* 11: 66), and when he does finally breach the sanctuary and enter Wessex he turns this destruction of identity into a destruction of the refuge and the hope that the island represents.

The changes that Paul brings to the island are signalled by a change in the weather. The summer idyll, a fragment of the Mediterranean relocated in southern England, is replaced by cold and wind and rain, noticeably similar to the unpleasant weather Julia had left in her present at the beginning of the book. Paul is symbolically bringing all the ills of the present, including the psycho-sexual ills of his relationship with Julia, into the idealised island escape of the future. The change in climate is followed by a change in the purpose and character of Wessex, the warm holiday retreat is replaced by an unwelcoming and environmentally heedless industrialisation: "The smoke from the oil-refinery poured over the town, dark and depressing and greasy" (*DW* 22: 143). When Julia and David triumph in the end the oil refineries and factory chimneys disappear from the view, sunshine returns. This is not only a restoration of the Wessex of their original idyll, but a healing as great in its way as if Julia had been able to correct the unseasonal weather that opens the novel. It signals the completeness of their engagement with each other and with their world.

> She had ceased to be an organic part of the real world from the day she had first entered the projection. She belonged to the future; life could never again be stable except in the Wessex of her mind (*DW* 26: 174).

Whether it is now a projection of their imaginations or reality is irrelevant, such distinctions have been removed. "It would be real, or *real-seeming*. It made no difference. It would be as it was, or as she expected it to be [...] and it therefore was of no importance" (*DW* 26: 179).

This question of the reality of Wessex is, of course, important in any consideration of the island as a representation of the identity of the characters. When one of the participants is out of the projector they leave a doppelgänger in Wessex, like a bookmark preserving their place in the story of the island. This persona is shadowy, so that when David continues his romance with Julia's doppelgänger "he did not *experience* her. He remembered her into existence" (*DW* 20: 119) but when she returns to the projection "[r]eality began at this instant, at every instant, and the past became false" (*DW* 20: 124). How real the world is depends on how thoroughly one interacts with it. Significantly, mirrors are used to recall people from the projection, you see yourself and hence see where you belong; but the mirrors do not work on David, he sees himself and knows himself in Wessex. He is so thoroughly engaged with this world that it is no longer a projection, it has become his reality, an echo of what we will later see in the shift to virtual reality in *The Extremes*.

Then David discovers a newspaper article. It is important to note the rôle that texts play in Priest's work. Only the fictional work, *The Affirmation*, in his story "The Negation", unequivocally reveals the truth about the world. Every non-fiction, from Destaine's Directive in *Inverted World* to the various texts that make up *The Separation*, may seem to state a simple fact about the world but actually serves to undermine our notion of what is reality. As Peter Sinclair says in *The Affirmation*:

> If I could find the right words, then with the proper will I could by assertion write all that was true. I have since learned that words are only as valid as the mind that chooses them, so that of essence all prose is a form of deception (A 1: 1).

So it is with the clipping David finds in which the project is described thus: "we are *imagining* a future world, which is made palpable to us by the Ridpath projector" (*DW* 22: 138). The photographs of himself and Julia accompanying the article force David to confront what Helward Mann has already faced in *Inverted World*, and that other of Priest's protagonists will also face: the fact that his reality may be a creation. It is notable that it is only after this discovery, after David's faith in his world is shaken, that the degradation of Wessex that marks Paul's assault on the identity of Julia and of David, begins to be noticeable.

When Paul inverts this world, sending the participants back through the Ridpath projector, they emerge severely damaged: "The loss of memory was like the loss they all experienced inside the projection: a total severance from their real lives" (*DW* 26: 177). Only Julia emerges intact because, through her love for David, she is now grounded in the reality of Wessex. And it is the strength of this engagement with each other and with the world that allows them to overcome Paul and remake Wessex.

At the end of *A Dream of Wessex*, as Julia and David possess their newly remade world, there is a lingering question about its status: "Where was the present from which Wessex was being projected? Were they the same ... or was the system now closed?" (*DW* 27: 188; Priest's ellipsis). Priest has created a loop, the real world feeds into the dream, the dream world feeds into the real, engagement with another equates with engagement with the world. This turn in the Möbius strip which makes it impossible to tell where one reality ends and another begins is a pattern that will become familiar in the ending of books such as *The Extremes*, *The Separation* and especially in *The Affirmation*.

In many ways it seems that *A Dream of Wessex* set a pattern, or rather a series of patterns, which have been further explored and elaborated in the novels that followed. The triangular relationship between Julia, David and Paul, for instance, is repeated in *The Glamour*, and echoed also in *The Extremes* and *The Separation*. More significantly, as is evidenced from the way that references to *The Affirmation* have wound themselves inextricably through this discussion of *A Dream of Wessex*, is the way Wessex would transform into the Dream Archipelago.

The Dream Archipelago, the setting for some of the most darkly unsettling of Priest's fictions, first appeared in a series of four stories published in 1978, the year after *Wessex*. A fifth story, "The Miraculous Cairn" (1980), appeared in *Granta* in 1983 as part of the promotion of the Best of Young British Writers in which Priest was featured. These stories were all slightly revised for the collection *The Dream Archipelago* in 1999, with a brief scene-setting piece, "The Equatorial Moment", added. A further novelette, "The Discharge", was published in France in 2000 and subsequently appeared online in an English version. Each of these stories, along with Priest's novel *The Affirmation*, appears to share the same geographical setting: the archipelago is always an innumerable swathe of islands that girdle the equator, so many that there are always several other islands visible from whichever island you are on; they separate a technologically sophisticated northern continent whose nations are involved in a seemingly endless war, from a barren southern continent where the war is fought (the North Africa campaign of the Second World War seems to be the model here); the northern city of Jethra and various islands such as Muriseay recur. Yet for all these repetitions, the infinitude of islands seems to be deliberately exploited to allow an infinitude of settings. The religious institution in "The Miraculous Cairn" does not cohere with the funeral rites of "The Cremation" (1978), whose sexual predation is very different from the sexual predation of "Whores" (1978), while the refuge to soldiers in that latter story seems a world away from the refuge to civilians offered in "The Watched" (1978). And so it goes; what really ties these stories together is their insularity, the island setting allows Priest to separate his protagonists from the familiarity of their world and cast them away in a place where their own darker imaginings come to haunt them. Where the Dream Archipelago resembles Wessex is in its evocation of Greece, a realm of sunshine, of moral and sexual liberty. But where this liberty allowed David and Julia to discover love, freedom and escape, these self-same liberties in the Dream Archipelago lead to nightmare as the various protagonists discover that freedom on their terms means freedom on other people's terms also, and they are not equipped to cope with that.

It is notable that the main point of "The Equatorial Moment" is to point up a curious temporal effect experienced by those flying over the archipelago (most of the minor changes made to the stories for *The Dream Archipelago* introduced passing references to this effect). In other words, like the Planalto in *Indoctrinaire* and the observatory in "Real-Time World", the Dream Archipelago is isolated not just by the sea and by the forced neutrality of war but also by time:

With a sense of future removed the past became irrelevant and those who came to the Archipelago, choosing the permanence of neutrality, made a conscious decision to abandon their former lives (DA 191).

In fact, the isolation of those who visit the islands is stressed all through these stories. In the stories of Moylita Kaine in "The Negation" it is a place of walls. Graian Sheeld in "The Cremation" finds "a sheltered, oppressive place" (DA 73) where everything is exotic and difficult and "[h]e felt isolated and cast adrift in the islands" (DA 72). This is partly a cultural effect; Alanya's frank stories "only helped to cut him off further from the other guests" (DA 76) so that in the end Sheeld becomes the victim of "the general paralysis of his culture shock and social alienation" (DA 78).

The islands are places of allure only to those who have not been there (Dik in "The Negation'), but to those who do go there they become places of mystery, of inexplicable threat, of alienation. But it is an alienation that cannot be escaped: the law says that those who move to the islands cannot return, and in fact they offer no opportunity to return for there will always be some new seduction that leads on to the grave. Even if you get back to Jethra, as the narrator in "The Mysterious Cairn" does, some lotus-eating experience will have changed you forever. Significantly, as islands always reflect the identity of Priest's characters, those who seek out the islands do so to escape a troubled life, and bring their trouble with them amplified by the magic of the islands. Graian Sheeld, for instance, is fleeing "the mounting confusion and emotional fall-out" (DA 88) caused by his infidelities. It is fitting, therefore, that what he finds in the islands is a sexually predatory woman who becomes implicit in his gruesome death. Similarly Yvann Ordier, in "The Watched", leaves behind his involvement with the microscopic spying devices known as scintillas, only to find himself emotionally trapped by his own voyeurism which leads eventually to him taking the place of the one he was watching.

The narrator of "The Miraculous Cairn" is typical, seeing the Dream Archipelago at once as a place of escape and of retribution. A sexually nervous middle-aged teacher – we discover only at the mid-point of the story that she is female and a lesbian – revisits the island of Seevl where, as a teenager, she had her first sexual encounter. As a child, even though she knew the island, she half-shared the popular impression that:

> Seevl was populated by bogeymen and creeping horrors, while the actual landscape was thought to be a nightmare terrain of crevasses and volcanic pools, sulphurous mists, steaming craters and shifting rocks (DA: 117).

Curiously, the nightmare is not far from what she actually discovers there. Led on by a carefree older girl, her first sexual encounter is unconsummated, but marked by an extraordinary incident in which her arm is caught in the jaws of a monstrous beast she never sees, and when she escapes its bite she finds it has left no mark on her flesh. Now, years later, she discovers that the ruined tower in which this strangely formative experience occurred does not actually exist. The island, like that childhood nightmare, is a place of psycho-sexual terror where fears of one's sexuality are externalised and turned into creatures of irrational punishment. And in that, as invariably occurs within Priest's fiction, lies the key to her identity, or lack of it.

> Everything I am, that I have been as an adult, began here at the seminary. I gained my identity here. If I hadn't come back I would still feel that I had that identity, but now it's gone. I am not sure of anything (*DA* 184).

The result is the existential doubt that marks so many of Priest's characters, and which we will encounter most notably in Peter Sinclair. And as with Sinclair, that doubt is identified with the islands.

Sinclair starts out with certainties, the clearest way of recognising that his identity is made up of uncertainties:

> This much I know for sure:

> My name is Peter Sinclair, I am English and I am, or I was, twenty-nine years old. Already there is an uncertainty, and my sureness recedes. Age is a variable; I am no longer twenty-nine (A 1: 1).

It is a litany that calls to mind Whitman's statement of identity at the beginning of *Fugue*, and in exactly the same way it prefigures doubts, hesitations and a profound remaking of who Peter Sinclair is. (The other Peter Sinclair, writing a parallel narrative in the Dream Archipelago, will later have the same hesitation at Lotterie-Collago when he claims to be 29 though the records state he is 31.) At this point Peter's life is breaking apart. How much is his fault we are never entirely sure, but we know he loses his job, his girlfriend and his father in short order. When a friend of his father offers him a cottage in the country he deliberately cuts himself off from what remains of his life: "I wanted to be unencumbered after my move" (A 1: 8). This is a deliberate isolation from reality: "in London I had been extensively aware of the world [... N]ow I was cut off from all that" (A 2: 11). This is exactly the loss of news experienced by the scientists in "Real-Time World", but in this more sophisticated working out of the Tolneuve Theory there is no guarantee that Sinclair will follow the same bell curve. His loss of identity quickly becomes apparent: "One day I looked in the bloom-spotted mirror in the kitchen and saw the familiar face staring back at me, but I could not identify it with anything I knew of myself" (A 2: 13). The mirror which reaffirmed the real identity of the inhabitants of Wessex clearly does not work here.

To reclaim his identity, therefore, Peter Sinclair starts to write his autobiography. When Julia is brought back into a recursive present in *A Dream of Wessex*, the event which destroys the mind of her fellow participants, she is able to retain her grip on reality and hence defy Paul by clinging onto the reality of her memories of Wessex and of David. Similarly, Sinclair now decides "I could only regain my sense of identity through my memories" (A 2: 14). Looking upon his autobiography he declares: "I had imagined myself into existence" (A 3: 15) and later, as his manuscript changes through the invention of the Dream Archipelago and "to achieve total truth I must create total falsehood" (A 3: 23): "I had found myself, explained myself, and in a very personal sense of the word I had *defined* myself" (A 3: 25). These islands "represented a form of wish, or of escape" (A 3: 24), but they are also the metaphor that he lives. This is surely what Helward Mann is doing in *Inverted World* and David and Julia in *Wessex*, living a metaphor; and the metaphor is an island separated from mundane reality. But the island of release, of identity, of escape, also implies a mainland, and the mainland is the place of confusion and anarchy, but also the place of connection and reality. In *Inverted World*, *Wessex* and *The Extremes*, even back in *Indoctrinaire* and "Real-Time World", the protagonists turn their backs on reality and find escape in the dream island. But they do so at a cost, which may be isolation or madness or even non-existence (*Wessex*, *The Extremes*) which is what madness and isolation amount to. In *The Affirmation* we discover the madness and isolation early in the way Sinclair splits his reality even while still wholly in this world.

Charged by the owners of the cottage to redecorate it, Sinclair realises that "[t]o visualize the rooms newly painted, made clean and tidy, was in a sense half the work already done" (A 2: 12), and from that moment we are unsure if what we are told is real or only what he imagines. Then his sister, Felicity, visits, and having exclaimed about the filthiness of this supposedly pristine cottage, begins to wash up.

"Is there no hot water?"

"Yes [...] it's hot." I could see the steam cascading around her arms (A 4: 30).

But this doubling of reality is not a problem for Sinclair, it was "Felicity's failure, not mine. She was perceiving it wrongly" (A 4: 33).

Throughout it all – the breakdown in the cottage, the enforced stay with Felicity, renewed contact with his suicidal girlfriend, Gracia – Sinclair clings to his manuscript which tells of Peter Sinclair in the Dream Archipelago. Meanwhile Peter Sinclair sets sail among the islands of the Dream Archipelago carrying a manuscript he wrote two years before during a long summer in the country while he had been unemployed. This manuscript, we will eventually discover, tells of a Peter Sinclair who lives in the imaginary city of London. Only the fact that *The Affirmation* opens in London gives Peter Sinclair the Londoner any precedence over the Jethran Peter Sinclair: each invents the other, and either or neither could be real. The Jethran Sinclair is travelling to claim a prize he won in a lottery, athanasia treatment, which will give him prolonged life. Just as there has been a consistent temporal element in the island settings Priest has created from *Indoctrinaire* to the Dream Archipelago stories, this treatment too is a way of isolating Sinclair in time: "My friends, my family, would move on into biological future, while I would be fixed, or petrified" (A 9: 83). The symbolism of this is emphasised when Sinclair and Seri visit a village where objects are left in running water to become petrified, an event echoed in this world when Sinclair goes with Felicity's family to visit Castleton in the Peak District where there is a "pool which could turn things to stone" (A 10: 88). As a result of one visit Sinclair and Seri become lovers, as a result of the other Sinclair and Gracia are reunited.

When Sinclair leaves Sheffield to move back to London and Gracia:

> I was moving from one island to another. Beside me was Seri, behind me were Kalia and Yallow. Through them I could discover myself in the glowing landscape of the mind. I felt that at last I saw a way to free myself from the confinements of the page. There were now two realities, and each explained the other (A 11: 100).

This is a potent a statement as can be found of the rôle islands play in Priest's fiction. Islands are the "glowing landscape of the mind", the second of two realities that Priest's protagonists inhabit. But because the two realities, islands and the mainland, as it were, each explain the other, they cannot be independent; there must be movement each way. (It is noticeable how often there is an interdiction on travel between the worlds, from the supposed temporal dislocation of "Real-Time World" to the restrictions on movement in *Fugue* and the Dream Archipelago stories.) Each reality is necessary: in the island of the imagination is to be found individual identity; in the mainland of the outside world is social, political and cultural connection. Alone, the island is a place of madness; alone, the mainland is a place of anarchy and turmoil. Too often, however, Priest's protagonists choose one world over the next. Sinclair, in this brief moment of self-knowledge, might recognise that "through them I could discover myself", but he makes no discoveries "through them". He might wish to free himself "from the confinements of the page", but that is something he will prove unable to do. Indeed, as *The Affirmation* ends with the same broken sentence that Sinclair's manuscript has twice reached, there is a recursion that turns us back, glancingly at an odd angle, into the novel. Neither Sinclair nor the reader can, in the end, escape the page; quite the opposite, when Sinclair is asked to write his life story as part of the athanasia treatment it is "so that afterwards I could be made into the words I had written" (A 13: 117). Reality is trapped within the novel as it is also in *The Prestige* and *The Separation*. Though as Seri tells Sinclair towards the end of the novel, "There's no such thing as truth. You are living by your manuscript, and everything in it is false" (A 24: 208).

What happens throughout the second half of *The Affirmation* is a progressive breaking down of the walls that separate the two worlds of the imagination. Mostly this revolves round the character of Seri/Gracia, with each Peter Sinclair finding it increasingly difficult to know which was which. "I knew that Seri must be more than a fictional analogue of Gracia. She was too real, too complete, too motivated by her own personality" (A 16: 143), as Sinclair acknowledges. After this, Seri and Gracia change places during lovemaking, a scene uncomfortably reminiscent of the invisible rape in *The Glamour*. Later, as each Sinclair moves restlessly between London and Jethra without really connecting with either, Seri becomes specifically linked to the islands: "To her, each island represented a different facet of her personality, each one vested in her a sense of identity. She was incomplete without islands, she was spread across the sea" (A 21: 183). Seri has become the Dream Archipelago. Sinclair had hoped to find his own identity within the islands, but finds only the identity of his girlfriend, or the avatar of his girlfriend; and in the end he is unable to commit himself to her. His final abandonment of Gracia/Seri, which leaves the novel uncompleted, is also his abandonment of the islands and hence of his own identity. He had been promised: "For you, the islands will be a redemption" (A 17: 150), but there can be no redemption now. He has turned back into the words on the page, into an imagination that does not connect with reality. That is to abandon the world.

Others will follow this trajectory to more or less the same effect, Niall in *The Glamour*, Angier in *The Prestige*, Teresa in *The Extremes*. They follow routes that involve duplicates of themselves, as Peter Sinclair's duplication is echoed by Borden in *The Prestige* and by J. L. Sawyer in *The Separation*. It is a route that takes them away from the world, into islands of invisibility or virtual reality or alternate worlds. Again and again Priest follows his protagonists on their journeys into the islands, whether it be the Planalto or Earth City, Wessex or the Dream Archipelago. Sometimes they might find their identity there, as David and Julia did in *A Dream of Wessex*; sometimes they might lose it, as Peter Sinclair does. Conflating Seri with the islands of the Dream Archipelago, Sinclair recognises at one point: "She offered only escape [...] but escape from, not to, so there was nothing to replace what I left behind" (A 21: 186). Though the focus may be on the escape, Christopher Priest's island stories are always really about what is left behind.

Bibliographies

1 Works by Christopher Priest

1a Novels

Indoctrinaire (London: Faber, 1970; New York: Harper & Row, 1970; London: NEL, 1971; New York: Pocket Books, 1971; rev. edn London: Pan, 1979).

Fugue for a Darkening Island (London: Faber, 1972; London: NEL, 1973; London: Pan, 1978).

— As *Darkening Island* (New York: Harper & Row, 1972; New York: Manor, 1974).

Inverted World (London: Faber, 1974; London: NEL, 1975; London: Pan, 1979; London: Gollancz, 1987).

— As *The Inverted World* (serialised *Galaxy* December 1973-March 1975; New York: Harper & Row, 1974; New York: Popular Library, 1975).

— Extract "The Inverted World", in *Beyond This Horizon*, ed. Christopher Carrell (London: Ceolfrith, 1973).

— Extract "The Inverted World", in *New Writings in SF 22*, ed. Kenneth Bulmer (London: Sidgwick & Jackson, 1973).

The Space Machine: A Scientific Romance (London: Faber, 1976; New York: Harper & Row, 1976; London: Futura, 1977; New York: Popular Library, 1978; London: Pan, 1981; London: Gollancz, 1988).

A Dream of Wessex (London: Faber, 1977; London: Pan, 1978; London: Abacus, 1987; London: Abacus, 1991).

— As *The Perfect Lover* (New York: Scribner's, 1977; New York: Dell, 1979).

The Affirmation (London: Faber, 1981; New York: Scribner's, 1981; London: Arena, 1983; London: Gollancz, 1988; London: Touchstone, 1996).

The Glamour (London: Cape, 1984; Rev. edn Garden City, New York: Doubleday, 1985; Rev. edn London: Abacus, 1985; Rev. edn London: Touchstone, 1996).

The Quiet Woman (London: Bloomsbury, 1990; London: Abacus, 1991; Helicong, PA: Wildside, 2005).

The Prestige (London: Simon and Schuster/Touchstone, 1995; London: Simon and Schuster, 1996; New York: St Martin's Press, 1996; New York: Tor, 1997).

— Extract: "In a Flash", *Interzone* 99 (September 1995).

The Extremes (London: Simon and Schuster, 1998; New York: Touchstone, 1998; St. Martin's Press: New York, 1999).

eXistenZ (New York: HarperEntertainment, 1999).

The Separation (London: Simon and Schuster, 2002; London: Gollancz, 2003).

1b Collections

Real-Time World (London: NEL, 1974; London: NEL, 1976).

An Infinite Summer (London: Faber, 1979; New York: Scribner's, 1979; London: Pan, 1980; New York: Dell, 1981).

— As *The Dream Archipelago* [revised contents] (London: Earthlight, 1999).

Christopher Priest Omnibus 1 [*The Space Machine: A Scientific Romance* and *A Dream of Wessex*] (London: Earthlight, 1999).

Christopher Priest Omnibus 2 [*Fugue for a Darkening Island* and *Inverted World*] (London: Earthlight, 1999).

1c Selected Short Fiction

"The Run", *Impulse* (May 1966) [*RTW*].

"The Ersatz Wine", *New Worlds* 171 (1967).

"The Interrogator", in *New Writings in SF 15*, ed. John Carnell (London: Dobson, 1969).

"The Perihelion Man", in *New Writings in SF 16*, ed. John Carnell (London: Dobson, 1969) [*RTW*].

"Fire Storm", *Quark* 1, eds. Samuel R. Delany and Marilyn Hacker (New York: Paperback Library, 1970) [*RTW*].

"Double Consummation", in *The Disappearing Future*, ed. George Hay (London: Panther, 1970) [*RTW*].

"Breeding Ground", *Vision of Tomorrow* (January 1970) [*RTW*].

"Real-Time World", in *New Writings in SF 19*, ed. John Carnell (London: Dobson, 1971) [*RTW*].

"Sentence in Binary Code", *Fantastic* (August 1971) [*RTW*].

"The Head and the Hand", in *New Worlds Quarterly* 3, ed. Michael Moorcock (London: Sphere, 1972) [*RTW*].

"Transplant", *Worlds of If* (January/February 1974) [*RTW*].

"A Woman Naked", *Science Fiction Monthly* 1: 1 (February 1974) [*RTW*].

"The Invisible Men", in *Stopwatch*, ed. George Hay (London: NEL, 1974).

"Men of Good Value", in *New Writings in SF 26*, ed. Kenneth Bulmer (London: Sidgwick & Jackson, 1975).

"An Infinite Summer", in *Andromeda* 1, ed. Peter Weston (London: Futura 1976) [*IS*].

"The Negation", in *Anticipations*, ed. Christopher Priest (London: Faber, 1978) [*IS/DA*].

"The Watched", *Fantasy and Science Fiction* (April 1978). [*IS/DA*].

"Whores", in *New Dimensions 8*, ed. Robert Silverberg (New York: Harper & Row, 1978) [*IS/DA*].

"The Cremation", in *Andromeda* 3, ed. Peter Weston (London: Futura, 1978) [*DA*].

"Palely Loitering", *Fantasy and Science Fiction* (January 1979) [*IS*].

The Making of the Lesbian Horse (Birmingham: Novacon, 1979).

"The Miraculous Cairn", in *New Terrors* 2, ed. Ramsey Campbell (London: Pan, 1980) [*DA*].

"I, Haruspex", *The Third Alternative* 16 (1998).

"The Equatorial Moment", (1999) [*DA*].

"The Cage of Chrome" *Interzone* 154 (April 2000).

"Retour au foyer" (2001).

— As "The Discharge", *Sci Fiction* (2002). Online at: http://www.scifi.com/ scifiction/originals/originals_archive/priest/.

—, and Redd, David, "The Agent", in *Aries* 1, ed. John Grant (London: David and Charles, 1979).

1d Edited Anthologies

Anticipations (London: Faber, 1978; New York: Scribners, 1978; London: Pan, 1980).

—, and Holdstock, Robert, *Stars of Albion* (London: Pan, 1979).

1e Book-Length Non-Fiction

The Book on the Edge of Forever (The Lost Deadloss Visions) (Seattle, WA: Fantagraphics, 1994).

—, and Gunnell, Sally, *Running Tall* (London: Bloomsbury, 1994).

—, and Sharman, Helen, *Seize the Moment: The Autobiography of Helen Sharman* (London: Gollancz, 1993).

1f Selected Reviews and Articles

[Items marked with * are credited as by Chris Priest, but note that this is not always consistent within a specific issue of a publication]

* "Science Fiction Magazine Survey 1963", *Zenith Science Fiction* 5 (June/July 1964), pp. 17-20.

"New Wave – Prozines", *Zenith Speculation* 8 (March 1965), pp. 9-11.

Reviews of Harry Harrison, *Plague from Space* and Brian Aldiss, *The Saliva Tree*, *Zenith Speculation* 13 (July 1966a), pp. 35-36.

Review of Dan Morgan, *The Richest Corpse in Show Business*, *Vector* 40 (Autumn 1966b), pp. 29-30.

Review of Philip K. Dick, *The Three Stigmata of Palmer Eldritch*, *Vector* 40 (Autumn 1966c), pp. 31-32.

Review of Keith Roberts, *The Furies*, *Vector* 42 (January 1967), pp. 29-30.

"Death of a Fairy Queen [Review of Keith Roberts, *Pavane*]", *Vector* 51 (October 1968), pp. 15-16, 21.

"View of Suburbia: The Chris Priest Column: On Book Reviewing", *Speculation* 23 (July/August 1969a), pp. 12-13.

"View of Suburbia", *Speculation* 24 (September/October 1969b), pp. 35-39.

"View of Suburbia: Open Letter to David Rome", *Speculation* 25 (January/ February 1970a), pp. 12-16.

"View of Suburbia", *Speculation* 26 (May 1970b), pp. 10-14.

"View of Suburbia (six)", *Speculation* 27 (September/October 1970c), pp. 40-43.

"View of Suburbia", *Speculation* 28 (January/February 1971), pp. 32-34.

* Letter re. Tony Sudbery's review of *Indoctrinaire*, *Speculation* 30 ("Spring" [June] 1972), pp. 49-50.

Review of Lester Del Rey, *Pstalemate*, *Foundation* 3 (March 1973a), pp. 76-77.

Review of John Rankine, *The Ring of Garamas*, *Foundation* 3 (March 1973b), pp. 77-78.

Review of Dick Morland, *Heart Clock*, *Vector* 65 (May/June 1973c), pp. 34-35.

Review of Bob Shaw, *Tomorrow Lies in Ambush*, *Foundation* 4 (July 1973d), pp. 77-79.

Review of Arthur C. Clarke, *Rendezvous With Rama*, *Foundation* 5 (January 1974a), pp. 91-94.

Review of David Gerrold, *The Man Who Folded Himself*, *Vector* 67-68 (Spring 1974b), pp. 29-32.

Letter re. inspiration for *The Space Machine*, *Vector* 79 (March 1976), p. 51.

Letter re. Ian Watson, *Vector* 79 (January/February 1977a), p. 15.

Review of Ben Bova, *Notes to a Science Fiction Writer* and L. Sprague De Camp and Catherine Crook De Camp, *Science Fiction Handbook*, *Foundation* 11/12 (March 1977b), pp. 187-191.

"The Suburbs My Destination", in *The View from the Edge*, ed. George Turner (Melbourne: Nostrilia Press, 1977c).

"The Profession of Science Fiction: 13: Overture and Beginners", *Foundation* 13 (May 1978a), pp. 51-56.

Letter re. reviews of reprints and attitudes of writers, *Vector* 87 (May/June 1978b), pp. 47-48.

Letter re. economics and bookselling, *Vector* 79 (July/August 1978c), pp. 52-53.

"Foreword: Swimming Against the Stream", in *Envisaged Worlds*, ed. Paul Collins (London: Void, 1978d), pp. 1-2.

"Introduction", in *Anticipations*, ed. *Christopher Priest* (London and Boston: Faber, 1978e), pp. 1-7.

"New Wave: A Radical Change in the 1960s", in *Encyclopedia of Science Fiction*, ed. Robert Holdstock (London: Octopus, 1978f), pp. 162-173.

"News for High-Octane Water-Lilies", *Matrix: The Newsletter of the British Science Fiction Association 22* (February 1979a), pp. 3-7.

"Short story contracts", *SFWA Bulletin* 14 (Spring 1979b), pp. 6-16, 56-59.

Review of Anthony Burgess, *1985*, *Foundation* 16 (May 1979c), pp. 55-58.

"Writing a Novel? Do!", *Focus: An SF Writers' Magazine* 1 (Autumn 1979d), pp. 10-11.

"Afterword", in *Stars of Albion*, eds. Robert Holdstock and Christopher Priest (London: Pan, 1979e), p. 233.

"British Science Fiction", in *Science Fiction: A Critical Guide*, ed. Patrick Parrinder (London and New York: Longman, 1979f), pp. 187-202.

"We do it, too! British SF, 1965-1979", in *World Science Fiction Convention, 1979. Seacon 79 Programme Book* (Brighton: Seacon 1979g), pp. 50-53.

"Outside the Whale", *Vector* 97 (April 1980a), pp. 5-14

"Outside the Whale", *SF Commentary* 54 (April 1980b), pp. 1-3, 15-16.

"Meetings with Remarkable Men", *Vector* 98 (June 1980c), pp. 4-11.

"Outside the Whale", *Science Fiction Review* 9 (August 1980d), pp. 17-21.

"Landscape Artist: The Fiction of J. G. Ballard", in *The Stellar Gauge*, ed. M. J. Tolley (Carlton: Norstrilia, 1980e), pp. 187-196.

"'It' Came From Outer Space", *Foundation* 21 (February 1981a), pp. 53-63.

"The Authentic Voice", *Focus: An SF Writers' Magazine* 4 (Spring 1981b), pp. 4-5.

Letter re. critical standards in sf, *Vector* 101 (April 1981c), pp. 47-48.

Letter 29 December 1980 on Rottensteiner and science fiction, *SF Commentary* 62/63/64/65/66 (June 1981d), pp. 54-55.

Letter to the Reviews Editor, *Foundation* 24 (February 1982a), pp. 79-80.

* "Into the Arena: The Barrel", *Vector* 109 (August 1982b), pp. 22-25.

"Novel Contracts", *Focus: The Writers' Magazine of the British Science Fiction Association* 6 (Autumn 1982c), pp. 15-19.

"Crouching in Cheadle", *Vector* 112 (February 1983a).

Review of Norman Spinrad, *Staying Alive*, *Foundation* 29 (November 1983b), pp. 65-69.

Letter re. Colin Greenland's review of Mary Gentle, *Vector* 118 (February 1984a), p. 40.

Letter re. BSFA's treatment of writers, *Vector* 119 (April 1984b), pp. 48-49.

"Mucking About in Bytes", *Focus: An SF Writers' Magazine* 10 (February 1985a), pp. 26-28.

"Leave the Forgotten to the Night", *Vector* 127 (August/September 1985b), pp. 9-10.

Letter re. Wyndham and Shaw, *Vector* 135 (December 1986/January 1987), p. 5.

* "Layout: Chris Priest Corrects", *Focus: The Writers' Magazine of the British Science Fiction Association* 15 (July/August 1988), p. 5.

"Peoria My Destination!", *Interzone* 26 (November/December 1988), pp. 33-34.

Review of Nicholas Ruddick, *Christopher Priest*, *Foundation* 50 (Autumn 1990a), pp. 94-101.

* "Without a Suit", *Focus: An SF Writers' Magazine* 22 (December 1990b), pp. 3-5.

"One or Two Things I Know About Him", in *A is for Brian*, eds. Frank Hatherley, Margaret Aldiss and Malcolm Edwards (Oxford: Avernus, 1990c), pp. 79-85.

"Out of the Temple", *Interzone* 86 (August 1994a), pp. 37-39.

"Pax Ortygia", *Interzone* 88 (October 1994b), p. 52.

"Author's Note", in Christopher Priest, *The Affirmation* (London: Touchstone, 1996).

"A Retreat from Reality", *SFWA Bulletin* 32 (Spring 1999a), pp. 15-17.

"A Retreat from Reality", *Vector* 206 (July/August 1999b), pp. 10-13.

"Yes . . . Or Then Again, No", *Steam-Engine Time* 3 (December 2001), pp. 9-14.

"A Meeting with Richard Cowper", *Matrix: The Newsletter of the British Science Fiction Association* 156 (July/August 2002), pp. 19-21.

Favourite Slipstream Books, top10s, Guardian Unlimited Website, online at: http://books.guardian.co.uk/top10s/top10/0,6109,965598,00.html (2003a).

"The Scars of War", *The Guardian Review* (14 June 2003b), p. 31.

— and Watson, Ian, "Science Fiction: Form Versus Content", *Foundation* 10 (June 1976), pp. 55-65.

2. Secondary Materials

Agamben, Giorgio, *Infancy and History: Essays on the Destruction of Experience*, translated by Liz Heron (London: Verso, 1993 [1978]).

—, *Homo Sacer: Sovereign Power and Bare Life*, translated by Daniel Heller-Roazen (Stanford, Ca.: Stanford University Press, 1998 [1995]).

Aldiss, Brian, *Billion Year Spree: The History of Science Fiction* (New York: Doubleday, 1973).

—, and Wingrove, David, *Trillion Year Spree: The History of Science Fiction* (London: Gollancz, 1986).

Austin, J. L., *How to do Things with Words* (Oxford: Oxford University Press, 1980).

Badiou, Alain, *Ethics: An Essay on the Understanding of Evil*, translated by Peter Hallward (New York: Verso, 2001 [1993]).

—, *Saint Paul: The Foundation of Universalism*, translated by Ray Brassier (Stanford, CA: Stanford University Press, 2003 [1997]).

Baetens, Jan, "La novellisation, un genre contaminé?", *Poétique* 138 (2004), pp. 235-251.

—, and Lits, Marc, "La novellisation: au-delà des lieux communs", in *La novellisation: du film au livre/Novelization: From Film to Novel*, eds. Jan Baetens and Marc Lits (Leuven: Leuven University Press, 2004), pp. 9-18.

Ballard, J. G., "Which Way to Inner Space?", *New Worlds* 188 (1962a), pp. 2-3, 116-118.

—, *The Wind from Nowhere* (New York: Berkely, 1962b).

—, *The Crystal World* (London: Cape, 1966)

—, *Crash* (London: Cape, 1973).

—, *Concrete Island* (London: Cape, 1974).

Baudelaire, Charles, *Baudelaire: Selected Verse*, ed. Francis Scarfe (Harmondsworth, Middlesex: Penguin, 1961).

Beevor, Antony, *Stalingrad* (London: Viking, 1998).

—, *Berlin: The Downfall 1945* (London: Viking, 2002).

Benjamin, Walter, "An Outsider Attracts Attention: on *The Salaried Masses* by S. Kracauer", in Siegfried Kracauer, *The Salaried Masses*, translated by Quinton Hoare (London: Verso, 1998 [1930]), pp. 109-114.

Bolter, Jay David and Grusin, Richard, *Remediation: Understanding New Media* (Cambridge, Mass.: MIT Press, 1999).

Boon, Richard, Brenton: *The Playwright* (London: Methuen, 1991).

Bould, Mark, "Film and Television", in James and Mendlesohn 2003, pp. 79-95.

Bradbury, Ray, "And the Rock Cried Out", in *The Day It Rained Forever* (Harmondsworth, Middlesex: Penguin, 1963), pp. 199-223.

Braudel, Fernand, *On History* (Chicago: University of Chicago Press, 1980).

Brenton, Howard, "The Churchill Play", in *Brenton: Plays One* (London: Methuen, 1986), pp. 107-177.

—, *H.I.D. (Hess is Dead)* (London: Hern, 1989).

Brin, David, "To Read *The Separation*", *New York Review of Science Fiction* 185 (January 2004), pp. 1, 8-11.

Broderick, Damien, *Reading By Starlight: Postmodern Science Fiction* (London and New York: Routledge, 1995).

Brooks, Peter, *Reading for the Plot: Design and Intention in Narrative* (Oxford: Oxford University Press, 1984).

Burelbach, Frederick M., "Christopher Priest", in *Dictionary of Literary Biography, Vol. 261: British Fantasy and Science-Fiction Writers Since 1960*, ed. Darren Harris-Fain (Detroit: Gale, 2002), pp. 327-335.

Butler, Judith, *Gender Trouble: Feminism and the Subversion of Identity* (New York: Routledge, 1989).

—, *Bodies That Matter: On the Discursive Limits of "Sex"* (New York and London: Routledge, 1993).

—, *The Psychic Life of Power: Theories in Subjection* (Stanford, Ca: Stanford University Press, 1997).

Byatt, A. S., *Possession* (London: Chatto & Windus, 1990).

Calder, Angus, *The People's War: Britain 1939-45* (London: Cape, 1969).

Christopher, John, *The Long Winter* (New York: Fawcett, 1962).

Clarke, Arthur C., *Childhood's End* (New York: Ballantine, 1953).

—, *Rendezvous with Rama* (New York: Harcourt, Brace, Jovanovich, 1973).

—, "Technology and the Future", in *Report on Planet Three and Other Speculations*, [1972] (London: Pan, 1984), pp. 146-159.

Clute, John, Review of Christopher Priest, *An Infinite Summer*, *Foundation* 18 (January 1980), pp. 62-64.

—, *Look at the Evidence: Essays and Reviews* (Liverpool: Liverpool University Press, 1995).

—, *Scores: Reviews 1993-2003* (Harold Wood: Beccon Publications, 2003a).

—, "Science Fiction from 1980 to the Present", in James and Mendlesohn, pp. 64-78.

Clute, John and Nicholls, Peter, eds., *The Encyclopedia of Science Fiction* (London: Orbit, 1993).

Conrad, Joseph, *Heart of Darkness*, ed. D .C. R. A. Goonetilleke (Peterborough, ON and Orchard Park, NY:, 1995 [1898]).

Costello, John, *David Cronenberg* (Harpenden: Pocket Essentials, 2000).

Cowper, Richard, *The Twilight of Briareus* (London: Gollancz, 1974).

de Baecque, Antoine, *La cinéphilie: invention d'un regard, histoire d'une culture (1944-1968)* (Paris: Fayard, 2003).

Deighton, Len, *SS-GB Nazi-Occupied Britain, 1941* (London: Cape, 1978).

Deleuze, Gilles and Guattari, Félix, *Kafka: Toward a Minor Literature*, foreword by Réda Bensmaïa, translated by Dana Polan (Minneapolis: University of Minnesota Press, 1986 [1975]).

—, A *Thousand Plateaus*, Capitalism and Schizophrenia, 2, translated by Brian Massumi, (Minneapolis: University of Minnesota Press, 1987 [1980]).

del Rey, Lester, *Science Fiction 1926-1976 - The History of a Subculture* (New York: Del Rey, 1979).

Dick, Philip K., *The Three Stigmata of Palmer Eldritch* (Garden City, New York: Doubleday, 1964).

Disch, Thomas M., "Casablanca", in *Under Compulsion* (London: Rupert Hart-Davis, 1968), pp. 197-220.

Donne, John, *Poetical Works*, ed. Sir Herbert Grierson (Oxford: Oxford University Press, 1937).

Ellison, Harlan, ed., *Dangerous Visions* (Garden City, New York: Doubleday, 1967).

Ford, Bob, "The BSFA Award Winners: Bob Shaw, *Orbitsville*", *Vector* 192 (March/April 1997), p. 10.

Foucault, Michel, *The Archaeology of Knowledge and the Discourse on Language*, translated by A. M. Sheridan Smith (New York: Pantheon Books, 1972 [1969]).

—, *The Use of Pleasure*, The History of Sexuality 2, translated by Robert Hurley, (New York: Vintage, 1990 [1984]).

—, *The Order of Things: An Archaeology of the Human Sciences* (New York: Vintage, 1994 [1966]).

—, "Nietzsche, Genealogy, History", in *Aethestics, Method and Epistemology*, ed. J. D. Faubion (New York: New Press, 1998 [1971]).

Fowles, John, *The Magus* (St Albans: Triad Panther, 1978 [1966, rev. 1977]).

Frayn, Michael, *Spies* (London: Faber, 2002).

Freud, Sigmund, "Remembering, Repeating and Working-Through [1914]", in *The Standard Edition of the Complete Psychological Works of Sigmund Freud: Volume XII*, ed. James Strachey (London: Hogarth Press, 1958a), pp. 147-156.

—, "Observations on Transference-Love [1915]", in *The Standard Edition of the Complete Psychological Works of Sigmund Freud: Volume XII*, ed. James Strachey (London: Hogarth Press, 1958b), pp. 159-171.

—, "On Narcissism [1914]", in *On Metapyschology*, Penguin Freud Library 11, ed. Angela Richards (Harmondsworth, Middlesex: Penguin, 1984a), pp. 65-97.

—, "Beyond the Pleasure Principle [1920]", in *On Metapsychology*, Penguin Freud Library 11, ed. Angela Richards (Harmondsworth, Middlesex: Penguin, 1984b), pp. 275-338.

—, "The Uncanny", in *Art and Literature*, Penguin Freud Library 14, ed. James Strachey (Harmondsworth, Middlesex: Penguin, 1990), pp. 335-376.

Fry, Stephen, *Making History* (London: Hutchinson, 1996).

Gee, Maggie, *The Ice People* (London: Richard Cohen, 1998).

Genette, Gérard, "Introduction to the Paratext", *New Literary History* 22 (1991), pp. 261-272.

Gernsback, Hugo, "A New Sort of Magazine", *Amazing* 1 (1926), p. 3.

Grant, Michael, ed., *The Modern Fantastic: The Films of David Cronenberg* (Trowbridge: Flicks, 2000).

Green, Henry, *Caught: A Novel* (London: Hogarth, 1943).

—, *Back: A Novel* (London: Hogarth, 1946).

Greene, Graham, *The Ministry of Fear: An Entertainment* (London: William Heinemann, 1943).

Gribbin, John, Review of Christopher Priest, *The Prestige*, *New Scientist* (1996), p. 52.

Gunn, James, "On the Lem Affair", *Science Fiction Studies* 4 (November 1977), pp. 314-316.

—, Letter re. the Aesthetic Fallacy 11 July 1977, *Foundation* 13 (May 1978), pp. 56-58.

Hamilton, Patrick, *Hangover Square: A Story of Darkest Earl's Court* (London: Constable, 1941).

Harris, Robert, *Fatherland* (London: Arrow, 1993 [1992]).

Harrison, M. John, Letter re. Fearn, *Speculation* 25 (January 1970), p. 43.

—, *The Committed Men* (London: Hutchinson New Authors, 1971).

Herr, Michael, *Kubrick* (London: Picador, 2000).

Hilton, James, *Random Harvest* (London: Macmillan, 1941).

Hubble, Nick, "'An Artificial Restoration of Normal Life in an Abnormal State': Five English Disaster Novels, 1951-1972", *Foundation* 95 (forthcoming, 2005a).

—, "Virtual Histories and Counterfactual Myths: Christopher Priest's The Separation", *Extrapolation* (forthcoming, 2005b).

Hutcheon, Linda, *A Poetics of Postmodernism: History, Theory, Fiction* (London: Routledge, 1988).

Iser, Wolfgang, "The Reading Process: A Phenomenological Approach", in *Modern Criticism and Thought: A Reader*, ed. David Lodge (London: Longman, 1988), pp. 212-228.

Jack, Ian, "Introduction", *Granta: The Magazine of New Writing* 81 (Spring 2003), pp. 9-14.

James, Edward and Mendlesohn, Farah, eds., *The Cambridge Companion to Science Fiction* (Cambridge: Cambridge University Press, 2003).

Jauss, Hans Robert, "Literary History as a Challenge to Literary Theory", in *Toward an Aesthetic of Reception* (Minneapolis: University of Minnesota Press, 1982), pp. 3-45.

Jones, Gwyneth, *Deconstructing the Starships: Science, Fiction and Reality* (Liverpool: Liverpool University Press, 1999).

Jones, Langdon, ed., *The New SF: An Original Anthology of Modern Speculative Fiction* (London: Hutchinson, 1969).

Joyard, Olivier and Tesson, Charles, "L'aventure Intérieure: Entretien avec David Cronenberg", *Cahiers Du Cinéma* 534 (1999), pp. 67-73.

Keen, Suzanne, *Romances of the Archive in Contemporary British Fiction* (Toronto: University of Toronto Press, 2001).

Keller, Donald G., Review of Christopher Priest, *The Quiet Woman*, *New York Review of Science Fiction* 25 (September 1990), pp. 10-11.

Kincaid, Paul, "Only Connect: Psychology and Politics in the Work of Christopher Priest", *Foundation* 52 (Summer 1991), pp. 42-58.

—, "Throwing Away the Orthodoxy: A Conversation about Sex, Innocence and Science Fiction", *Vector* 206 (July/August 1999a), pp. 4-10.

—, "Mirrors, Doubles, Twins: Patterns in the Fiction of Christopher Priest, 1, In the Dreamtime", *Vector* 206 (July/August 1999b), pp. 10-13.

—, "Mirrors, Doubles, Twins – Patterns in the Work of Christopher Priest. Part 2: In the Realtime", *Vector* 209 (January/February 2000), pp. 10-15.

King, Nicola, "'We Come After': Post-Holocaust National Identity in Recent Popular Fiction: Fatherland and Eve's Tattoo", in *Contemporary Writing and National Identity*, eds. Tracey Hill and Williams Hughes (Bath: Sulis Press, 1995), pp. 81-91.

Langford, David, *Critical Assembly* (Reading: Ansible Information, 1992).

—, "Christopher Priest", in *Science Fiction Writers*, ed. Richard Bleiler (New York: Scribner's, 1999).

Lashku, Ludmila, "The Marriage of Fantasy and Psychology in the Works of Christopher Priest", *Foundation* 50 (Autumn 1990), pp. 52-60.

Le Guin, Ursula K. and Suvin, Darko, "The Lem Affair", *Science Fiction Studies* 4 (March 1977), pp. 100-103.

Lem, Stanislaw, "Science-Fiction: A Hopeless Case With Exceptions", in *Philip K. Dick: Electric Shepherd*, ed. Bruce Gillespie (Carlton, Victoria and Melbourne: Norstrilia, 1975a), pp. 69-94.

—, "Philip K. Dick: A Visionary Among the Charlatans", *Science Fiction Studies* 2 (March 1975b), pp. 54-67.

—, "Looking Down on Science Fiction", *Science Fiction Studies* 4 (July 1977), pp. 127-128.

Lethem, Jonathan, ed., *The Vintage Book of Amnesia* (New York: Vintage, 2000).

McEwan, Ian, *Atonement* (London: Jonathan Cape, 2001).

—, "Mother Tongue", in *On Modern British Fiction*, ed. Zachary Leader (Oxford: Oxford University Press, 2002), pp. 34-44.

McFarlane, Brian, *Novel to Film: An Introduction to the Theory of Adaptation* (Oxford: Clarendon Press, 1996).

McHale, Brian, *Postmodernist Fiction* (London and New York: Methuen, 1987).

Mendlesohn, Farah, "Introduction", in James and Mendlesohn 2003, pp. 1-12.

Merril, Judith, ed., *England Swings SF: Stories of Speculative Fiction* (Garden City, New York: Doubleday, 1968).

Miall, David S. and Kuiken, Donald, "What Is Literariness? Three Components of Literary Reading", *Discourse Processes* 28 (1999), pp. 121-138.

Milton, John, *Paradise Lost*, ed. Alastair Fowler (London: Longman, 1971).

Mitchell, Timothy, "The Limits of the State: Beyond Statist Approaches and Their Critics", *American Political Science Review* 85 (1991), pp. 77-96.

Moine, Raphaëlle, "Cinéma, genres et novellisation dans l'espace éditorial français contemporain", in *La novellisation: du film au livre/Novelization: From Film to Novel*, eds. Jan Baetens and Marc Lits (Leuven: Leuven University Press, 2004), pp. 85-94.

Montgomerie, Lee, Review of Christopher Priest, *A Dream of Wessex*, *Foundation* 14 (September 1978), pp. 68-69.

Moorcock, Michael, *The Black Corridor* (London: Mayflower, 1969).

Mullen, R. D., Review of Nicholas Ruddick, *Christopher Priest*, *Science Fiction Studies* 18 (1991), pp. 453-454.

Nicholls, Peter, Review of Christopher Priest, *Inverted World*, *Foundation* 7/8 (March 1975), pp. 185-188.

Niven, Larry, *Ringworld* (New York: Ballantine, 1970).

Offutt, Andrew, "How It Happened: One Bad Decision Leading to Another", *Science Fiction Studies* 4 (July 1977), pp. 138-143.

Paling, Chris, *After the Raid* (London: Cape, 1995).

Raymond, Derek, *A State of Denmark, or A Warning to the Incurious* (London: Hutchinson, 1970).

Rimbaud, Jean Arthur, *Rimbaud: Collected Poems*, ed. Oliver Bernard (Harmondsworth, Middlesex: Penguin, 1962).

Roberts, Adam, *Science Fiction* (London: Routledge, 2000).

Roberts, Keith, *The Furies* (London: Hart-Davis, 1966).

—, *Pavane* (London: Hart-Davis, 1968).

Rubin, Gayle, "Thinking Sex: Notes for a Radical Theory of the Politics of Sexuality", in *Pleasure and Danger: Exploring Female Sexuality*, ed. Carol S. Vance (Boston: Routledge, 1984), pp. 267-319.

Ruddick, Nicholas, *Christopher Priest* (Mercer Island, WA: Starmont, 1989).

—, *Ultimate Island: On the Nature of British Science Fiction* (Westport, Ct.: Greenwood Press, 1993).

—, "The Search for a Quantum Ethics: Michael Frayn's Copenhagen and Other Recent British Science Plays", *Journal of the Fantastic in the Arts* 11 (2001), pp. 415-431.

Sarban, *The Sound of his Horn* (London: Davies, 1952).

Sargent, Pamela, "Why It Happened: Comments and Conclusions", *Science Fiction Studies* 4 (July 1977), pp. 134-136.

Sargent, Pamela and Zebrowski, George, "How It Happened: A Chronology", *Science Fiction Studies* 4 (July 1977), pp. 129-134.

Sawyer, Andy, "Christopher Priest", in *Dictionary of Literary Biography, Vol. 207: British Novelists Since 1960*, Third Series, ed. Merritt Moseley (Detroit: Gale, 1999), pp. 213-220.

—, Butler, Andrew M. and Mendlesohn, Farah, eds., *A Celebration of British Science Fiction* (Guildford: SFF, 2005).

Scholes, Robert, *Structural Fabulation: An Essay on Fiction of the Future* (Notre Dame: University of Notre Dame Press, 1975).

Shaw, Bob, *Tomorrow Lies in Ambush* (London: Gollancz, 1973).

—, *Orbitsville* (London: Gollancz, 1975).

Shelley, Mary, *Frankenstein; or, The Modern Prometheus*, eds. D. L. Macdonald and Kathleen Scherf. 2nd Edn (Peterborough, ON and Orchard Park, NY: Broadview Press, 2001).

Shippey, Tom, Review of Bob Shaw, *Orbitsville*, *Foundation* 9 (November 1975), pp. 87-90.

Sladek, John, *Love Among the Xoids* (Polk City, Iowa: Drumm, 1984).

Steele, Robert, Letter re. Hurst on Wyndham, *Vector* 134 (October/November 1986), p. 3.

Stevenson, Robert Louis, *The Strange Case of Dr Jekyll and Mr Hyde*, ed. Martin A. Danahay (Peterborough, ON and Orchard Park, NY: Broadview Press, 1999).

Stiegler, Bernard, *Technics and Time, 1: The Fault of Epimetheus*, translated by George Collins and Richard Beardsworth (Stanford: Stanford University Press, 1994).

Suvin, Darko, *Metamorphoses of Science Fiction: On the Poetics and History of a Literary Genre* (New Haven: Yale University Press, 1979).

Thomas, Hugh, *Hess: A Tale of Two Murders* (London: Hodder and Stoughton, 1988).

Tressell, Robert, *The Ragged Trousered Philanthropists*, introduced by Alan Sillitoe (London: Granada, 1965).

Tuve, Rosemond, *Elizabethan and Metaphysical Imagery: Renaissance Poetic and Twentieth-Century Critics* (Chicago and London: University of Chicago Press, 1962 [1947]).

Tynjanov, Jurij, "On Literary Evolution", in *Readings in Russian Poetics: Formalist and Structuralist Views*, eds. Ladislav Matejka and Krystyna Pomorska (Cambridge, Mass: MIT Press, 1971), pp. 66-78.

Watson, Ian, Review of Christopher Priest, *The Affirmation*, *Foundation* 23 (October 1981), pp. 82-84.

Waugh, Patricia, *Metafiction: The Theory and Practice of Self-Conscious Fiction* (London and New York: Methuen, 1984).

Wellek, René, "The Crisis of Comparative Literature", in *Concepts of Criticism*, ed. Stephen G. Nichols Jr. (New Haven: Yale University Press, 1963), pp. 282-295.

Wells, H. G., "Preface", in *Seven Famous Novels* (New York: Knopf, 1934), p. viii.

—, *The Island of Doctor Moreau* (Harmondsworth, Middlesex: Penguin, 1973 [1896]).

—, *Love and Mr Lewisham: The Story of a Very Young Couple*, ed. Jeremy Lewis (London: Everyman, 1993 [1900]).

—, *The Time Machine: An Invention*, ed. Nicholas Ruddick (Peterborough, Ontario: Broadview Press, 2001 [1895]).

—, *The War of the Worlds*, ed. Martin A. Danahay (Peterborough, Ontario: Broadview Press, 2003 [1898]).

White, Hayden, *The Content of the Form: Narrative Discourse and Historical Representation* (Baltimore: Johns Hopkins University Press, 1987).

Williams, Liz, Review of *The Separation*, *Foundation* 89 (Autumn 2003), pp. 103-105.

Williams, Raymond, *Television: Technology and Cultural Form* (London: Routledge, 1990).

Wingrove, David, "Legerdemain: The Fiction of Christopher Priest", *Vector* 93 (May/June 1979), pp. 3-9.

Wymer, Rowland, "How 'Safe' Is John Wyndham? A Closer Look at His Work, With Particular Reference to *The Chrysalids*", *Foundation* 55 (Summer 1992), pp. 25-36.

Wyndham, John, "Time to Rest", *New Worlds*, 2: 5 (1949), pp. 82-92 [as John Benyon].

—, *The Day of the Triffids* (London: Jonathan Cape, 1951).

3. Other Media

Borràs, Laura, "*eXistenZ*, by David Cronenberg: Cyber-Fictions for a Post-Humanity", *Digithum* 5 (2003). Available at: http://www.uoc.edu/humfil/articles/eng/borras0303/borras0303.html.

Broxton, Jonathan, "Howard Shore Questions his Own *eXistenZ*", *Movie Music U.K.* (1999). Available at: http://www.moviemusicuk.us/shoreint.htm.

Cronenberg, David, *eXistenZ* (Momentum Pictures, 1999). Available on DVD, various regions.

Gevers, Nick, "The Interrogation: An Interview with Christopher Priest", *Infinity Plus* (2002). Available at: http://www.infinityplus.co.uk/nonfiction/intcpriest. htm. [Reproduced from *Interzone* 183 (October 2002).]

Langford, David, Christopher Priest Interview. (1995) Available at: http://www. ansible.demon.co.uk/writing/cpriest.html.

Roberts, Adam, Review of Edward James and Farah Mendlesohn, eds., *The Cambridge Companion to Science Fiction*, *The Alien Online* (2003). Available at: http://www.thealienonline.net/ao_060. asp?baa=1&tid=2&scid=21&iid =2093.

Shore, Howard, *eXistenZ, Music from the Motion Picture* (RCA Victor, 1999). Available on CD.

Sterling, Bruce, "Slipstream". Available at: http://moshkow.rsl.ru/koi/ STERLINGB/catscan05.txt.

Van Parys, Thomas, Jansen, Lien and Vanhoutte, Elisabeth, "eXistenZ, a Different Novelization?: An Interview with Christopher Priest", *Image & Narrative* 9 (2004). Available at: http://www.imageandnarrative.be.

Vernet, Xavier, "Interview de Christopher Priest", *ActuSF* (2001). Available at: http://www.actusf.com/SF/interview/itw_priest.htm.

Notes on Contributors

Andrew M. Butler was the features editor of *Vector* 1995-2005 and teaches Media and Cultural Studies at Canterbury Christ Church University College. He is the author of Pocket Essentials on *Philip K. Dick* (2000), *Cyberpunk* (2000), *Terry Pratchett* (2001), *Film Studies* (2002; 2nd Edn 2005) and *Postmodernism* (2003, with Bob Ford). He is the co-editor, with Edward James and Farah Mendlesohn, of *Terry Pratchett: Guilty of Literature* (2000; 2nd edn 2004), and, with Farah Mendlesohn, *The True Knowledge of Ken MacLeod* (2003). In 2004 he won the SFRA's Pioneer Award. If he had any spare time, he would collect shiny trousers.

Gilles Dumay is the French publisher of the series *Lunes d'encre* (Denoël), where he publishes four British writers: Christopher Priest, Robert Holdstock, Mary Gentle and Michael Moorcock. He will soon be publishing a fifth, one of the most powerful writers of the moment: Ian R. MacLeod. He's 33 and divides his life between France, where he works, and Cambodia, where he lives with his wife. This interview is part of a much longer one between Christopher Priest and Gilles Dumay, which will be published in France in 2005.

Nick Hubble is a Research Fellow at the Centre for Suburban Studies, Kingston University and is currently compiling a suburban mythology for the Twenty-First Century based on participant observation in Bromley, Brighton and Pease Pottage Service Station. His book *Mass-Observation and Everyday Life: Culture, History, Theory* is being published by Palgrave in late 2005. His essay "'An Artificial Restoration of Normal Life in an Abnormal State': Five English Disaster Novels, 1951-1972" will appear in *Foundation* 95.

Paul Kincaid is the administrator of the Arthur C. Clarke Award. His essays and reviews have appeared in *Extrapolation, Foundation, Science Fiction Studies, New York Review of Science Fiction* and various other journals, reference books and collections. His own collection of essays, *What It Is We Do When We Read Science Fiction*, is published by Borgo Press, and he is currently co-editing (with Andrew M. Butler and Maureen Kincaid Speller) a collection of essays on the Clarke Award winners.

Nicholas Ruddick is Professor of English and Director of the Humanities Research Institute at the University of Regina. He teaches undergraduate courses on science fiction, fairy tales, and horror fiction, and graduate courses on Darwinism's influence on the literary and cultural history of the later nineteenth century. He is the author of *Christopher Priest* (1989), *British Science Fiction: A Chronology 1478-1990* (1993), and *Ultimate Island: On the Nature of Brit-*

ish Science Fiction (1993), and the editor of *State of the Fantastic* (1992), *The Time Machine* by H. G. Wells (2001), *Caesar's Column* by Ignatius Donnelly (2003), and *The Woman Who Did* by Grant Allen (2004). The subjects of some of his recent essays include Margaret Atwood's *The Handmaid's Tale*, Charles Perrault's "Bluebeard", Oscar Wilde's *The Picture of Dorian Gray*, and Michael Frayn's *Copenhagen*. He was appointed University of Regina President's Scholar, 2002-04.

Andy Sawyer is the librarian of the Science Fiction Foundation Collection at the University of Liverpool Library, and Course Director of the MA in Science Fiction Studies offered by the School of English. He has published on children's/young adult sf, John Wyndham, Telepathy, *Babylon 5*, "Reverse-Time Narratives" and Terry Pratchett. He co-edited the collection *Speaking Science Fiction* (Liverpool University Press, 2000). He is also Reviews Editor of *Foundation: the International Review of Science Fiction* and Advisory Editor of *The Greenwood Encyclopedia of Science Fiction and Fantasy: Themes, Works, and Wonders* (Greenwood Press). In his spare time he investigates the arcane history of Liverpool Fandom.

Graham Sleight lives in London. He writes regularly for the *New York Review of Science Fiction* and *Foundation*, and is Assistant Editor of *Foundation*. He has also contributed to *Interzone, SF Weekly, Science Fiction Studies*, and infinityplus.co.uk . His essays appear in *Snake's-Hands: The Fiction of John Crowley* (eds. Alice K. Turner and Michael Andre-Driussi), *Supernatural Fiction Writers* (2nd Edn ed. Richard Bleiler), and the forthcoming *Polder: A Festschrift for John Clute and Judith Clute* (ed. Farah Mendlesohn).

Victoria Stewart is Senior Lecturer in the School of English and Drama, University of the West of England, Bristol. As well as articles on the representation of history in the works of contemporary writers including John Banville and Michael Frayn, she has published *Women's Autobiography: War and Trauma* (Palgrave, 2003) and is currently working on *Narratives of Memory: British Writing of the 1940s*.

Thomas Van Parys has recently graduated in Germanic Languages and Literatures at the University of Leuven in Belgium. The subject of his MA thesis concerned the science fiction novelisation from 1950 to 2000. In 2004 he published an interview with Christopher Priest on the novelisation of *eXistenZ* in *Image [&] Narrative* (www.imageandnarrative.be).

Matthew Wolf-Meyer is a Ph.D. candidate in Sociocultural Anthropology at the University of Minnesota, specialising in medical anthropology and the social study of science and technology. He holds Masters of Arts degrees from the University of Liverpool (in Literature and Science Fiction Studies) and Bowling Green State University (in American Cultural Studies). He is the co-editor of the online cultural studies journal, *Reconstruction: Studies in Contemporary Culture*, and the author of a number of articles on science fiction, contemporary cultural theory, and the social study of science, medicine and technology; his current research focuses on the intersection of medical and legal discourses of "abnormal" bodies, the temporal regimes of capitalism, modernist theories of the city, and the idea of the "everyday".

Index